Stevens Greek Workbook

Stevens Greek Workbook

A Companion to the Accordance Module

Gerald L. Stevens

PICKWICK *Publications* · Eugene, Oregon

STEVENS GREEK WORKBOOK
A Companion to the Accordance Module

Pickwick Publications
An Imprint of Wipf and Stock Publishers
199 W. 8th Ave., Suite 3
Eugene, OR 97401

www.wipfandstock.com

PAPERBACK ISBN: 978-1-5326-1919-9
HARDCOVER ISBN: 978-1-4982-4538-8
EBOOK ISBN: 978-1-4982-4537-1

Cataloging-in-Publication data:

Names: Stevens, Gerald L.
Title: Stevens Greek workbook : a companion to the Accordance module / Gerald L. Stevens
Description: Eugene, OR : Pickwick Publications, 2017 | Includes bibliographical references and index.
Identifiers: ISBN 978-1-5326-1919-9 (paperback) | ISBN 978-1-4982-4538-8 (hardcover) | ISBN 978-1-4982-4537-1(ebook)
Subjects: LCSH: Bible. N.T.—Language, style. | Greek language, Biblical—Grammar.
Classification: LCC PA258 S73 2017 (print) | LCC PA258 (ebook)

Manufactured in the U.S.A.

Cover image: Columns of the inner sanctuary of Trajan's temple on the Upper Acropolis at the ancient site of Pergamum, Turkey. Begun in the time of Trajan and completed by Hadrian, this imperial temple built in the *peripteros* style (having a surrounding portico with a single colonnade) was nine columns in length and six columns in width. Altars to the emperors stood to the side of the temple. Pergamum was designated a *neokoros* city, a coveted, honorific title granted to cities by the Roman emperor for building imperial temples or maintaining cults dedicated to members of the imperial family. Pergamum was declared a *neokoros* city twice, once for being the first city in Asia Minor to erect a temple dedicated to the emperor, granted by Augustus in 29 BC, and the second time for this temple. Among ancient cities, only about forty held this *neokorate* title, but being granted the *neokoros* honor twice was quite rare. (Smyrna was second in Asia Minor, building an imperial temple in AD 26, and Ephesus was third, in AD 89–90.) Worship of the Roman emperors became an increasing social, economic, and religious problem for Christian believers. © 2017 Gerald L. Stevens. All rights reserved.

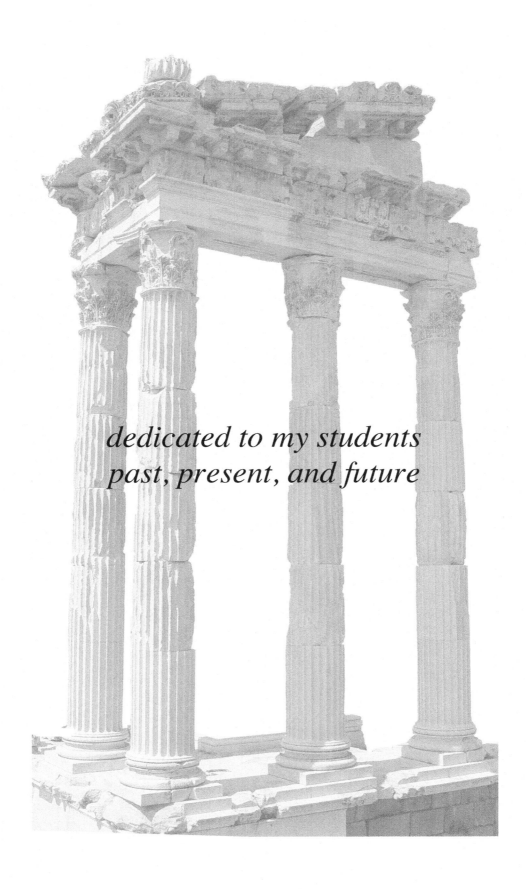

*dedicated to my students
past, present, and future*

CREDITS AND PERMISSIONS

CONTENTS

FIGURES

PREFACE

THIS *WORKBOOK* CONTAINS PROGRAMMED learning material supplementing the Greek grammar presented in the text, *New Testament Greek, Second Edition*, which was incorporated as a module into the Accordance program by OakTree Software.[1] Users of Accordance software brought to the attention of the author the usefulness of a workbook as a companion to the Accordance module both for independent study and as a learning tool for those incorporating Accordance into their classroom activities. This simple idea inspired the present publication.

In this *Workbook,* students have three major responsibilities: (1) vocabulary, (2) paradigms, and (3) exercises. Vocabulary is designed carefully to speed the way into the New Testament text. Frequency lists have been consulted so that students learn words that occur most frequently first. Words are chosen to illustrate grammar being studied. Vocabulary study on iPhones and iPads can access the *NOBTS Vocab* app on the Apple iTunes App Store. This app incorporates two preprogrammed modules that, in essence, work through all the vocabulary of the *New Testament Greek* text Accordance module and this workbook.

Translation exercises, with few exceptions, are taken directly from the Greek New Testament, with occasional, minor adjustments. Students begin translating the text of 1 John toward the later chapters of the grammar. Sentences to translate are chosen with two purposes in mind: (1) to use assigned vocabulary in its native setting in the New Testament, which helps cement the word in memory, and (2) to illustrate the grammar of that chapter.

Since almost all sentences are taken directly from the Greek New Testament, students are exposed to idiomatic expressions. The footnotes try to explain these as they are encountered. Early exposure to idiomatic Greek is crucial to mastering the New Testament language. This way, students are not in shock the moment they leave the sheltered environment of a controlled workbook.

Some lessons are divided into two assignment sets ("Assignment 1" and "Assignment 2"). These assignment sets subdivide the material into logical sections

---

[1]OakTree Software, Inc., 222 S. Westmonte Drive, Suite 211, Altamonte Springs, FL 32714. The Accordance module is entitled "Stevens' NT Greek Grammar," with the short name, "Stevens Greek." Gerald L. Stevens, *New Testament Greek, Second Edition* (Lanham, MD: University Press of America, 1994). All rights of the grammar and its workbook returned to the author in 2007.

for the purpose of taking more time to absorb important morphology paradigms before attempting to work on translation exercises. For example, the first lesson on verbs (Lesson 3), in which students first hit verb inflection, is divided into morphology mastery first (Assignment 1) and then translation (Assignment 2). Likewise, the first lesson on noun inflection (Lesson 4) is subdivided similarly.

Because students are working directly with the Greek text, exercise support is provided by:

κἀγὼ[1] πέμπω ὑμᾶς ["you"] [John 20:21]

[1] Crasis for καὶ ἐγώ, here something on the order of "I also," "Even I."

(1) brackets giving translations for unknown words, (2) brackets in early lessons showing the passages from which the Greek has been taken as a self-monitoring check, and (3) footnotes. For example, a verb may be identified in a note to help stimulate memory, even though a principal part has been covered. Moreover, sentences being translated in one lesson sometimes are selected because they also contain grammar that will be covered in the next lesson. The footnotes anticipate this connection. As students read the notes, they already are getting a preview of these coming attractions. Thus, the footnotes not only reinforce current grammar being studied but also prepare the way for new material.

Grammar tables lay out the paradigms. Paradigms are assigned to memorize, but short cuts are suggested to help. The paradigms are presented in an order that builds upon the others. Sometimes entire paradigms have only one or two differences from a previous one.

The workbook includes an answer key at the back covering the odd-numbered questions in the exercises. The intent is to reinforce right answers and to spur on more study for a missed question. The student should be cautioned to prevent the answer key from becoming a crutch.

A word to the student. Keep in mind a vital principle of learning: *never done, never learned*. Using someone else's answer will torpedo your own boat. *An honest wrong answer is a faster path to understanding than a copied right answer*. If you can, find ways to study together. Some find the group method quite helpful. At the same time, let the exercises be truly yours. Never copy. Remember: never done, never learned. Focus on one day at a time. Every person who crosses the finish line always gets there one step at a time.

Gerald L. Stevens
New Orleans, Louisiana
Easter 2017

LESSON 1

(εἷς)

Writing and Pronouncing Greek

εἷς, *one*,[1] **henotheism** (belief in one god without denying the existence of others; literally, "one god"), **hyphen** (a punctuation mark used to connect the parts of a compound word; literally, "under one")

ἐγώ, *I*, **ego** (the self), **egocentric** (self-centered or selfish), **egoism** (the ethical doctrine that morality has its foundations in self-interest), **egomania** (an obsessive preoccupation with the self), **egotism** (excessive reference to oneself in speaking or writing), cf. Latin *ego*

θεός, *God*, **atheism** (the belief that there is no God; literally, "no god"), **henotheism** (belief in one god without denying the existence of others; literally, "one god"), **monotheism** (belief in only one God; literally, "only god"), **pantheism** (belief that God is the sum of all things; literally, "all is God"), **pantheon** (a temple for all the gods; literally, "all the gods"), **polytheism** (the belief in many gods; literally, "many gods"), **theocracy** (a government of religious leaders claiming to rule by divine authority; literally, "the power of God"), **theodicy** (a vindication of divine justice), **theology** (the study of the nature of God and religious truth; literally, "the study of God"), **theophany** (a divine manifestation; literally, "the appearance of a god"), **Theophilus** (literally, "loved of God"), **theotokos** (a theological term for Mary, the mother of Jesus; literally, "God bearer"), cf. Latin *deus*, *dei* (deify, deity)

---

[1]These derivatives, taken from "Derivatives of Commonly-Used Greek Words" compiled by Jeff Cate, have been included to assist the student in learning Greek vocabulary. English words that etymologically are derived from vocabulary words have been given with a short definition and an etymological connection. Not every Greek word in each vocabulary will have an English derivative, of course. Many derivatives actually are from related cognate groups, but these still function to aid vocabulary retention. Definitions and etymologies are based on numerous reference works including: Ernest Klein, *Klein's Comprehensive Etymological Dictionary of the English Language* (New York, Oxford, Amster-dam: Elsevier Scientific Publishing Company, 1971); E. G. Withycombe, *The Oxford Dictionary of English Christian Names*, 2d ed. (Oxford: Clarendon Press, 1950); *The American Heritage Dictionary*, 2d ed. (Boston: Houghton Mifflin Company, 1991); C. T. Onions, ed., *The Oxford Dictionary of English Etymol-ogy* (Oxford: Clarendon Press, 1966); *Webster's New World Dictionary*; and Frederic M. Wheelock, *Latin*, 3d ed. (New York: Barnes & Noble Books, 1963).

Greek Letters   (Aα-Mμ)

A alpha

α (iota subscript) α

B beta

β

Γ gamma

γ

Δ delta

δ

E epsilon

ϵ

Z zeta

ζ

H eta

η (iota subscript) η

Θ theta

θ

I iota

ι

K kappa

κ

Λ lambda

λ

M mu

μ

Greek Letters   (Νν-Ωω)

N nu

ν

Ξ xi

ξ

O omicron

ο

Π pi

π

P rho

ρ

Σ sigma

σ

(final sigma)

ς

T tau

τ

Υ upsilon

υ

Φ phi

φ

Χ chi

χ

Ψ psi

ψ

Ω omega

ω

(iota subscript)
ῳ

breathing (rough)
ῥ
(smooth)
ἰ

OBJECTIVE QUESTIONS

1. Identify the diphthongs by type of opening vowel:

alpha (α)	omicron (o)	epsilon (ε)	upsilon (υ)	rare	improper

2. The short vowels are _____, _____, and, when final, _____ and _____.

3. The long vowels are _____, _____, and all _____.

4. The variable vowels are _____, _____, and _____.

5. Specify with the equivalent English letters how to pronounce:

$$\gamma\gamma = \_\_\_\_\_, \gamma\kappa = \_\_\_\_\_, \gamma\xi = \_\_\_\_\_, \gamma\chi = \_\_\_\_\_$$

6. Capital letters are referred to as _____ or _____.

7. Small letters are referred to as _____.

8. _____ _____ is an ancient writing style using all capital letters, no word divisions, and no accents or punctuation.

9. Earlier New Testament manuscripts are _____ style; later manuscripts are _____ style.

10. Be ready to name the marks, punctuation, or accents in the following lines:

ἵνα ὁ λόγος Ἠσαΐου τοῦ προφήτου
πληρωθῇ ὃν εἶπεν· κύριε, τίς ἐπίστευσεν
τῇ ἀκοῇ ἡμῶν; καὶ ὁ βραχίων κυρίου τίνι
ἀπεκαλύφθη;

11. κἀγώ This word is a merger of the two words καί and ἐγώ; this process is called _____; the mark over the alpha (α) is called a _____.

12. ἐπ᾽ αὐτόν The first word actually is spelled ἐπί; the vowel iota is dropped in a process called _____, and an apostrophe after the pi (π᾽) indicates this missing letter. The first mark over the epsilon (ἐ) looks the same, but this actually is the mark indicating _____ _____.

13. Quotations in Greek are indicated two ways:

   A. _____

   B. _____

14. Define *literary* Hellenistic Greek: _____

   _____

15. Define *non-literary* Hellenistic Greek: _____

   _____

16. Check the type of Greek represented in the New Testament:

   ☐ Literary   ☐ Non-literary

17. _____ is the scholar associated with the discovery of the nature of the Greek in the New Testament documents.

18. Check the approximate time of this discovery, that is, the beginning of the:

   ☐ 1700's   ☐ 1800's   ☐ 1900's

19. Check the kind of major scholarly output that resulted from this discovery:

   ☐ lexicons   ☐ systematic theologies   ☐ philosophy

20. Convert the following transliteration back into Greek. Do not worry about accent marks, but *include* breathing marks. After you are finished, use Col. 2:20–23 (UBS[5], 669–70) to check your work. Mark carefully what you missed, but try to figure out why.

2.20 Ei apethanete syn Christōi apo tōn stoicheiōn tou

———————————————————————————————

kosmou ti hōs zōntes en kosmōi dogmatizesthe?

———————————————————————————————

2.21 Mē hapsēi mēde geusēi mēde thigēis, 2.22 ha estin

———————————————————————————————

panta eis phthoran tēi apochrēsei, kata ta entalmata kai

———————————————————————————————

didaskalias tēn anthrōpōn, 2.23 hatina estin logon men

———————————————————————————————

echonta sophias en ethelothrēskiāi kai tapeinophrosynēi

———————————————————————————————

[kai] apheidiāi sōmatos, ouk en timēi tini pros

———————————————————————————————

plēsmonēn tēs sarkos.

———————————————————————————————

21. Convert the following from Greek into English transliteration. Do not worry about accent marks or elision (like apostrophe), but do note rough breathing. After you are finished, turn to the last page of this lesson to check your work. Mark mistakes and observe carefully what you missed.

2.13 καὶ ὑμᾶς νεκροὺς ὄντας [ἐν] τοῖς

παραπτώμασιν καὶ τῇ ἀκροβυστίᾳ τῆς

σαρκὸς ὑμῶν, συνεζωοποίησεν ὑμᾶς σὺν

αὐτῷ, χαρισάμενος ἡμῖν πάντα τὰ

παραπτώματα. 2.14 ἐξαλείψας τὸ καθ᾽

ἡμῶν χειρόγραφον τοῖς δόγμασιν ὃ ἦν

22. Circle the number by those Greek letters in each column that when pronounced as *Greek* sounds *sound like* the English word at the top of the column:

buyer	pouting	cave	fool	tweed
1. γυφεη	1. ρουτιην	1. χειφ	1. φωλ	1. τυιδ
2. γυιεη	2. ρουτιηγ	2. χεφε	2. φουλ	2. τοιεδ
3. βαιερ	3. πουτιην	3. κενε	3. ξευλ	3. τωεεδ
4. βυηρ	4. παυτιγγ	4. κανε	4. ξωλ	4. τωεεζ

23. Be prepared to read aloud the text in question 21 above in class.

(Answer to Question #21—Transliteration)

2.13 kai hymas[1] nekrous[2] ontas [en] tois paraptōmasin kai tēi[3] akrobystiāi tēs sarkos hymōn, synezōopoiēsen hymas syn autōi charisamenos[4] hēmin panta ta paraptōmata 2.14 exaleipsas to kath' hēmōn cheirographon tois dogmasin ho ēn

BONUS (Transliteration):

ἐνέγκαι = _____

Ἰακώβ = _____

---

[1] Upsilon by itself is "y"; see *NTG*, 3 n. 9.
[2] Upsilon in combination with another vowel (i.e., diphthongs) is "u"; see *NTG*, 3 n. 9.
[3] Long vowels with iota subscript require a stroke over vowel, then "i"; see *NTG*, 3 n. 4.
[4] Remember: some Greek letters require two English letters, so χ is "ch"; cf. φ = ph, ψ = ps.

LESSON 2
(δύο)
Consonants, Syllables, and Accents

δύο, *two*, **duet** (a musical composition for two people), **duo** (a pair or a couple), **dyad** (two units regarded as a pair), **dyothelitism** (the theological doctrine that in Christ there were two wills, both human and divine; literally, "two wills"), cf. Latin *duo*

ἄνθρωπος, *man*, **anthropocentric** (regarding humankind as the central fact or final aim of the universe), **anthropology** (the study of humankind), **anthropogenesis** (the scientific study of the origin of humankind; literally, "the beginning of man"), **anthropoid** (resembling humans, such as apes), **anthropomorphic** (ascribing human features to a non-human object or being; literally, "the form of man"), **anthropophagus** (a cannibal or an eater of human flesh; literally, "human eater"), **misanthrope** (a person who hates or mistrusts people; literally, "human hater"), **philanthropy** (a desire to help humankind; literally, "human lover")

λόγος, *word*, **alogi** (early opponents of the Logos doctrine in the Johannine literature; literally, "without the Logos"), **alogia** (inability to speak; literally, "without words"), **analogy** (a correspondence between subjects otherwise dissimilar), **apologetics** (the branch of theology which deals with the defense and proof of Christianity), **biology** (the science of living organisms and life processes; literally, "the study of life"), **decalogue** (the Ten Commandments; literally, "the ten words"), **dialogue** (a conversation between two persons; literally, "words between"), **epilogue** (a short addition to the conclusion of a literary or dramatic work), **logic** (the science of correct reasoning), **monologue** (a long speech given by only one person; literally, "the only word"), **syllogism** (a form of deductive reasoning consisting of a major premise, a minor premise, and a conclusion), **trilogy** (a group of three dramatic or literary works related in subject or theme)

ἀκούω, *I hear*, **acoumeter** (an instrument for measuring hearing), **acoustics** (pertaining to sound or hearing)

γράφω, *I write*, **agrapha** (sayings of Jesus not recorded in the gospels; literally, "unwritten things"), **autograph** (a person's own signature or handwriting; literally, "self written"), **bibliography** (a list of books), **biography** (a written account of a person's life; literally, "life writing"), **calligraphy** (the art of fine handwriting; literally, "beautiful writing"), **chronograph** (the recording of time intervals; literally, "time writing"), **epigraph** (an inscription, as on a statute or building), **geography** (the study of the earth and its features), **graph** (a drawing that exhibits a numerical relationship), **graphic** (pertaining to written representation), **graphite** (the allotrope of carbon used in lead pencils), **Hagiographa** (the third of three divisions of the Old Testament; literally, "the sacred writings"), **lithography** (a printing process which uses a large flat surface; literally, "stone writing"), **opistograph** (an ancient document written on both the front and back sides; literally, "writing behind"), **paragraph** (a division in a writing which expresses a complete thought. Originally, a mark was placed in the margin *beside* the new section), **phonograph** (a device which reproduces sound from a record; literally, "sound writing"), **photograph** (an image or picture recorded on a light-sensitive surface; literally, "light writing"), **pornography** (sexually explicit writings or pictures; literally, "immoral writings"), **pseudepigrapha** (spurious writings falsely attributed to an important person; literally, "falsely ascribed"), **seismograph** (an instrument used to record earthquake measurements; literally, "earthquake writings"), **topography** (the graphical representation of the physical features of a region; literally, "place writing")

λέγω, *I say*, **dialect** (a certain form of a spoken language; literally, "to speak across or through"), **hapax legomenon** (a word which only occurs one time in the Greek New Testament; literally, "spoken once"), **lecture** (a spoken exposition of a given subject for instructional purposes), **legend** (an unverified popular story handed down from earlier times), **prolegomenon** (a critical introduction; literally, "to say beforehand")

λύω, *I loose*, **analysis** (the separation of a subject into its constituent parts for study), **catalyst** (a substance which increases the rate of a chemical reaction without being consumed in the process), **electrolysis** (a chemical change produced by an electric current), **Hippolytus** (literally, "letting horses loose"), **litholysis** (treatment for a kidney stone; literally, "to break up stones"), **paralysis** (loss or impairment of the movement of a part of the body)

OBJECTIVE QUESTIONS

1. List the *liquid* consonants: _____, _____, _____, _____.

2. Circle the liquids in the following line:

    ἑωράκαμεν τοῖς ὀφθαλμοῖς ἡμῶν

3. List the *labial* stops: _____, _____, _____.

4. Circle the labial stops in the following line:

    ἡμεῖς οὖν ὀφείλομεν ὑπολαμβάνειν

5. List the *palatal* stops: _____, _____, _____.

6. Circle the palatal stops in the following line:

    χρῖσμα ἔχετε ἀπὸ τοῦ ἁγίου καὶ

7. List the *dental* stops: _____, _____, _____.

8. Circle the dental stops in the following line:

    τῷ σκότει περιπατῶμεν, ψευδόμεθὰ

9. List the *sibilant* consonants: _____, _____, _____, _____.

10. Circle the sibilants in the following line:

    ποιήσεις προπέμψας ἀξίως τοῦ

11. Divide the following words into syllables. Specify the main syllable principle illustrated by each word. (More than one principle can be

illustrated, but what one *main* principle does each word best illustrate to you?)

Word	Division	Principle
τέσσαρες		
θνῄσκω		
βλέπω		
εἰμί		
στίγμα		
ἀκούω		
διϋλίζω		
γνῶσις		
Λύστρα		
ὄρθριος		
ἐκλύω (compound)		
ἐχθρός		

12. The names of the three last syllables of a Greek word are _____, _____, and _____.

13. Syllable quantity is the length of the _____ or _____ in that syllable.

14. The circumflex accent is limited to _____ syllables only and cannot stand over the _____ syllable.

15. The grave accent position is found only on the _____ syllable and can sustain a maximum of only one syllable of _____ quantity.

16. The antepenult cannot be accented if the ultima is _____.

17. If the ultima is short, a long penult, if accented, will have _____ accent.

18. The accented antepenult always will receive the _____ accent.

19. Noun accents are said to be _____, that is to say that _____
    _____

20. Verb accents are said to be _____, that is to say that _____
    _____

21. Specify the accent for the following verb forms:

21.1 ἀκουωσιν*   ἀκουετε   ἀκουετω

21.2 βλεπομεν   βλεπει   βλεπομενη

21.3 λεγωμεν   λεγομενοι   λεγομενοις
    *Consider the iota short.

22. Write the correct accent for the following noun forms of ἄνθρωπος, λόγος,
    and κύριος.

22.1 ἀνθρωποι   ἀνθρωπου   ἀνθρωπον

22.2 λογοι   λογοις   λογῳ

22.3 κυριοι   κυριου   κυριον

23. Specify what is wrong with the following accents:

    23.1 γραφόμεν   _____
    23.2 βλῖπουσιν   _____
    23.3 λὲγει   _____
    23.4 ἄκουσει   _____
    23.5 λῖγεις   _____
    23.6 ἀνθρῶπου   _____
    23.7 ἀνθρώπον   _____

23.8 κυριοῖς   _____

23.9 κύριου   _____

23.10 λογοῦς   _____

LESSON 3

(τρεῖς)

Present Active Indicative

Vocabulary 3

τρεῖς, *three*, **triad** (a group of three), **triangle** (a figure with three sides and three angles; literally, "three angles"), **trigonometry** (the mathematical study of triangles; literally, "the measurement of triangles"), **trio** (a musical composition for three), **tripod** (a three-legged stand; literally, "three feet"), cf. Latin *tres, tria* (trident, triumvirate, trivia)

ἄγγελος, *angel*; **angel** (a heavenly messenger), **evangelist** (a messenger of good news, particularly the Christian gospel)

ἀδελφός, *brother*, **Philadelphia** (literally, "brotherly love")

ἀπόστολος, *apostle*, **apostle** (a missionary of the early church; literally, "one sent out"), **apostolic** (having to do with the Apostles)

οἶκος, *house*, **ecocide** (the destruction of an environment; literally, "house killer"), **ecology** (the science of the relationships between organisms and their environment), **economy** (the management of the resources of a community; literally, "household law"), **ecosystem** (an ecological community with its environment, considered as a unit), **ecumenical** (universal or worldwide in range)

γινώσκω, *I know*, **agnostic** (someone who believes that God's existence cannot be known), **diagnosis** (a critical analysis of the nature of something; literally, "to know through"), **gnomic** (characterized by brief statements of truth), **Gnosticism** (the early Christian sect which centered on spiritual knowledge), **physiognomy** (the face or countenance as an index to character; literally, "physically known"), **prognosis** (a prediction or a forecast; literally, "to know beforehand")

διδάσκω, *I teach*, **didactic** (intended to teach or instruct), **Didache** (an early Christian writing among the Apostolic Fathers; literally, "The Teaching of the Twelve Apostles")

ἔχω, *I have*, **epoch** (a particular period of history; literally, "to hold upon")

λαμβάνω, *I take*, *receive*, **analeptic** (restorative or stimulating, especially of a medicine; literally, "to take up"), **epilepsy** (a disorder characterized by attacks of seizures; literally, "to take or seize upon"), **syllable** (a single uninterrupted sound of a spoken language; literally, "to take together")

INDICATIVE TENSES

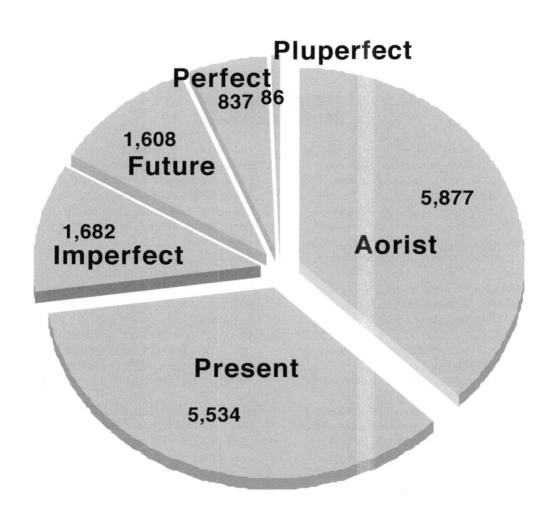

ASSIGNMENT
1

OBJECTIVE QUESTIONS

1. Greek verbs have _____ (how many?) principal parts that are determined by the formation of tense _____.

2. The "first principal part" has two tenses, _____ and _____.

3. "Thematic verbs" have a _____ _____ before the ending.

4. The equation for a Greek verb is tense = time + _____.

5. The present tense is _____ kind of action.

6. Action that has on-going results or consequences is called _____ action.

7. _____ indicates the relationship of a verb's subject to the verb's action.

8. English has no counterpart to the Greek _____ voice.

9. The verb _____ has no voice component.

10. The _____ voice is the subject receiving the action.

11. Mood expresses degree of _____ and _____ of action.

12. The _____ mood indicates that the reality of the statement is assumed to be true. The negative used is _____.

13. Primary tenses involve _____ and _____ time.

14. Primary tenses take _____ endings. Secondary tenses take _____ endings.

15. Define "inflection": _____

16. Endings showing person and number are called _____ _____.

17. What is obscured in the primary active endings? _____
_____

18. The letter nu (ν) on the end of 3d person plural is called _____ ____,
which smooths pronunciation when the next word begins with a
_____ (what type of letter).

19. _____ stems result from adding a prefix, infix, or suffix to verb
stems.

20. The thematic vowel pattern is: ____, ____, ____ (sg.) and ____, ____, ____
(pl.).

21. To form the primary active indicative, take the present tense stem, add the
appropriate thematic vowel, and then the _____ _____.

22. Give primary active indicative endings and equivalent meanings:

Number	Person	Form	Translation
singular	1st		
	2nd		
	3rd		
plural	1st		
	2nd		
	3rd		

23. Complete the following conjugations—present, active, indicative:

ἀκούω	
Form	Translation

λέγω	
Form	Translation

βλέπω	
Form	Translation

ἔχω	
Form	Translation

24. Define "conjugate": _____

_____

25. To "locate" a verb, what do you specify? _____

_____

26. Locate the following:

ἔχουσιν

Tense	Voice	Mood	Person	Number	Lexical

λαμβάνεις

Tense	Voice	Mood	Person	Number	Lexical

ASSIGNMENT
2

TRANSLATION

27. Translate the following:

27.1 ἀκούουσιν = _____   27.7 διδάσκει = _____

27.2 βλέπει   = _____   27.8 ἔχουσιν = _____

27.3 γράφετε   = _____   27.9 λαμβάνεις = _____

27.4 λέγεις   = _____   27.10 ἀκούετε = _____

27.5 λύομεν   = _____   27.11 βλέπω   = _____

27.6 γινώσκω   = _____   27.12 γράφομεν = _____

28. Translate the following, using the translation aids provided below:

○   *Translation Aids*   ○

ὁ, Greek article, *the*, but not translated when used with God

-ος, -οι, noun endings for the subject; the first is singular, the second plural

τόν, *the*, another form of the Greek article, used with the noun that is direct object

-ον, noun ending for the word that is direct object

ἡμῶν, *us*, first personal pronoun, in this context translated "our"

Τιμόθεον, *Timothy*

-α, noun ending for the word that is subject or direct object; here, the direct object

πατέρα, *father*; direct object

ὀρθῶς, *correctly*, *right*; adverb here used with the compound verbs; think of our word "orthodontist," a person who corrects abnormally positioned teeth

πρόσωπον, *face*; direct object, but the word is part of an idiom in Greek; read the footnote provided

28.1   ὁ θεός βλέπει

_____

28.2 ἀδελφός καὶ ἀπόστολος διδάσκουσιν

28.3 λαμβάνετε καὶ διδάσκετε

28.4 τρεῖς οἶκοι καὶ δύο ἄγγελοι

28.5 πέμπεις καὶ γινώσκομεν

28.6 ἀκούουσιν τὸν λόγον [Mark 4:20]

28.7 Γινώσκετε τὸν ἀδελφὸν ἡμῶν Τιμόθεον [Heb. 13:23]

28.8 τὸν πατέρα καὶ τὸν υἱὸν ἔχει [2 John 9]

28.9 ὀρθῶς λέγεις καὶ διδάσκεις καὶ οὐ λαμβάνεις πρόσωπον[1] [Luke 20:21]

29. Diagram the following three sentences from the translation exercises in the space provided:

29.1 ὁ θεός πέμπει.

---

[1]Literally, "receive face": an idiomatic expression about showing partiality; notice the negative οὐ. English custom is to use the auxiliary verbs "do" or "did" in front of the negative. Be able to locate λαμβάνεις. To understand the problem of idioms, read the Appendix, "On the Art of Translation," *NTG*, 373–76.

29.2 ἀδελφός καὶ ἀπόστολος διδάσκουσιν.

29.3 λαμβάνετε καὶ διδάσκετε.

LESSON 4

(τέσσαρες)

Second Declension

τέσσαρες, *four*, **Diatessaron** (Tatian's harmony of the four gospels; literally, "through four"), **tetragon** (a four-sided polygon; literally, "four angles"), **Tetragrammaton** (the four Hebrew letters usually transliterated as YHWH which are used as a proper name for God; literally, "four letters"), **tetrahedron** (a solid figure with four triangular faces; literally, "four bases"), **tetrarch** (a governor of one of the four divisions of a country, especially in the Roman Empire; literally, "four rulers")

γάμος, *marriage*, **bigamy** (being married to two persons; literally, "two marriages"), **gamete** (a sex cell which combines with another sex cell to produce a new organism), **misogamy** (hatred of marriage; literally, "marriage-hate"), **monogamy** (being married to only one person; literally, "only marriage"), **polygamy** (being married to more than one person at the same time; literally, "many marriages")

θάνατος, *death*, **Athanasius** (Greek patriarch of Alexandria; literally, "deathless"), **euthanasia** (killing or allowing a person to die for merciful reasons; literally, "good death"), **thanatopsis** (meditation upon death; literally, "seeing death"), **Thanatos** (death as a personification or as a philosophical notion)

κόσμος, *world*, **cosmic** (pertaining to the universe), **cosmogony** (the study of the evolution of the universe; literally, "world creation"), **cosmology** (the study of the universe), **cosmonaut** (an astronaut, especially one from the former Soviet Union; literally, "world sailor"),

cosmopolitan (common to the whole world; literally, "world citizen"), **cosmorama** (an exhibition of scenes from all over the world; literally, "world view"), **cosmos** (the universe as an orderly, harmonious whole), **microcosm** (a diminutive system representative of a larger system; literally, "small world")

νόμος, *law*, **agronomy** (soil and plant management), **antinomian** (a Christian sect that emphasized faith without the law; literally, "against the law"), **autonomous** (self-governing or self-ruling; literally, "self law"), **Deuteronomy** (the Old Testament book which contains the second giving of the Mosaic law; literally, "second law"), **economy** (the management of the resources of a community; literally, "household law"), **gastronomy** (the management of good eating; literally, "stomach law"), **taxonomy** (the science and principles of classification; literally, "arrangement law")

οὐρανός, *heaven*, **Uranium** (a heavy, radioactive element; literally, "heavenly"), **uranography** (the scientific study of celestial bodies; literally, "writing the heavens"), **Uranus** (the seventh planet rotating around the sun; literally, "heavenly")

υἱός, *son*, Mark Antony made a pun regarding the well-known brutality of Herod the Great: "It is better to be his pig (ὕς) than his son (υἱός)."

Χριστός, *Christ*, **Christ** (the English transliteration of the Greek word *christos* which was used for the Hebrew word *Messiah* meaning "anointed one"),

Christology (the study of Christ's person and qualities), cf. χρίω ("to anoint"; hence, "christen")

δῶρον, *gift*, **Dorothy** (or Dorothea; literally, "gift of God"), **Pandora** (in Greek mythology, the first mortal woman who opened a box releasing all evil into the world; literally, "all giving"), **Theodore** (literally, "God's gift")

ἔργον, *work*, **allergy** (an adverse reaction to a substance; literally, "other work"), **energy** (power for work), **erg** (a measurable unit of energy or work), **ergonomics** (the study of workers), **George** (literally, "earth worker"), **metallurgy** (the science of metal working), **synergism** (the action of two or more subjects which achieve an effect of which each is individually incapable; literally, "work together"), **thaumaturge** (a performer of miracles or magic feats; literally, "miracle worker")

εὐαγγέλιον, *gospel, good news*, **evangelism** (the process of proclaiming the gospel), **evangelist** (a proclaimer of the gospel), **evangelize** (to proclaim the gospel)

ἱερόν, *temple*, **hierophant** (an interpreter of sacred mysteries; literally, "a revealer of sacred things"), **Hierapolis** (an ancient city of Asia Minor; literally, "sacred city"), **hierarchy** (a body of persons organized according to rank of authority; literally, "priestly rule"), **hieroglyphics** (a pictorial system of writing in ancient Egypt; literally, "sacred carvings"), **Jerome** (or Hieronymos [Ἱερώνυμος]; the biblical scholar of the fourth to fifth centuries; literally, "sacred name")

πρόσωπον, *face*, **prosopography** (a description of a person's appearance or character; literally, "face writing")

τέκνον, *child*, **theotokos** (a theological term for Mary, the mother of Jesus; literally, "God bearer")

ἄγω, *I lead*, **demagogue** (a person who stirs up people to gain power; literally, "a people leader"), **pedagogue** (a school teacher or educator; literally, "child leader"), **stratagem** (a military maneuver designed to surprise an enemy; literally, "to lead an army"), **synagogue** (a building for Jewish gatherings; literally, "assembly" or "to lead together"; cf. σύν + ἄγω), cf. Latin *ago* (agenda, agent, agile, agitate)

βαπτίζω, *I baptize*, **baptism** (the Christian sacrament or ordinance involving immersion into or sprinkling of water), **Baptists** (the Protestant denomination which emphasizes the ordinance of baptism)

εὑρίσκω, *I find*, **eureka** (an exclamation of triumph or discovery; literally, "I found it"; Archimedes supposedly exclaimed *eureka* when he discovered how to measure the volume of an irregular solid and thereby determine the purity of a gold object), **heuristic** (pertaining to an educational method in which the student learns by discovery)

κηρύσσω, *I preach*, **kerygma** (the theological term for the message proclaimed by the early church)

NOUNS

Vocative 634

Dative 4,381

Accusative 8,825

Genitive 7,686

Nominative 7,787

ASSIGNMENT
1

OBJECTIVE QUESTIONS

1. English meaning is determined in two basic ways, _____
    _____ and _____. In contrast, Greek meaning is
    determined by _____.

2. English *sometimes* shows inflection to indicate gender, number, and case:

    2.1 **Gender**. To distinguish feminine from masculine, one might add
        suffixes, such as -*ess*, as in host to _____, or -*ine*, as in hero
        to _____. One might change the word, as in man to
        _____. Or, one might make a compound form, as manservant
        to _____.

    2.2 **Number**. For example, one might add -*s*, -*es*, convert *f* to *v* before -*es*,
        -*en*, -*y* after vowel just -*s*, -*y* after consonant convert to -*ies*, change the
        vowel, or make no change at all. Provide the English plural forms for
        the following:

Singular	*Plural*	*Singular*	*Plural*
book	_____	mouse	_____
church	_____	piano	_____
wife	_____	hero	_____
ox	_____	key	_____
man	_____	sky	_____
goose	_____	sheep	_____

    2.3 **Case.** Provide English case forms for the following nouns or pronouns
        ("student," "I," "he," "she"), observing inflection (or lack thereof):

	Singular	*Plural*	*Singular*	*Plural*
Nominative	**student**		**I**	
Possessive				
Objective				

	Singular	*Plural*	*Singular*	*Plural*
Nominative	he		she	
Possessive				
Objective				

2.4   **Observation**. Notice: whenever an English word is *not* inflected (e.g., nouns), word order is crucial to the meaning: (1) John hit the *ball*. (2) The *ball* hit John. Yet, whenever an English word *is* inflected (e.g., pronouns), word order is not crucial to meaning: (1) I hit *him*! (2) *Him*, I hit! Thus, because Greek is so highly inflected, word order is not crucial to meaning.

3.   Fill in the following table clarifying *Greek* case and function:

Case	Function	Relationship

4.   A verb can have two accusatives, a situation referred to as a _____ accusative or an _____ complement.

5.   True or False

_____   1.   Gender must be memorized as part of vocabulary.

_____   2.   The Greek article is not always a good guide to the gender of a word.

_____   3.   All nouns with the lexical ending -ος are masculine.

_____   4.   Any noun whose lexical ending is -ον is neuter.

_____   5.   If the second item in a dictionary entry is "-ος," the noun is second declension.

_____   6. If the third item in a dictionary entry is "τό," the noun is neuter
gender.

6. Add correct second declension endings to these noun stems, with accent:

νόμος		
Case	Singular	Plural
N	νομ	νομ
G	νομ	νομ
D	νομ	νομ
A	νομ	νομ
V	νομ	νομ

ἀδελφός		
Case	Singular	Plural
N	ἀδελφ	ἀδελφ
G	ἀδελφ	ἀδελφ
D	ἀδελφ	ἀδελφ
A	ἀδελφ	ἀδελφ
V	ἀδελφ	ἀδελφ

7. Add correct second declension endings to these noun stems, with accent:

τέκνον		
Case	Singular	Plural
N	τεκν	τεκν
G	τεκν	τεκν
D	τεκν	τεκν
A	τεκν	τεκν
V	τεκν	τεκν

ἱερόν		
Case	Singular	Plural
N	ἱερ	ἱερ
G	ἱερ	ἱερ
D	ἱερ	ἱερ
A	ἱερ	ἱερ
V	ἱερ	ἱερ

8. A word with no accent of its own that "leans forward" in accent (as if the
first syllable of the following word) is called a _____. The two
forms of the masculine article that illustrate this principle are _____ and
_____.

9. Oxytones have an acute accent in the _____ (what syllable?).

10. One principle of oxytone accent is that the _____ cases take the
circumflex accent on the _____.

11. The basic function of the Greek article is to _____.

12. The _____ construction means "with the article." The _____ construction means "without the article."

13. True or False

    _____ 1. Every article in the Greek text must be translated.

    _____ 2. The article always is right next to its associated noun.

    _____ 3. The article belongs to the masculine declension only.

    _____ 4. The Greek article always must be present in the Greek text to be used in translation.

14. Concord is agreement in _____, _____, and _____.

15. Supply the correct article form with accent, then translate:

Case	Form	Translation
N	ἔργον	
G	ἔργου	
D	ἔργῳ	
A	ἔργον	
V	ἔργον	

16. The _____ (gender) plural can take a *singular* verb.

17. Noun accent is _____ (tries to stay in the syllable of the lexical form).

18. Correctly accent the following forms of θάνατος and δοῦλος:

18.1 θανατος θανατοι   18.2 δουλος δουλοι

      θανατου θανατων   δουλου δουλων

      θανατῳ   θανατοις   δουλῳ   δουλοις

      θανατον θανατους   δουλον δουλους

19. Locate the following:

ἀγγέλοις

Case	Gender	Number	Lexical	Meaning
↓	↓	↓	↓	↓

ἀποστόλων

Case	Gender	Number	Lexical	Meaning
↓	↓	↓	↓	↓

δῶρα

Case	Gender	Number	Lexical	Meaning
↓	↓	↓	↓	↓

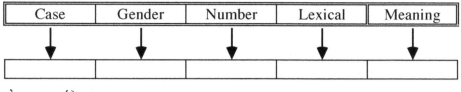

ASSIGNMENT 2

TRANSLATION

20. Translate the following words, noting inflection:

1. κηρύσσομεν _____
2. σῴζει _____
3. εὐαγγελίου _____
4. κόσμῳ _____
5. εὑρίσκετε _____
6. ἀνθρώπους _____
7. θανάτου _____
8. ἐργῶν _____
9. πιστεύεις; _____
10. ἄγει _____
11. οὐρανῶν* _____
12. δούλους _____
13. ἱεροῖς _____
14. υἱός _____
15. εὑρίσκουσιν _____
16. πρόσωπον _____
17. λαμβάνεις _____
18. δῶρα _____
19. βαπτίζετε _____
20. πέμπω _____

*Some habitually plural Greek words translate as singular in English.

21. Translate the following, using the translation aids provided below:

○   *Translation Aids* ○

ἀρνίον, τό, *lamb*
κἀγώ, crasis for καὶ ἐγώ, here
    something on the order of "I
    also," "Even I."
ὑμᾶς, *you* (2d pers. pronoun, acc.
    pl.)

Φίλιππον, *Philip* (acc. sg.)
αὐτῷ, *to him* (3d pers. pronoun,
    dat. sg.)
Ἰησοῦς, *Jesus* (nom. sg.)

21.1   οἱ τέσσαρες ἄγγελοι [Rev. 9:15]

21.2   ὁ γάμος τοῦ ἀρνίου

21.3   κἀγὼ πέμπω ὑμᾶς [John 20:21]

21.4   τὸν Χριστὸν κηρύσσουσιν

21.5   καὶ εὑρίσκει Φίλιππον καὶ λέγει αὐτῷ ὁ Ἰησοῦς
       [John 1:43]

21.6   ἀκούει τὰ τέκνα τὸ εὐαγγέλιον.

21.7   οἱ ἀπόστολοι τοῦ κυρίου τῷ οἴκῳ διδάσκουσιν
       ἀδελφούς τὸν λόγον.

---

22. Diagram sentences six and seven above, repeated below:

22.1   ἀκούει τὰ τέκνα τὸ εὐαγγέλιον.
22.2   οἱ ἀπόστολοι τοῦ κυρίου τῷ οἴκῳ διδάσκουσιν ἀδελφούς τὸν λόγον.

FIGURE 1. Bouleuterion at Gortyn. The ancient site of Gortyn on the island of Crete was a prominent city of the southern district of the island even into Roman times. Behind the bouleuterion is a structure enclosing the famous law code of Gortyn.

FIGURE 2. Law Code of Gortyn. The law code of Gortyn is an inscription covering the entire inner, circular wall of a building behind the bouleuterion, running about thirty feet long and five feet high. The content preserves the ancient law code of Gortyn. The law code of Gortyn is written in an ancient form of the Dorian dialect prominent in central Crete, including the famous site of Knossos.

FIGURE 3. Dorian Dialect. The Gortyn inscription documents an important stage in the development of the Greek language before the classical age of Pericles (d. 429 BC). Ancient Greek was written right to left like Hebrew (see comment on an inscription related to king Agamemnon in Pausanias 5.25.9). This Dorian inscription is an example of a transitional period mixing two directions. The lines alternate direction, turning around at the end of one line and continuing the opposite direction on the next line (like an ox plowing rows, hence, called the βουστροφηδόν, *boustrophēdon*, style). Further, right to left lines have mirror reverse letters. By about 500 BC, writing direction had standardized to the left to right direction. Topics in the Gortyn law code include slave ownership disputes, rape and adultery, rights of divorcees and widows, child custody, inheritance, property laws, ransom, mixed marriages, and adoption. Typical of ancient society, social classes are distinguished, so legal rights corresponded directly to social class. The Gortyn law code provides a rare glimpse into the social structure of pre-Hellenistic Greek society.

LESSON 5

(πέντε)

First Declension

πέντε, *five*, **pentagon** (a figure with five sides and five angles; literally, "five angles"), **pentagram** (a five-pointed star usually used in magic), **pentamerous** (having five similar parts; literally, "five parts"), **pentameter** (a line of verse containing five metrical feet), **Pentateuch** (the first five books of the Bible; literally, "five books"), **pentathlon** (an athletic competition consisting of five events)

ἁμαρτία, *sin*, **hamartiology** (the theological study of the doctrine of sin)

βασιλεία, *kingdom*, **Basil** (a Greek church father of the fourth century; literally, "kingly"), **basilica** (a type of a Roman building used as a court or place of assembly later used as churches; literally, "kingly")

ἐκκλησία, *church*, **ecclesia** (the political assembly of citizens of an ancient Greek city-state), **ecclesiastical** (pertaining to the church), **ecclesiology** (the theological study of the doctrine of the church)

ἡμέρα, *day*, **ephemeral** (lasting only one day), **ephemerid** (a mayfly which is a short-lived insect), **ephemeris time** (in astronomy, time based on the rotation of the earth), **hemerocallis** (a day lily)

καρδία, *heart*, **cardiac** (pertaining to the heart), **cardio-pulmonary** (pertaining to the heart and lungs), **cardiogram** (the curve traced by a cardiograph to diagnose heart defects), **cardiology** (the medical study of the diseases and functions of the heart)

ὥρα, *hour*, **horologe** (a timepiece), **horology** (the science or art of measuring time or making timepieces), **horoscope** (the aspect of the planets and stars at the time of a

person's birth), **hour** (one of the 24 parts of the day)

ἀγάπη, *love*, **agapanthus** (a genus of plants which includes the African lily; literally, "flower lover"), **Agape** (the fellowship meal of the early church; literally, "love [feast]")

γραφή, *writing*, *Scripture*, **agrapha** (sayings of Jesus not recorded in the gospels; literally, "unwritten"), **autograph** (a person's own signature or handwriting; literally, "self written"), **bibliography** (a list of books), **biography** (a written account of a person's life; literally, "life writing"), **calligraphy** (the art of fine handwriting; literally, "beautiful writing"), **chirography** (penmanship; literally, "hand writing"), **chronograph** (an instrument that records time intervals; literally, "time writing"), **epigraph** (an inscription, as on a statute or building; literally, "written upon"), **geography** (the study of the earth and its features), **graph** (a drawing that exhibits a numerical relationship), **graphic** (pertaining to written representation), **graphite** (the allotrope of carbon used in lead pencils), **Hagiographa** (the third of three divisions of the Old Testament; literally, "the sacred writings"), **lithography** (a printing process which uses a large flat surface; literally, "stone writing"), **opistograph** (an ancient document written on both the front and back sides; literally, "writing behind"), **paragraph** (a division in a writing which expresses a complete thought. Originally, a mark was placed in the margin *beside* the new section), **phonograph** (a device which reproduces sound from a record; literally, "sound writing"), **photograph** (an image or picture recorded a light-sensitive surface; literally, "light writing"), **pornography** (sexually explicit writings or pictures; literally, "immoral writings"), **pseudepigrapha** (spurious writings falsely attributed to important people; literally, "falsely ascribed"), **seismograph** (an instrument used to record earthquake measurements; literally, "earthquake writings"), **topography** (the graphical representation of the physical features of a region; literally, "place writing")

διδαχή, *teaching*, **Didache** (an early Christian writing among the Apostolic Fathers; literally, "The Teaching of the Twelve Apostles")

εἰρήνη, *peace*, **eirenicon** (a proposal for peace), **Irenaeus** (literally, "peaceful"), **Irene** (literally, "peace"), **irenic** (conciliatory or promoting peace)

ζωή, *life*, **Mesozoic** (the third era of geologic time; literally, "middle of life"), **protozoa** (a one-celled, primitive form of animal life; literally, "first life"), **Zoe** (literally, "life"), **zoo** (a park where animals are kept), **zoology** (the scientific study of animals)

παραβολή, *parable*, **parable** (a simple story to illustrate a lesson or moral; literally, "to throw alongside" or "to compare")

φωνή, *voice* (sound), **euphony** (a pleasant combination of agreeable sounds; literally, "good sound"), **megaphone** (a device used to amplify the voice; literally, "loud sound"), **phoneme** (the smallest unit of speech), **phonetics** (the linguistical study of sounds), **phonics** (the study of sound

and speech), **symphony** (a harmonious combination of musical sounds; literally, "to sound together"), **telephone** (a device that transmits sounds from one location to another; literally, "end sound"), **xylophone** (a wooden musical percussion instrument; literally, "wood sound")

ψυχή, *life*, *soul*, **psyche** (the soul or spirit), **psychiatry** (the medical study and treatment of mental illness; literally, "soul healing"), **psychology** (the science of mental processes and behavior; literally, "study of the soul"), **psychopath** (a person with a personality disorder), **psychosis** (a severe mental disorder), **psychosomatic** (a physical disorder originating in or aggravated by the mind; literally, "mind-body")

γλῶσσα, *tongue*, **epiglottis** (the cartilage that covers the windpipe during swallowing; literally, "upon the tongue"), **glossary** (an explanatory list of difficult terms), **glossolalia** (an uttering of unintelligible sounds; literally, "tongue speaking"), **polyglot** (a speech or writing in several languages; literally, "many tongues")

δόξα, *glory*, **doxology** (a liturgical formula of praise to God; literally, "to speak glory"), **heterodox** (not in agreement with accepted belief; literally, "other opinion"), **orthodox** (in agreement with accepted belief; literally, "correct opinion"), **paradox** (a seemingly contradictory statement that still may be true; literally, "against opinion")

θάλασσα, *sea*, **thalassic** (pertaining to seas or oceans)

OBJECTIVE QUESTIONS

1. First declension nouns have three basic stem types, _____, _____ and _____. Regardless of classification, all plural forms are _____.

2. The basic endings will show some form using either the vowel _____ or _____.

3. Give the endings only of the three basic singular inflection patterns for first declension, and the one plural pattern.

Case	Singulars by Stem Type			Plurals
	-ε, -ι, -ρ	Nom. in -η	Sibilant	
N				
G				
D				
A				

4. Fill in the following table for the feminine article:

Case	ἡ		
	Sing.	Plural	Meaning
N			
G			
D			
A			

5. Without the Greek article's form to help location, the feminine ending that could be confusing occurs with _____ stems in the form of _____, which could be either _____ singular or _____ plural. The Greek article makes the _____ (case) _____ (num.) form distinctive.

6. For the following table, supply the correct article form with accent for the given case, gender, and number, and then the correct inflectional ending pattern according to stem type, with accent, then translate:

Case	Form	Translation
Singular		
N	γλωσσ	
G	γλωσσ	
D	γλωσσ	
A	γλωσσ	
Plural		
N	γλωσσ	
G	γλωσσ	
D	γλωσσ	
A	γλωσσ	

7. Locate the following:

ὥρας

Case	Gender	Number	Lexical	Meaning

ψυχάς

Case	Gender	Number	Lexical	Meaning

ἡμέραν

Case	Gender	Number	Lexical	Meaning

θάλασσαι

Case	Gender	Number	Lexical	Meaning

TRANSLATION

8. Translate the following inflections of vocabulary words. If more than one location is possible, use any valid translation option.

1. γλῶσσα = _____
2. ἀλήθεια = _____
3. ἐντολῶν = _____
4. φωναῖς = _____
5. δόξης = _____
6. ἁμαρτίας = _____
7. διδαχῆς = _____
8. γραφάς = _____
9. εἰρήνη = _____
10. θάλασσαν = _____
11. ὥρας = _____

12. ἐντολή = _____
13. ψυχαῖς = _____
14. παραβολῶν = _____
15. ζωῆς = _____
16. καρδίαι = _____
17. βασιλεία = _____
18. ἀγάπης = _____
19. ἐκκλησίαν = _____
20. ἡμέρας = _____
21. χαρᾷ = _____
22. χαρᾶς* = _____

*Be careful with the accent!

9. Translate the following, using the translation aids provided below:

○ *Translation Aids* ○

εἰμί, *I am*; forms are εἰμί, εἶ, ἐστίν, ἐσμέν, ἐστέ, εἰσίν
φόβος, *fear*
μετά, *with* (used with the genitive of χαρά = genitive of attendant circumstances)
πρῶτον, *first*
λέγετε, a command (imperative mood, but the form is exactly the same as the indicative)

τούτῳ, *this* (demonstrative pronoun in concord with and modifying οἴκῳ)
αὐτοῦ, *his*, modifying ἐντολή (#6); ἐντολῆς (#9)
αἰώνιος, *eternal*, modifying ζωή
ἐν, *in* (#7, #9 twice); *with* (#8)
ἐκ, *from*
αὐτῶν, *their*, modifying καρδίας
βιβλίον, τό, *book*

9.1   Ἐγώ εἰμί ὁ ἄρτος τῆς ζωῆς. [John 6:35]

_____

9.2   φόβος οὐκ ἔστιν ἐν τῇ ἀγάπῃ

_____

9.3   ἡ ὥρα τῆς δόξης ἐστὶν ἡ ὥρα θανάτου.

_____

9.4   μετά χαρᾶς εὑρίσκομεν εἰρήνην καὶ ζωήν.

_____

9.5   πρῶτον λέγετε, Εἰρήνη τῷ οἴκῳ τούτῳ   [Luke 10:5]

_____

9.6   ἡ ἐντολὴ αὐτοῦ ζωὴ αἰώνιός ἐστιν.

_____

9.7   ἐν ταῖς ἡμέραις τοῦ υἱοῦ τοῦ ἀνθρώπου [Luke 17:26]

_____

9.8   πέμπει ὁ θεός πέντε ἀγγέλους τῆς ἐκκλησίας καὶ
      τὰς ἀληθείας τῆς βασιλείας κηρύσσουσιν ἐν
      παραβολαῖς.

_____

_____

_____

9.9   σῴζει γὰρ ψυχάς ἀνθρώπων ὁ υἱος τοῦ ἀνθρώπου
      ἐκ ἁμαρτίας ἐν ταῖς καρδίαις αὐτῶν καὶ
      γράφουσιν τὰς διδαχὰς τῆς ἐντολῆς αὐτοῦ ἐν
      βιβλίῳ.

_____

_____

10. Diagram the following:

10.1 σῴζει γὰρ ψυχάς ἀνθρώπων ὁ υἱος τοῦ ἀνθρώπου ἐκ ἁμαρτίας ἐν ταῖς καρδίαις αὐτῶν καὶ γράφουσιν τάς διδαχὰς τῆς ἐντολῆς αὐτοῦ ἐν βιβλίῳ.

FIGURE 4. Alexander Mosaic at Naples. The Alexander Mosaic, about sixteen feet by eight feet and held in the Naples National Archeological Museum, originally decorated a floor in the House of the Faun in Pompeii before its destruction in the eruption of Mount Vesuvius. The mosaic is thought to be based on a third-century BC Hellenistic painting. The war scene depicts Alexander's famous defeat of the Persian general Darius III at the battle of Issus in 333 BC. This victory cleared the way for Alexander to conquer the rest of the known world and engage a program of Hellenization that revolutionized culture, politics, society, and language. His moment in history begins the movement from the classical Greek of the age of Pericles to the Koine Greek of the New Testament.

LESSON 6

(ἕξ)

Adjectives and Εἰμί

Vocabulary 6

ἕξ, *six*, **hexagon** (a figure with six sides and six angles; literally, "six angles"), **hexameter** (a line of verse containing six metrical feet), **Hexapla** (Origen's compilation of the Old Testament which consisted of six Hebrew and Greek texts written side by side), **Hexateuch** (the designation for the first six books of the Bible; literally, "six books"), cf. Latin *sex* (sextet, sextant)

εἰμί, *I am*, **Homoiousion** (a fourth-century, Arian teaching that Jesus the Son and God the Father were of similar but different substance; literally, "similar essence"), **ontogeny** (the development of an individual organism from origin to death), **ontology** (the branch of philosophy that deals with being), **parousia** (the theological term for the second coming of Christ; cf. παρά, + εἰμί), cf. εξουσία

ἀγαθός, *good*, **Agatha** (literally, "good"), **agathism** (the doctrine that all things tend towards good)

ἀγαπητός, *beloved*, **agapanthus** (a genus of plants which includes the African lily; literally, "flower lover"), **Agape** (the fellowship meal of the early church; literally, "love [feast]")

ἄλλος, *other*, **allegory** (a symbolic representation; literally, "speaking the other"), **allergy** (an adverse reaction to a substance; literally, "other work"), **allotropy** (the variation of physical properties without change of substance, e.g., charcoal and diamonds; literally, "other kind")

βασιλικός, *royal*, **Basil** (a Greek church father of the fourth century; literally, "kingly"), **basilica** (a type of Roman building used as a court or place of assembly later used as churches; literally, "kingly")

δίκαιος, *righteous*, **syndicate** (a combination control of a business; literally, "together equals"), **theodicy** (a vindication of divine justice; literally, "justice of the gods")

ἔσχατος, *last*, **eschatology** (the theological study of the end times)

ἕτερος, *another*, **heterodox** (not in agreement with accepted belief; literally, "other opinion"), **heterosexual** (characterized by attraction to the opposite sex)

ἴδιος, *one's own*, **idiom** (an expression peculiar to its own language), **idiosyncrasy** (a behavior characteristic to a particular individual; literally, "one's own mixture together"), **idiot** (a foolish or stupid person; literally, "a person concerned with his own interests")

καινός, *new*, **Cenozoic** (the last era of geological time; literally, "new life")

κακός, *bad*, **cacodyl** (a poisonous oil with an obnoxious smell; literally, "bad odor"), **cacography** (bad handwriting or spelling; literally, "bad writing"), **cacophony** (a jarring, disconcordant sound; literally, "bad sound")

καλός, *good*, **calisthenics** (exercises to develop muscles and well-being; literally, "beautiful strength"), **calligraphy** (the art of fine handwriting; literally, "beautiful writing"), **kaleidoscope** (a tubular instrument that makes changing designs for the eyes; literally, "to see beautiful forms")

μακάριος, *blessed*, **macarize** (to pronounce happy or blessed; literally, "to bless") μικρός, *small*, **microbe** (a minute life form; literally, "small life"), **microbiology** (the study of microorganisms), **microcosm** (a diminutive system representative of a larger system; literally, "small world"), **microscope** (an optical instrument that enlarges images; literally, "to see the small"), **omicron** (the fifteenth letter of the Greek alphabet; literally, "the small O")

νεκρός, *dead*, **necrology** (a list of people who have died), **necromancy** (divination by means of a corpse; literally, "divination of the dead"), **necrophobia** (a morbid fear of death or corpses; literally, "fear of the dead"), **necrophilia** (an obsessive fascination with death or corpses; literally, "to love death"), **necropolis** (a cemetery, especially a large one of an ancient city; literally, "city of the dead"), **necrosis** (the death or decay of tissue in part of a body or plant)

OBJECTIVE QUESTIONS

1. Adjectives are inflected in _____ genders in Greek and show _____ with the noun modified.

2. A majority of adjectives in the New Testament follow first and second declension patterns, with the feminine forms either showing an _____ pure type ending or an _____ pure type in the singular forms. Oxytone patterns show a _____ accent in the interior cases.

3. Adjectives are used three ways: (1) _____, (2) _____, and (3) _____.

4. Explain the following terms:

    "articular adjective":   _____

    "anarthrous adjective":   _____

    An articular adjective is said to be in _____ position. An anarthrous adjective is in _____ position. The _____ position requires a form of the verb "to be."

5. Translate the following adjective uses:

    5.1 ἡ διδαχὴ καλή =   _____

    5.2 ἡ καινὴ καρδία =   _____

    5.3 οἱ ἄγγελοι οἱ κακοί =   _____

    5.4 ὁ ἀγαπητός ὁ υἱός =   _____

    5.5 δίκαια τὰ τέκνα =   _____

6. Define "enclitic":   _____

7. Accent the following enclitic forms and state the rule illustrated by each:

    7.1   ἀγαθος ἐστιν

          Rule # ___ = _____

7.2   δωρα ἐισιν

        Rule # ___ = _____

7.3   δικαιοι ἐισιν

        Rule # ___ = _____

8. Give the present indicative paradigm of the verb εἰμί:

Number	Person	Form	Translation
Singular	1st		
	2nd		
	3rd		
Plural	1st		
	2nd		
	3rd		

9. Locate the following:

πιστούς

Case	Gender	Number	Lexical	Meaning

ἰδίᾳ

Case	Gender	Number	Lexical	Meaning

μικρόν

Case	Gender	Number	Lexical	Meaning

10. Two nominatives with a linking verb means one is the subject of the verb and the other is a _____ _____. A hierarchy of precedence known as "Colwell's Rule" helps to determine which is subject, based on the three levels: (1) _____, (2) _____ _____, and (3) _____.

TRANSLATION

11. Translate the following, using the translation aids provided below:

○ *Translation Aids* ○

μου, *my*; first personal pronoun, translated as possessive, modifying υἱός in #1, τέκνον in #7

ἦν, *was*, imperfect, 3s, of εἰμί
Ἰησοῦς, *Jesus* (nominative)
πρόβατον, τό, *sheep*
ὅς, *who*, relative pronoun

11.1 ὁ υἱός μου νεκρὸς ἦν [Luke 15:24]

_____

11.2 ὁ υἱός ὁ ἔσχατος πιστός ἐστίν

_____

What grammatical function is πιστός? _____

11.3 ὁ λόγος ἐστὶν Ἰησοῦς

_____

What grammatical function is Ἰησοῦς? _____

What level of precedence is illustrated? _____

11.4 ἄλλα πρόβατα ἔχω

_____

11.5 ἔρχεται ὁ πονηρὸς [Matt. 13:19]

_____

11.6 καλὸς ὁ νόμος

_____

11.7 ὅς ἐστίν μου τέκνον ἀγαπητὸν καὶ πιστὸν ἐν κυρίῳ

[1 Cor. 4:17]

_____

11.8 παραβολάς τὰς μακαρίας λέγουσιν οἱ ἔξ δίκαιοι
καὶ πιστοί ἄνθρωποι τῇ ἐκκλησίᾳ τῇ μικρᾷ καὶ
ἀκούομεν τὸ εὐαγγέλιον.

_____

_____

_____

12. Diagram sentence two above, repeated below:

12.1 ὁ υἱός ὁ ἔσχατος πιστός ἐστίν.

LESSON 7

(ἑπτά)

Contract Verbs and Conjunctions

ἑπτά, *seven*, **heptagon** (a figure with seven sides and seven angles; literally, "seven angles"), **heptameter** (a unit of verse consisting of seven feet), **heptarchy** (rule of seven people), **heptathlon** (an athletic competition consisting of seven events), cf. Latin *septem* (September, septuagenarian, Septuagesima, Septuagint)

εὐλογέω, *I bless*, **eulogize** (to praise or commend; literally, "to speak well of"), **eulogy** (a spoken or written tribute; literally, "good word")

θεωρέω, *I observe*, **theorem** (an idea that is demonstrably true), **theory** (an idea based on limited information)

καλέω, *I call*, **ecclesia** (the political assembly of citizens of an ancient Greek city-state, cf. ἐκ + καλέω), **ecclesiastical** (pertaining to the church), **ecclesiology** (the theological study of the doctrine of the church), **Paraclete** (a theological designation for the Holy Spirit, cf. παρά, + καλέω)

λαλέω, *I speak*, **glossolalia** (an uttering of unintelligible sounds; literally, "tongue speaking")

παρακαλέω, *I comfort*, **Paraclete** (a theological designation for the Holy Spirit)

περιπατέω, *I walk*, **peripatetic** (pertaining to walking, such as Aristotle's teaching method of philosophizing while walking)

ποιέω, I do, *make*, **onomatopoeia** (formation of words by making their sounds; literally, "making a name"), **pharmacopoeia** (an official book listing drugs and their formulas; literally, "making drugs"), **poem** (a literary composition; literally, "something that is made")

φιλέω, *I love*, **bibliophile** (one who loves and collects books; literally, "book lover"), **hemophilia** (a disorder characterized by excessive bleeding; literally, "blood lover"), **Philadelphia** (literally, "brotherly love"), **philander** (to engage in casual love affairs; literally, "a loving man"), **philanthropy** (a desire to help humankind; literally, "human lover"), **philharmonic** (devoted to or appreciating music; literally, "harmony loving"), **philhellene** (one who loves Greece or the Greeks; literally, "Greek lover"), **Philip** (literally, "lover of horses"), **philodendron** (a tropical American vine; literally, "loves trees"), **philosophy** (pursuit of wisdom by intellectual means; literally, "the love of wisdom")

πληρόω, *I fulfill*, **pleroma** (in Valentinian Gnosticism, the *pleroma* was the fullness of the spiritual world composed of pairs of aeons; literally, "fullness")

ἀγαπάω, *I love*, **agapanthus** (a genus of plants which includes the African lily; literally, "flower lover"), **Agape** (the fellowship meal of the early church; literally, "love [feast]")

τιμάω, *I honor*, **Timothy** (cf. Τιμόθεος; literally, "honor of God")

OBJECTIVE QUESTIONS

1. The table gives another way to look at contraction results in the present
active indicative, showing six basic results: either ῶ, ᾶ, ᾳ, or the diphthongs
οῖ, εῖ, οῦ. Then, when working with exercise two below, notice: (1) *any*
alpha result is an alpha contract, (2) οῖ is omicron contract *only*, (3) εῖ is
epsilon contract *only*, (4) οῦ is either omicron or epsilon contract.

| Result | Contract | Person | | Contraction |
		Singular	Plural	
ῶ	any	1st		εω, οω, αω
	-α		1st, 3rd	αο, αου ("o" sounds)
ᾶ	-α		2nd	αε ("e" sounds, as also αη)
ᾳ	-α	2nd, 3rd		αει (or any ι form, as also αη)
οῖ	-ο	2nd, 3rd		οει (or any ι form, as also οη)
εῖ	-ε	2nd, 3rd	2nd	εει, εε ("e" sounds)
οῦ	-ο		1st, 2d, 3d	οο, οε, οου (ε or "o" sounds)
	-ε		1st, 3rd	εο, εου ("o" sounds)

2. Specify the original vowels involved prior to contraction and translate:

2.1 εὐλογεῖτε = _____ + _____ = _____

2.2 ἀγαπᾷς =   _____ + _____ = _____

2.3 ζητεῖ =   _____ + _____ = _____

2.4 πληροῦσιν = _____ + _____ = _____

2.5 ἀγαπῶμεν = _____ + _____ = _____

2.6 ἐρωτᾶτε =   _____ + _____ = _____

2.7 ποιεῖς =   _____ + _____ = _____

2.8 πληροῦμεν = _____ + _____ = _____

2.9 σταυρῶ =   _____ + _____ = _____

2.10 γεννᾷ =   _____ + _____ = _____

2.11 καλοῦμεν = _____ + _____ = _____

2.12 δηλοῦτε =   _____ + _____ = _____

2.13 λαλεῖ =   _____ + _____ = _____

2.14 ζῶσιν =   _____ + _____ = _____

2.15 φιλοῦσιν =   _____ + _____ = _____

2.16 ὁμολογῶ =   _____ + _____ = _____

2.17 πληροῖς =   _____ + _____ = _____

2.18 δηλοῖ =   _____ + _____ = _____

2.19 τιμῶ =   _____ + _____ = _____

TRANSLATION

3. Translate the following, using the translation aids provided below:

◯ *Translation Aids* ◯

μου, *my*; 1st per. pronoun, used possessively (literally, "of me"), modifying ψυχήν

Δαυίδ, *David* (nominative)

αὐτόν, *him* (accusative), 3d per. pronoun

σύ, *you*, 2d per. pronoun (nominative)

σέ, *you*, 2d per. pronoun (accusative)

σύν, *with* (preposition)

αὐτῷ, *him* (dative/instr. of association), 3d per. pronoun

λῃστής, ὁ, *thief*, follows inflection pattern of μαθητής (Table 8.2, *NTG*, 85)

οὐκέτι, *no longer* (οὐ, *not* + ἔτι, *still*)

ἐν, *in* (preposition)

ἐμοί, *me*, 1st per. pronoun (dative/loc.)

οὖν, *therefore* (conjunction)

ὑμᾶς, *you*, 2d per. pronoun (accusative)

Ἰησοῦ, *Jesus* (dat., Table 8.10, *NTG*, 91)

Τί, *why?*

με, *me*, 1st per. pronoun, alternate enclitic form (accusative)

ἅ, *the things which*, relative pronoun (acc., neu., pl.)

ἐμέ, *me*, 1st per. pronoun, accented form (accusative); compare με above

περὶ αὐτοῦ, *against it*, preposition and 3d per. pronoun (neuter)

αὐτοῦ, *its*, 3d per. pronoun, used possessively (literally, "of it")

3.1   οὐ τιμᾷ τὸν πατέρα [John 5:23]

_____

3.2   εὐλογοῦμεν τὸν κύριον

_____

3.3   ζητοῦσιν τὴν ψυχήν μου [Rom. 11:3]

_____

3.4   ἀγαπῶμεν τοὺς ἀδελφούς

_____

3.5   Δαυὶδ καλεῖ αὐτὸν κύριον [Matt. 22:45]

_____

3.6   σὺ γινώσκεις ὅτι φιλῶ σε

_____

3.7   τὰς ἐντολὰς αὐτοῦ τηροῦμεν

_____

3.8   σὺν αὐτῷ σταυροῦσιν δύο λῃστάς

_____

3.9   ζῶ δὲ οὐκέτι ἐγώ, ζῇ δὲ ἐν ἐμοὶ Χριστός

_____

3.10   Τί δέ με καλεῖτε, Κύριε κύριε, καὶ οὐ ποιεῖτε ἃ λέγω;

_____

_____

3.11   οὖν, ἀδελφοί, ἐρωτῶμεν ὑμᾶς καὶ παρακαλοῦμεν ἐν κυρίῳ Ἰησοῦ

_____

_____

3.12 ἐμὲ δὲ μισεῖ, ὅτι ἐγὼ μαρτυρῶ περὶ αὐτοῦ ὅτι τὰ
ἔργα αὐτοῦ πονηρά ἐστιν

_____

_____

4. Diagram sentence twelve above, repeated below. Focus on identifying the particular uses of the subordinate clauses.

4.1 ἐμὲ δὲ μισεῖ, ὅτι ἐγὼ μαρτυρῶ περὶ αὐτοῦ ὅτι τὰ ἔργα αὐτοῦ πονηρά ἐστιν

FIGURE 5. Claudius Inscription at Berea. The Archeological Museum of Veroia (Berea) retains in its outer courtyard an important inscription documenting imperial travel in the region. The citizens of Berea in the province of Macedonia honored Claudius Caesar (emperor of Rome from AD 41–54) with an inscription when he visited the area. About that same time, Paul also visited Berea on the second missionary journey (ca. AD 49–52; cf. Acts 17:10–14). The first line of the inscription in the image above identifies the Bereans (ΒΕΡΟΙΑΙΩΝ = Βεροιαιων), and the second line identifies the emperor (ΚΛΑΥΔΙΟΥ ΚΑΙΣΑΡΟ[Σ] = Κλαυδιου Καισαρο[ς], "Claudius Caesar"). The rest of the inscription includes names of the leaders of the city.

LESSON 8

(ὀκτώ)

Gender, Contraction, Adverbs, Comparisons

ὀκτώ, *eight*, **octagon** (a figure with ei̯... sides and eight angles; literally, "eight angles"), **octopus** (a marine creature having eight legs; literally, "eight feet"), cf. Latin *octo* (octave, octavo, octet, October, octogenarian)

ὁδός, *way*, *road*, **anode** (a positively charge electrode; literally, "the way up"; cf. ἀνά, + ὁδός), **cathode** (a negatively charge electrode; literally, "the way down"; cf. κατά + ὁδός), **electrode** (a conductor through which an electric current passes; literally, "an electric path"), **episode** (an incident that is part of a narrative but forms a separate unit; literally, "upon into the way"; cf. ἐπί, + εἰς + ὁδός), **Exodus** (the journey of the Hebrew people out of Egypt; literally, "the journey out"), **method** (a means or manner of procedure; literally, "the way across"; cf. μετά + ὁδός), **odometer** (an instrument used to measure travel; literally, "a journey measure"), **period** (an interval of time; literally, "the way around"; cf. περί + ὁδός), **synod** (a council or assembly of churches; literally, "the way together"; cf. σύν + ὁδός)

ἔρημος, *wilderness*, **eremite** (a religious recluse), **hermit** (a person who has withdrawn from society), **hermitage** (a secluded retreat, e.g., Andrew Jackson's home)

παρθένος, *virgin*, **parthenocarpy** (the production of fruit without fertilization; literally, "virgin fruit"), **parthenogenesis** (reproduction by the development of an unfertilized ovum, seed, or spore; literally, "virgin beginning"), **Parthenon** (the ancient temple of the Greek goddess Athena Parthenos, "Athena the Virgin," on

... .n Athens; literally, "the virgin")

μαθητής, *disciple*, **mathematics** (the science of numbers and their relationships), **polymath** (a person learned in many fields; literally, "much learning")

μεσσίας, *messiah*, **Messiah** (the anticipated deliverer of the Jews), **messianic** (pertaining to the messiah)

προφήτης, *prophet*, **prophet** (a person who speaks by divine inspiration; literally, "to speak before"; cf. πρό + φημί)

γῆ, *earth*, *land*, **apogee** (point in an orbit farthest from the focus; literally, "away from the earth"), **geography** (the study of the earth and its features), **geology** (the scientific study of the earth), **geometry** (mathematics based on points, lines, angles, surfaces, and solids; literally, "earth measure"), **George** (literally, "earth worker"), **geothermal** (pertaining to the internal heat of the earth; literally, "earth heat"), **perigee** (point in an orbit closest to the focus; literally, "near the earth")

συκῆ, *fig tree*, **sycamore** (a certain broad leaf tree; literally, "mulberry fig"), **syconium** (the fleshy fruit of a fig), **sycophant** (a person who attempts to win favor or advance himself by flattering influential people; literally, "to show figs")

μόνος, *only*, *alone*, **monarch** (a sole hereditary ruler; literally, "only ruler"), **monk** (a man who secludes himself to a religious order; literally, "alone"), **monogamy** (being married to only one person; literally, "only marriage"), **monograph** (a book on a single subject; literally, "single writing"), **monolith** (a single large block of stone; literally, "single stone"), **monologue** (a long speech given by only one person; literally, "the only word"), **monorail** (a railway with a single rail serving as track; literally, "single rail"), **monotheism** (belief in only one God; literally, "only god"), **monothelitism** (the theological doctrine that in Christ there was only one will though two natures; literally, "only one will"), **monotone** (speaking words without changing pitch; literally, "only one tone")

νέος, *new*, **misoneism** (hatred of change; literally, "hate the new"), **Neolithic** (the last period of the stone age; literally, "the new stone age"), **Neon** (a gaseous element; literally, "new"), **neo-orthodoxy** (a modern theological movement which seeks to revive adherence to certain doctrines), **neophyte** (a new convert; literally, "a new plant"), **Neoplatonism** (a modified form of Platonism)

σοφός, *wise*, **philosophy** (pursuit of wisdom by intellectual means; literally, "the love of wisdom"), **Sophia** (literally, "wise"), **sophism** (a plausible but fallacious argument), **sophist** (a member of a philosophical school in ancient Greece), **sophisticated** (refinement or complexity), **sophomore** (a second-year student; literally, "a wise fool"), **sophomoric** (immature and overconfident; literally, "foolishly wise")

δικαίως, *justly* (adv.), **syndicate** (a combination control of a business; literally, "together equals"), **theodicy** (a vindication of divine justice; literally, "justice of the gods"), cf. δίκαιος

ἔξω, *outside* (adv.), **exoteric** (pertaining to the outside or external), **exotic** (from another part of the world)

κακῶς, *badly* (adv.), **cacodyl** (a poisonous oil with an obnoxious smell; literally, "bad odor"), **cacography** (bad handwriting or spelling; literally, "bad writing"), **cacophony** (jarring, disconcordant sound; literally, "bad sound"), cf. κακός

καλῶς, *well* (adv.), **calisthenics** (exercises to develop muscles and well-being; literally, "beautiful strength"), **calligraphy** (the art of fine handwriting; literally, "beautiful writing"), **kaleidoscope** (a tubular instrument that makes changing designs for the eyes; literally, "to see beautiful forms"), cf. καλός

πάλιν, *again* (adv.), **palimpsest** (a document which has been erased and rewritten; literally, "to scrape again"), **palindrome** (a word or sentence reading the same backwards and forwards; e.g., "level" or "a man, a plan, a canal, Panama"; literally, "to run again")

ταχέως (ταχύ), *soon* (adv.), **tachometer** (an instrument that measures rotational speed; literally, "speed measure"), **tachycardia** (excessively rapid heartbeat; literally, "swift heart"), **tachygraphy** (rapid writing or shorthand; literally, "fast writing"), **tachypnea** (excessively rapid respiration; literally, "fast breathing")

ADJECTIVE DEGREES

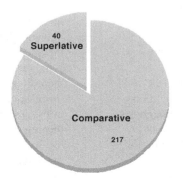

40 Superlative

Comparative 217

■■ OBJECTIVE QUESTIONS ■■

1. Nouns whose nominative singular form ends in _____ or _____ are first declension, but *masculine* in gender. The two paradigm patterns have the following endings (only endings):

Case	Singular	Plural	Singular	Plural
N				
G				
D				
A				

2. Specify the correct form of the Greek article to be in concord with the given noun:

2.1 _____ μεσσίᾳ   2.5 _____ μεσσίαι

2.2 _____ προφήτας   2.6 _____ προφήτης

2.3 _____ Ἰωάννῃ   2.7 _____ μεσσίαν

2.4 _____ μαθηταῖς   2.8 _____ μαθηταί

3. Some second declension nouns ending in _____ actually are *feminine*, so they will take the feminine article in concord.

4. The nouns _____, _____, and _____ are three "α pure" nouns that contract into two basic patterns. The two nouns _____ and _____ show a pattern having the letter _____ throughout. The noun _____ shows a pattern having the letter _____ throughout. Each pattern has a _____ accent betraying the previous contraction.

5. Adverbs can be used as _____, as _____, or as case _____. However, the primary use is as _____ qualifiers adding manner, time, and _____ ideas.

6. Comparisons have three degrees: _____, _____, and _____. The second degree uses the inflected ending _____,

_____, _____ and the third degree uses the inflected ending _____,
_____, _____ .

7. Comparisons are structured three ways in Greek. The first uses the
_____ case function. The second uses the _____ case with
the prepositions _____ and _____. The third simply uses the
conjunction _____ .

8. The genitive of relationship means that the proper name occurring in the
genitive case specifies some _____ or other type relationship that is
decided on the basis of _____ .

▰▰▰ TRANSLATION ▰▰▰

9. Translate the following, using the translation aids provided below:

○ *Translation Aids* ○

Σίμων, *Simon*

με, *me*, 1st per. pronoun,
    alternate enclitic form
    (accusative)

μου, *my*, 1st per. pronoun, used
    possessively (genitive) with
    μαθηταί

εἰς, *into*, preposition (used with
    acc.)

ἀσκούς, *wineskins* (acc., mas.,
    pl.)

πνεῦμα, *Spirit* (nom., neu., sg.)

αὐτόν, *him* (accusative), 3d per.
    pronoun

εἰς, *into* (preposition used with
    acc.)

ἡμῶν, *our*, 1st per. pronoun
    (genitive), used possessively
    modifying σωτηρία; literally,
    "of us"

ἤ, *than* (review Table 8.8, Table
    8.9, *NTG*, 89–90)

ὅτε, *when*

ἐπιστεύσαμεν, *we believed* (past
    tense of πιστεύω)

ἐν, *in*, preposition

μείζων, *greater*

9.1 μόνῳ σοφῷ θεῷ [Rom. 16:27]

_____

9.2 ἀληθῶς μαθηταί μού ἐστε

_____

9.3 Σίμων Ἰωάννου, ἀγαπᾷς με; [John 21:16]

9.4 οὐδὲ οἱ ἄγγελοι τῶν οὐρανῶν οὐδὲ ὁ υἱός

9.5 βάλλουσιν οἶνον νέον εἰς ἀσκοὺς καινούς [Matt. 9:17]

9.6 Καὶ εὐθὺς τὸ πνεῦμα αὐτὸν ἐκβάλλει εἰς τὴν ἔρημον

9.7 νῦν γὰρ ἐγγύτερον ἡμῶν ἡ σωτηρία ἢ ὅτε ἐπιστεύσαμεν [John 21:16]

9.8 ὁ δὲ μικρότερος ἐν τῇ βασιλείᾳ τῶν οὐρανῶν μείζων αὐτοῦ ἐστιν

---

10. Diagram the following two sentences taken from above. Focus on comparison structure and adverbs.

10.1 Καὶ εὐθὺς τὸ πνεῦμα αὐτὸν ἐκβάλλει εἰς τὴν ἔρημον

10.2 ὁ δὲ μικρότερος ἐν τῇ βασιλείᾳ τῶν οὐρανῶν
      μείζων αὐτοῦ ἐστιν

LESSON 9

(ἐννέα)

Prepositions and Compounds

Vocabulary 9

ἐννέα, *nine*, **ennead** (a group or set of nine)

ἀνά, *up*, **Anabasis** (a military advance, such as that of Cyrus the Younger into Asia Minor, as narrated by Xenophon; literally, "to go up"), **anabolic** (something which builds up living tissue; lit., "to throw up"), **analogy** (an affinity between two otherwise unrelated things), **analysis** (an examination of something by studying its component parts; lit., "to break up"), **anatomy** (the biological study of the body; lit., "to cut up" or "to dissect"), **anode** (a positively charge electrode; literally, "the way up"; cf. ἀνά, + ὁδός)

ἀντί, *against*, **anti-** (anything opposed to something else: Antibacterial, antibiotic, Antichrist, anticlimax, antidote, antifreeze, antinomian, anti-Semitism), **antonym** (a word opposite in meaning to another word; lit., "name against"), **antithesis** (direct contrast; literally, "set against")

ἀπό, *away from*, **apodosis** (the clause which states the consequence of a conditional statement; literally, "given back"), **apostasy** (abandoning something formerly believed; literally, "to stand away from"), **apostle** (one who is sent out; literally, "sent out"), **apostrophe** (a sign indicating the omission of letter(s); literally, "to turn away")

διά, *through*, **diabetes** (disease affecting urine passage; literally, "going through"), **diagnosis** (the process of determining the nature of a problem; literally, "known through"), **diagonal** (literally, a line going from angle to angle), **dialogue** (a conversation between two persons; literally, "words between"), **diameter** (the width of a circle; literally, "measure through"), **diaphanous** (being transparently thin; literally, "appears through"), **Diaspora** (the Dispersion of the Jews through the world beginning with the Babylonian captivity; literally, "to scatter through(out)")

εἰς, *into*, **eisegesis** (reading a meaning into a text; literally, "to lead into")

ἐκ, *out of*, **ecstasy** (a state of intense joy; literally, "to drive out of one's senses" or "to stand out"), **exegesis** critical analysis of a text to obtain meaning; literally, "to lead out"), **Exodus** (the journey of the Hebrew people out of Egypt; literally, "the journey out")

ἐν, *in*, **emblem** (an object which functions as a symbol; literally, "to insert" or "to throw in"), **embolism** (the obstruction of a blood vessel by a clot or air bubble; literally, "insertion" or "thrown in"), **embryo** (a fetus or unborn organism; literally, "that which grows in [the body]"), **empathy** (sympathetic understanding of another person; literally, "feeling within"), **emphasis** (speaking with the force of the voice on; literally, "speaking on"), **emporium** (a trading place; literally, "on the road"), **encephalitis** (an inflammation of the brain; literally, "in the head"), **enclitic** (a word which is dependent on the preceeding word; literally, "leaning on"), **encyclical** (something which is circular or general; literally, "in a circle"), **endemic** (something prevalent in a particular group; literally, "in or among the people")

ἐπί, *on, upon*, **epicenter** (the location directly above the center of an earthquake; literally, "on the center"), **epidemic** (a disease which strikes a large portion of a population;

literally, "on the people"), **epidermis** (the outer layer of skin; literally, "on the skin"), **epiglottis** (the cartilage which closes the windpipe during swallowing; literally, "on the tongue"), **epilepsy** (a chronic nervous disease characterized by convulsions; literally, "to seize upon"), **epilogue** (the conclusion of a writing or drama; literally, "a saying in addition" or "a word upon"), **epiphany** (a manifestation of the divine; literally, "to shine upon"), **episcopal** (governed by bishops or overseers; literally, "overseen"), **epitaph** (an inscription on a tomb; literally, "on a tomb"), **epithet** (a descriptive name or title; literally, "placed upon"), **epitome** (something which embodies or exemplifies a large whole; literally, "to cut upon")

κατά, *down*, **cataclysm** (a great flood; literally, "to wash against"), **catalog** (a list of items; literally, "word down"), **catastrophe** (a sudden change towards misfortune; literally, "a turn against"), **catechism** (oral instruction; literally, "to resound" or "to sound down"), **category** (a group of items; literally, "accused" or "judged down"), **catheter** (a medical tube to remove fluids from the body; literally, "to send down"), **cathode** (a negatively charge electrode; literally, "the way down")

μετά, *with*, **metabolism** (the physical and chemical processes involved in a living organism; literally, "thrown across"), metamorphosis, **metaphor** (a figure of speech; literally, "to carry across"), **metathesis** (the transposition of letters or sounds in a word; literally, "transposed" or "place after"), **method** (a means or manner of procedure; literally, "the way across")

παρά, *beside*, **parable** (a simple story to illustrate a lesson or moral; literally, "to throw alongside" or "to compare"), **paradigm** (a list of all inflectional forms of a word; literally, "shown alongside"), **paragraph** (a division in a writing which expresses a complete thought. Originally, a mark was placed in the margin *beside* the new section), paramedic, **parallel** (being equidistant apart; literally, "beside one another"), **parenthesis** (punctuation marks used to set off explanatory remarks; literally, "set in alongside")

περί, *around*, **pericope** (small section of a literary work; literally, "to cut around"), **perigee** (the point at which the moon is closest to the earth; literally, "around the earth"), **perihelion** (the point at which the earth is closest to the sun; literally, "around the sun"), **perimeter** (the circumference or outside outline of an object; literally, "measure around"), **periodontal** (occurring around a tooth or affecting the gums; literally, "around the tooth"), **periphery** (the outermost region of a precise boundary; literally, "to carry around"), **periphrastic** (circumlocution or round about way of saying something; literally, "to point around"), **periscope** (device used to aid vision when sight is blocked or limited; literally, "to look around")

πρό, *before*, **problem** (source of perplexity which needs a solution; literally, "thrown before"), **prognosis** (prediction or a forecast; literally, "to know before"), **program** (public notice; literally, "to write before"), **prolegomenon** (an introduction; literally, "spoken before"), **prolepsis** (anticipation; "to take before"), **prologue** (introduction to a literary work; literally, "a word before"), **prophylactic** (preventive precaution; literally, "to guard before"), **protasis** (the "if" clause of conditional sentences; literally, "to arrange before")

πρός, *near*, *toward*, **proselyte** (a convert to Judaism; literally, "one who has come to")

σύν, *with*, *together*, **asyndeton** (the omission of conjunctions in constructions which normally would need them; literally, "without being bound together"), **symbol** (something that represents something else; literally, "to throw together"), **symphony** (a harmonious combination of musical sounds; literally, "to sound together"), **symposium** (a meeting or conference for discussion of some topic; literally, "to drink together"), **symptom** (an indication of a condition or event; literally, "to fall together"), **synagogue** (a building for Jewish gatherings; literally, "assembly" or "to lead together"; cf. σύν + ἄγω), **synapse** (the point of contact where nerve impulses are transmitted from one neuron to another; literally, "to touch together"), **syndrome** (characteristics of a situation; literally, "run together"), **synchronize** (to occur at the same time; literally, "timed together"), **synod** (a council or assembly of churches; literally, "the way together"; cf.σύν + ὁδός), **synonym** (a word having the same meaning as that of another in the same language; literally, "name together"), **synoptic** (arranging similar items side by side; literally, "seen together"), **synthesis** (the combination of separate elements to form a whole; literally, "placed together")

ὑπέρ, *over*, *above*, **hyper-** (something that is overdone or exaggerated: hyperactive, hypercritical, hypersensi-tive), **hyperbola** (a geometrical curve; literally, "over thrown"), **hyperbole** (an exaggeration; literally, "over throw"), **hyperglycemic** (a diabetic condition of having too much sugar; literally, "over sugar")

ὑπό, *under*, **hypodermic** (a medical instrument used to inject substances below the skin; literally, "below the skin"), **hypoglycemic** (a diabetic condition of too little blood sugar; literally, "under sugar"), **hypostasis** (the substance or essence of something; literally, "standing under"), **hypotaxis** (the subordinate relationship of clauses with connectives), **hypotenuse** (the side of a right triangle opposite the right angle; literally, "stretched under"), **hypothesis** (an assumption or explanation; literally, "placed under")

ἔξω, *outside*, **exotic** (something foreign; literally, "from the outside")

μέσον, *in the midst of*, **Mesolithic** (the cultural period between the Paleolithic and Neolithic ages; literally, "the middle stone age"), **Mesopotamia** (the region between the Tigris and Euphrates rivers; literally, "between the rivers"), **mesosphere** (the layer of air between the stratosphere and thermosphere; also layer of the earth between the athenosphere and the earth's core; literally, "the middle sphere"), **Mesozoic** (the third era of geologic time; literally, "middle of life")

ὀπίσω, *after*, *behind*, **opistograph** (an ancient document written on both the front and back sides; literally, "writing behind")

συνάγω, *I gather together*, **synagogue** (a building for Jewish gatherings; literally, "assembly" or "to lead together"; cf. σύν + ἄγω)

PREPOSITIONS

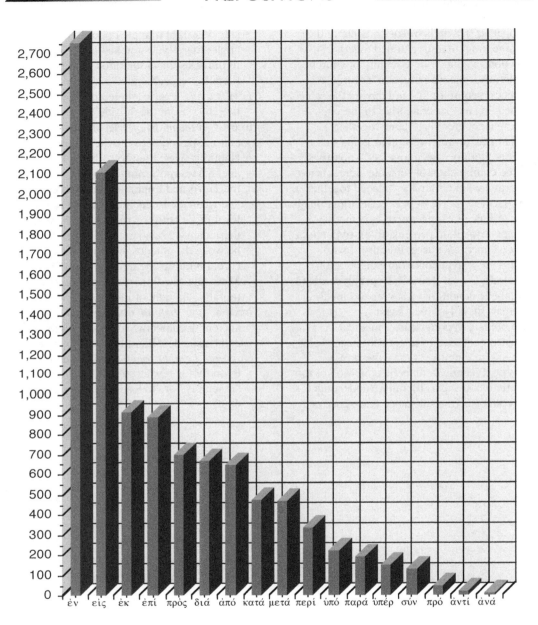

ASSIGNMENT
1

Vocabulary #1: ἐννέα and the boldface proper preposition definitions.

OBJECTIVE QUESTIONS

1. Prepositions are old _____ that have lost their original function.

2. Prepositional phrases function _____ to modify a noun or pronoun or _____ to modify a verb.

3. Give the root idea and one other meaning for the seventeen proper prepositions.

Preposition	Root Idea	Others	Preposition	Root Idea	Others
1.			10.		
2.			11.		
3.			12.		
4.			13.		
5.			14.		
6.			15.		
7.			16.		
8.			17.		
9.			-------	-------	-------

4. Specify seven prepositions used in one case (or function) only.

Preposition	Case	Preposition	Case
1.		5.	
2.		6.	
3.		7.	
4.			

5. Fill in the directional prepositions using the figure in the text:

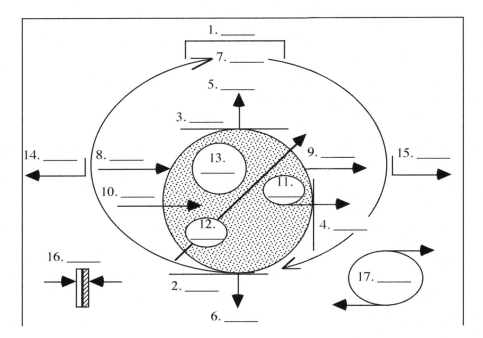

6. True or False

___ 1. A preposition's spelling never changes.

___ 2. Prepositions can be found compounded at the end of tense stems.

___ 3. A compounded verb may not necessarily have a different meaning than the uncompounded form.

___ 4. Sometimes one will find the preposition of a compounded verb repeated again in a phrase that follows.

___ 5. Prepositions may suffer elision of the final vowel in compounded contruction with verbs.

___ 6. Normally, the compounded preposition is treated as part of the tense stem in forming principal parts.

7. Recognition—provide the regular vocabulary form for the following:

7.1 ἀπ' = _____   7.4 δι' = _____   7.7 ἐφ' = _____

7.2 ὑφ' = _____   7.5 παρ' = _____   7.8 ἀφ' = _____

7.3 καθ' = _____   7.6 ἀνθ' = _____   7.9 κατ' = _____

ASSIGNMENT 2

Vocabulary #2: adverbial prepositions, verbs, and one other use for each of the proper prepositions.

8. Recognition—provide the non-compounded forms for the following:

8.1 ἀπάγω = _____   8.5 μετανοέω = _____

8.2 διέρχομαι = _____   8.6 κατεσθίω = _____

8.3 παρακαλέω =_____   8.7 ἐπερωτάω = _____

8.4 ὑποτάσσω = _____   8.8 ἀναγινώσκω =_____

TRANSLATION

9. Translate the following, using the translation aids provided below:

○   *Translation Aids* ○

ἔρχεται, *he is coming* (9.2; cf. 9.6 also)
κοινωνίαν, *fellowship* (accusative)
αὐτοῦ, *him* (genitive), 3d per. pronoun
καρπός, ὁ, *fruit*
αἰώνιον, adj., *eternal*, modifying ζωήν; for issues of concord, see Table 16.1, *NTG*, 172)
Ἱεροσόλυμα, *Jerusalem*
χάριν, *grace* (accusative)
τυφλός, adj., *blind*
χωλός, adj., *lame*
ὀφείλω, *I ought*

ἀποθανεῖν, *to die*
ἡμῶν, *our*, 1st per. pronoun (genitive), used possessively modifying κυρίου; literally, "of us"
τοὺς δούλους and τὰς δούλας, notice the Greek article showing a gender distinction
μου, *my*, 1st per. pronoun, used possessively (genitive)
ἐκείναις, *those*, remote demonstrative pronoun, modifying ἡμέραις (observe the concord)

9.1   μεθ' ἡμέρας ἓξ [Matt. 17:1]

9.2　ἔρχεται πρὸς τοὺς μαθητὰς

_____

9.3　κοινωνίαν ἔχομεν μετ' αὐτοῦ [1 John 1:6]

_____

9.4　συνάγει καρπὸν εἰς ζωὴν αἰώνιον

_____

9.5　"See that no one repays" κακὸν ἀντὶ κακοῦ [1 Thess. 5:15]

_____

9.6　Καὶ ἔρχονται πάλιν εἰς Ἱεροσόλυμα.

_____

9.7　οὐκ ἀκούετε, ὅτι ἐκ τοῦ θεοῦ οὐκ ἐστέ. [John 8:47]

_____

9.8　οὐ γάρ ἐστε ὑπὸ νόμον ἀλλὰ ὑπὸ χάριν.

_____

9.9　τυφλοὶ ἀναβλέπουσιν καὶ χωλοὶ περιπατοῦσιν
[Matt. 11:15]

_____

9.10　νόμον ἔχομεν, καὶ κατὰ τὸν νόμον ὀφείλει
ἀποθανεῖν

_____

9.11　εἰρήνην ἔχομεν πρὸς τὸν θεὸν διὰ τοῦ κυρίου ἡμῶν
Ἰησοῦ Χριστοῦ [Rom. 5:1]

_____

_____

9.12   ἐπὶ τοὺς δούλους μου καὶ ἐπὶ τὰς δούλας μου ἐν
       ταῖς ἡμέραις ἐκείναις

       _____

       _____

9.13   Παῦλος ἀπόστολος οὐκ ἀπ' ἀνθρώπων οὐδὲ δι'
       ἀνθρώπου ἀλλὰ διὰ Ἰησοῦ Χριστοῦ [Gal. 1:1]

       _____

       _____

10.   Diagram the sentence indicated below taken from the translation
       exercises.

10.1. εἰρήνην ἔχομεν πρὸς τὸν θεὸν διὰ τοῦ κυρίου ἡμῶν Ἰησοῦ Χριστοῦ

FIGURE 6. Proconsul Inscription at Ephesus. The image above is the top third of a proconsul inscription in the Ephesos Müzesi in Selçuk, Turkey. Note how the inscription uses all capital letters, has no punctuation, does not separate words, and can continue a word from the end of one line to the beginning of the next, writing customs that are much like our Greek uncial manuscripts of the New Testament. Even though inscriptions show spelling variations from region to region, as well as inflectional variations, you still probably can recognize several words. You probably can find the name "Gaius" (Γάϊος; cf. Acts 19:29; 20:4; Rom 16:23; 1 Cor 1:14; 3 John 1). What about γενόμενον, the aorist middle participle of γίνομαι, with an article sitting in front? Only Acts tells us about proconsuls, such as Sergius Paulus on Cyprus (Acts 13:7, 8, 12), Gallio in Corinth (Acts 18:12), and the reference to the tribunal of proconsuls in Ephesus (Acts 19:38). The word for "proconsul" is ἀνθύπατος. In what line is this word? Finally, the word for "benefactor" is εὐεργέτης (cf. Luke 22:25). In what line is this word?

LESSON 10

(δέκα)

Present Middle/Passive Indicative

Vocabulary 10

δέκα, *ten*, **decalogue** (the Ten Commandments; literally, "the ten words"), **decapolis** (the district of first-century Palestine comprised of ten hellenistic cities; literally, "ten cities"), **decade** (a period of ten years), **decathlon** (an athletic contest consisting of ten events), cf. Latin *decem* (December, decemvir, decimal, decimeter)

ἀγρός, *field*, **agronomy** (the management of land), cf. Latin *ager, agri* (agrarian, agriculture)

ἄνεμος, *wind*, **anemometer** (an instrument that measures wind; literally, "wind measurement"), **sea anemone** (a flower-like marine organism; literally, "sea wind")

βούλομαι, *I wish, am willing*, **abulia** (loss of the ability to decide or act independently; literally, "without a will"), **Aristobulus** (literally, "the best counselor"), **boule** (the senate of 400 founded in ancient Athens by Solon; literally, "council"), **bouleuterion** (a Greek senate house), cf. Latin *volo* (involuntary, volition, volitive, voluntary, volunteer, voluptuous)

γίνομαι, *I am (become, take place)*, **anthropogenesis** (the scientific study of the origin of humankind; literally, "the beginning of man"), **autogenous** (self-generated or self-produced; literally, "self

beginning"), **Genesis** (the first book of the Bible; literally, "the beginning"), **genetic** (pertaining to the origin or development of something), **parthenogenesis** (reproduction by the development of an unfertilized ovum, seed, or spore; literally, "virgin beginning"), **pyrogenous** (produced by or producing heat; literally, "fire producing"), **orogenesis** (the formation of a mountain; literally, "mountain beginning")

ἐργάζομαι, *I work (accomplish)*, **allergy** (an adverse reaction to a substance; literally, "other work"), **energy** (power for work), **erg** (a measurable unit of energy or work), **ergonomics** (the study of workers), **George** (literally, "earth worker"), **metallurgy** (the science of metal working), **synergism** (the action of two or more subjects which achieve an effect of which each is individually incapable; literally, "work together"), **thaumaturge** (a performer of miracles or magic feats; literally, "miracle worker")

λογίζομαι, *I account, reckon*, **logic** (the science of correct reasoning), **logical** (in accordance with reason)

πορεύομαι, *I go (proceed, travel)*, **pore** (an opening in the skin through which fluids pass)

VOICES

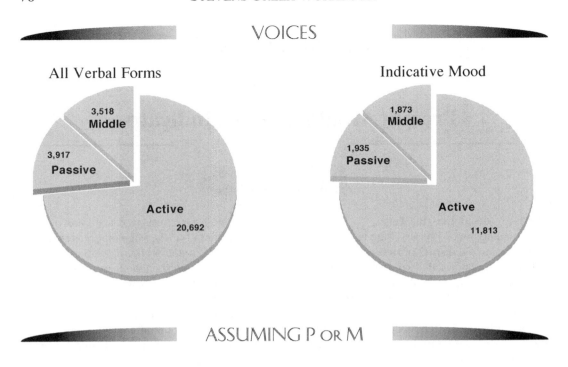

All Verbal Forms

3,518 Middle

3,917 Passive

Active 20,692

Indicative Mood

1,873 Middle

1,935 Passive

Active 11,813

ASSUMING P OR M

(Present, imperfect, perfect, and pluperfect tenses, minus -μαι verbs)

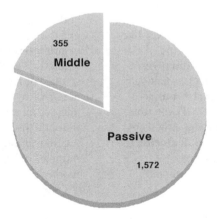

355 Middle

Passive 1,572

Thus, the advice, "assume a verb is passive unless context dictates middle," holds true about 77% of occurrences in the principal parts involved (first, fourth, fifth). You will be right three out of four times (except as unrecognized -μαι verbs—so-called "deponents"—cloud the issue).

OBJECTIVE QUESTIONS

1. Greek voice is used to indicate the relationship of the verbal action to the
   _____.

2. English has no middle voice, using _____ _____ instead.

3. In the Greek middle voice, the subject performs the action on itself, or has
   _____ _____ in the action. Circle the *primary* middle
   endings:

   -μαι, -μην, -μεθα, -νται, -ντο, -σαι, -σθε, -σο, -ται, -το

4. Identify the verbal components of the following:

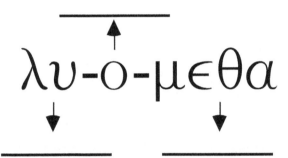

$$\lambda\upsilon\text{-}o\text{-}\mu\epsilon\theta\alpha$$

5. Give the paradigm for the present *passive* indicative of συνάγω.

Number	Person	Form	Translation
Singular	1st		
	2nd		
	3rd		
Plural	1st		
	2nd		
	3rd		

6. In the active voice, ἄρχω means _____, but as middle, ἄρχομαι
   means _____. Again, πείθω means _____, but πείθομαι

means _____. Finally, φοβέω means _____, but φοβέομαι is _____.

7. Middle form but active meaning is called _____. So, translate:

    7.1 βούλεται = _____   7.4 γίνεσθε = _____

    7.2 λογιζόμεθα = _____   7.5 ἔρχῃ = _____

    7.3 πορεύομαι = _____   7.6 προσεύχονται =

8. Complete the paradigm for the present *middle* indicative of ἀγαπάω.

Number	Person	Form	Translation
singular	1st		
	2nd		
	3rd		
plural	1st		
	2nd		
	3rd		

9. Since both middle and passive voice use the same form, what is the general procedure for translation?

    _____

10. *Personal* agency is expressed by the preposition _____ in the _____ case. Impersonal agency is expressed by the preposition _____ in the _____ case.

11. When God is assumed the agent of the passive voice construction, this is called a _____ _____ expression.

12. Translate the following, using Table 10.8 as a guide:

    12.1 ἀκούουσι τῆς φωνῆς = _____

    What case is φωνῆς? = _____

    What is the grammatical function of φωνῆς? = _____

12.2   πιστεύω γὰρ τῷ θεῷ = _____

What case is θεῷ? = _____

What is the grammatical function of θεῷ? = _____

12.3   γίνονται δοῦλοι = _____

What case is δοῦλοι? = _____

What is the grammatical function of δοῦλοι? = _____

12.4   δικαία ὑπάρχει = _____

What case is δικαία? = _____

What is the grammatical function of δικαία? = _____

TRANSLATION

13. Translate the following, using the translation aids provided below. New verbs in this vocabulary are lexical middle (so-called "deponent"). Thus, most sentences below will default to active voice. Assuming a verb is passive does not apply to lexical middle verbs, so that rule does not apply for many of these sentences.

O *Translation Aids* O

πνεῦμά, *spirit* (nominative)
μου, *my*, 1st per. pronoun
   (genitive), literally, "of
   me"; used possessively
Μακεδονίαν, *Macedonia*
   (accusative)

καρπός, ὁ, *fruit*
δένδρον, τό, *tree*
ἐνώπιον, *before*, adverbial
   preposition
ὑμῖν, *to you*, 2nd per. pronoun
   (dative)

13.1   ὁ δὲ ἀγρός ἐστιν ὁ κόσμος [Matt. 13:38]

_____

13.2   τὸ πνεῦμά μου προσεύχεται

_____

13.3   οὐ λογίζεται τὸ κακόν [1 Cor. 13:5]

13.4   μετὰ χαρᾶς δέχονται τὸν λόγον

13.5   ἀλλὰ ἔρχεται ὥρα, καὶ νῦν ἐστιν

13.6   Μακεδονίαν γὰρ διέρχομαι

13.7   εἰς τὴν βασιλείαν τοῦ θεοῦ εἰσπορεύονται [Luke 18:24]

13.8   ἐκ γὰρ τοῦ καρποῦ τὸ δένδρον γινώσκεται

13.9   Καὶ συνάγονται οἱ ἀπόστολοι πρὸς τὸν Ἰησοῦν

13.10 λέγω ὑμῖν, γίνεται χαρὰ ἐνώπιον τῶν ἀγγέλων τοῦ θεοῦ

LESSON 11

(ἕνδεκα)

Pronouns — A Summary

Vocabulary 11

ἕνδεκα, *eleven*, **hendecasyllabic** (a verse containing eleven syllables; literally, "eleven syllables")

ἐγώ, *I*, **ego** (the self), **egocentric** (self-centered; selfish), **egoism** (the ethical doctrine that morality has its foundations in self-interest), **egomania** (obsessive preoccupation with self), **egotism** (excessive reference to oneself in speaking or writing), cf. Latin *eg*

αὐτός, *he*, *him*, **autobiography** (a biography of a person written by that same person; literally, "writing one's own

life"), **autogenous** (self-generated or self-produced; literally, "self beginning"), **autograph** (a person's own signature or handwriting; literally, "self written"), **automatic** (acting in an independent manner; literally, "self-acting"), **automobile** (a self-propelled vehicle; literally, "self-moving"), **autonomous** (independent or self-governing; literally, "self law"), **autopsy** (examination of a corpse to determine the cause of death; literally, "self seeing")

PRONOUNS

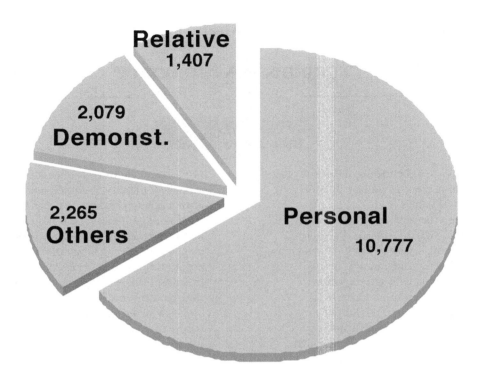

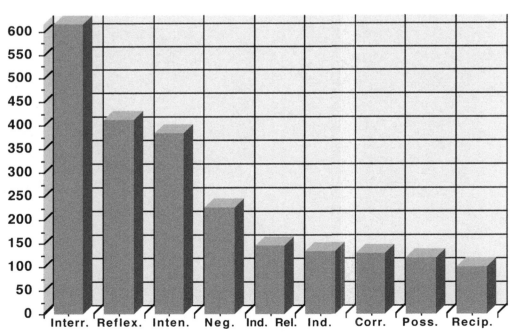

OBJECTIVE QUESTIONS

1. Fill in the following for the first and second personal pronouns:

First Personal Pronoun			
Singular	Meaning	Plural	Meaning

Second Personal Pronoun			
Singular	Meaning	Plural	Meaning

2. Pronouns are _____ which either can take the place of a _____ or can function as an _____. The word substituted for is called the _____.

3. Pronouns agree with the antecedent in _____ and _____, but the _____ depends upon the _____ _____ in the sentence.

4. When used as an adjective, the pronoun will maintain concord in _____, _____, *and* _____.

5. A prepositional phrase pronoun has the case called for by the _____.

6. True or False

   _____ The first and second personal pronouns ("I," "you") are inflected for all three genders in Greek.

_____ The plural form of the third personal pronoun in Greek is not inflected for gender, just as the English "they."

7. The subject of the verbal action is emphasized by including the appropriate personal pronoun in _____ position before or after the verb, using the _____ case. This is called the _____ use.

8. Add the correct personal pronoun (person, number) to make the following verbs emphatic and translate reflexively (use "myself," "yourself," etc.):

8.1 ἐργάζομαι = _____ = _____

8.2 βούλεσθε = _____ = _____

8.3 ἀποκρινόμεθα = _____ = _____

8.4 ἀσπάζῃ = _____ = _____

9. Greek has possessive pronouns, but the habit was to express possession with a personal pronoun in the _____ case.

10. Besides use as a personal pronoun, the *third* personal pronoun can have two special *intensifying* functions, one with the resultant meaning _____ when the pronoun is in _____ construction, and the other resultant meaning _____ when the pronoun is _____ in construction.

TRANSLATION

11. Translate the following, using the translation aids provided below:

○   *Translation Aids*   ○

εὐαγγελίζω, *I bring good news*
παρακαλέω, *I comfort*
κἀγώ, *and I*, crasis for καί +
   ἐγώ
Πέτρος, *Peter* (nominative)

ποιεῖτε, from ποιέω, *I do*, the
   form is imperative mood =
   command
ταύτην, *this* (accusative),
   demonstrative pronoun
   modifying παραβολήν

11.1   ἐμὲ δέχεται [Matt. 18:15]

_____

11.2   σὺ ἔρχῃ πρός με;

_____

11.3   ὁ κύριος ὑμῶν ἔρχεται [Matt. 24:42]

_____

11.4   λέγει αὐτῇ ὁ Ἰησοῦς, Ἐγώ εἰμι

_____

11.5   καὶ ἡμεῖς ὑμᾶς εὐαγγελιζόμεθα [Acts 13:32]

_____

11.6   παρακαλούμεθα αὐτοὶ ὑπὸ τοῦ θεοῦ

_____

11.7   καγὼ δέ σοι λέγω ὅτι σὺ εἶ Πέτρος [Matt. 16:18]

_____

11.8   Αὐτὸς δὲ ἐγὼ Παῦλος παρακαλῶ ὑμᾶς

_____

11.9   Καὶ οἱ κύριοι, τὰ αὐτὰ ποιεῖτε πρὸς αὐτούς [Eph. 6:9]

_____

11.10 Κύριε, πρὸς ἡμᾶς τὴν παραβολὴν ταύτην λέγεις;

_____

FIGURE 7. Roman Milestone at Side. The author stands next to a Roman milestone found during a hotel construction project in 1990 near the ancient port city of Side, on the coast of ancient Pamphylia. Side is about 38 miles from Perge where Paul and Barnabas stopped twice on the first missionary journey (Acts 13:13–14; 14:25). The simple limestone cylinder has no decoration or base, with a roughly dressed surface smoothed for the cut letters. The bilingual inscription (Latin followed by Greek) dates to 129–126 BC during the governorship of Manius Aquillius, first governor of Asia. (The inscription wrongly reads "governor of the Romans," which is not accurate.) The milestone records 331 Roman miles measured from the road's head at Pergamum: CCC (= 300) XXX (= 30) I (= 1); the Greek letters are T (=300) Λ (= 30) A (= 1). For a brief movie describing the inscription, see http://drkoine.com/movies/1mj/SideMilestone.mp4.

LESSON 12

(δώδεκα)

Imperfect Active Indicative

Vocabulary 12

δώδεκα, *twelve*, **dodecagon** (a polygon with twelve sides; literally, "twelve angles"), **dodecahedron** (a polyhedron with twelve faces; literally, "twelve bases"), **dodecaphonic** (pertaining to twelve-tone music; literally, "twelve sounds")

οὗτος, *this*, *these*, **tautology** (needless repetition of the same sense in different words; literally, "the same saying")

ἐξουσία, *authority*, cf. ἐκ + εἰμί

λαός, *people*, **Archelaus** (literally, "ruler of the people"), **laity** (common people collectively as distinguished from clergy or professionals), **Nicholas** (literally, "victory of the people")

ὄχλος, *crowd*, **ochlocracy** (government by the masses or mob rule; literally, "crowd power"), **ochlophobia** (an abnormal fear of crowds; literally, "crowd fear")

ἅγιος, *holy*, **Hagiographa** (the third of three divisions of the Old Testament; literally,

the sacred writings"), **hagiography** (biography of saints; literally, "writing of the saints"), **hagiology** (literature dealing with the lives of saints), **hagioscope** (a small opening in an interior wall of a church to view inside; literally, "to see the sacred")

ἀποστέλλω, *I send*, *send out*, **apostle** (a missionary of the early church; literally, "one sent out"), **apostolic** (having to do with the Apostles)

μαρτυρέω, *I witness*, *testify*, **martyr** (a person whose testimony is sealed by their death), **martyrdom** (the death of a martyr)

ὁράω, *I see*, **cosmorama** (an exhibition of scenes from all over the world; literally, "world view"), **diorama** (a view through a small opening), **panorama** (an open view in all directions; literally "seeing all")

INDICATIVE TENSES

OBJECTIVE QUESTIONS

1. The imperfect tense is classified as a _____ tense taking
   _____ endings. The imperfect is _____ kind of action in
   past time and is built on the _____ stem, so this is the *second* tense
   in the first principal part. Fill in the table below for primary and secondary
   verb endings:

		Primary		Secondary	
		Active	Mid./Pass.	Active	Mid./Pass.
Sing.	1st				
	2nd				
	3rd				
Plural	1st				
	2nd				
	3rd				

2. All past time tenses have an _____, a prefix to the tense stem
   indicating past time. With consonants, this prefix is the letter _____, called a
   _____ _____. With vowels, this prefix is a lengthened
   vowel, usually the letters _____ or _____, and is called a _____
   _____. For compounds, the prefix occurs (before or after?)
   _____ the preposition.

3. Identify the component parts of the imperfect tense below:

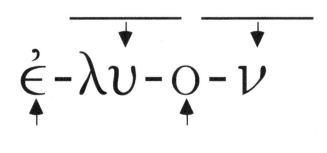

4. Translate imperfect usage as *descriptive, inceptive, conative, or customary.*

    4.1 ἐτιμᾶτε as *descriptive* imperfect =   _____

    4.2 ἐδίδασκεν as *inceptive* imperfect =   _____

    4.3 ἐλύομεν as *conative* imperfect =   _____

    4.4 ἤκουες as *customary* imperfect =   _____

5. Give the imperfect active indicative of ἀκούω.

Number	Person	Form	Translation
singular	1st		
	2nd		
	3rd		
plural	1st		
	2nd		
	3rd		

6. Give the imperfect indicative of εἰμί.

Number	Person	Form	Translation
singular	1st		
	2nd		
	3rd		
plural	1st		
	2nd		
	3rd		

7. The demonstrative pronoun "this" has the genitive masculine singular form
    _____. The genitive masculine plural for "these" is _____.
    All nominative forms of the demonstrative pronoun "this" in both masculine
    and feminine gender do not have the letter _____ as other forms have, but
    do have distinctive _____ breathing.

7.1 Translate: οὗτός ἐστιν = _____

7.2 Translate: τοῦ ἀνθρώπου τούτου = _____

7.3 Translate: τοὺς λόγους τούτους = _____

8. The demonstrative pronoun "that" and "those" is easy, because the form is a very distinctive spelling, _____ in nominative masculine singular and _____ in the plural.

8.1 Translate: ἐκεῖνός ἐστιν = _____

8.2 Translate: ἐν ἐκείναις ταῖς ἡμέραις = _____

9. The correlative pronoun "such" is distinctive with the three letters _____ prefixed to forms similar to the demonstrative pronoun.

9.1 Translate: ἀκούω τοιαῦτα = _____

10. Relative pronouns are easy once one remembers the phrase "relatives are _____." The acute accent distinguishes from forms of εἰμί.

10.1 Translate: περὶ οὗ ἀκούω = _____

10.2 Translate: τὰ σημεῖα* ἃ ἐποίει = _____

*From σημεῖον, τό, "sign," "miracle."

11. The key issue with relative pronouns is that their case is not determined by concord with the antecedent, but by their _____ in the relative clause.

TRANSLATION

12. Translate the following, using the translation aids provided below:

○   *Translation Aids* ○

καί, *also, even,* #12.2,
    adjunctive or ascensive use
    (*NTG*, 191–92)
σημεῖον, τό, *sign*
τίλλω, *I pluck, pick*
Γαλιλαία, *Galilee*
ἀκολουθέω, *I follow*
τίς, *who?*
διότι, *because*

θλῖψις, ἡ, *tribulation*
    (accusative)
παραλαμβάνω, *I take, take
    along*
διάβολος, *devil*
πόλις, ἡ, *city* (accusative)
ὁ ποιῶν, *the one who does*
    (nominative), participle
    form of ποιέω

12.1   αὐτὴ ἀπέθνῃσκεν [Luke 8:42]

12.2   καθὼς καὶ περιπατεῖτε

12.3   ἐμαρτύρει οὖν ὁ ὄχλος [John 12:17]

12.4   ἐθεώρουν τὰ σημεῖα ἃ ἐποίει

12.5   ἐγὼ ἀποστέλλω τὸν ἄγγελόν μου [Mark 13:24]

12.6   καὶ ἔτιλλον οἱ μαθηταὶ αὐτοῦ καὶ ἤσθιον

12.7   ὅτε ἦν ἐν τῇ Γαλιλαίᾳ ἠκολούθουν αὐτῷ [Mark 15:41]

12.8   τίς δέ ἐστιν οὗτος περὶ οὗ ἀκούω τοιαῦτα;

12.9　οἱ δὲ ὄχλοι ἔλεγον· οὗτός ἐστιν ὁ προφήτης [Matt. 21:11]

12.10　αἰτεῖτε καὶ οὐ λαμβάνετε διότι κακῶς αἰτεῖσθε

12.11　ὁ υἱὸς τοῦ ἀνθρώπου ἐξουσίαν ἔχει ἐπὶ τῆς γῆς
[Luke 5:24]

12.12　τῶν γὰρ τοιούτων ἐστὶν ἡ βασιλεία τῶν οὐρανῶν

12.13　Ἀλλὰ ἐν ἐκείναις ταῖς ἡμέραις μετὰ τὴν θλῖψιν ἐκείνην [Mark 13:24]

12.14　Τότε παραλαμβάνει αὐτὸν ὁ διάβολος εἰς τὴν ἁγίαν πόλιν

12.15　ὁ ποιῶν τὴν δικαιοσύνην δίκαιός ἐστιν, καθὼς ἐκεῖνος δίκαιός ἐστιν [1 John 3:7]

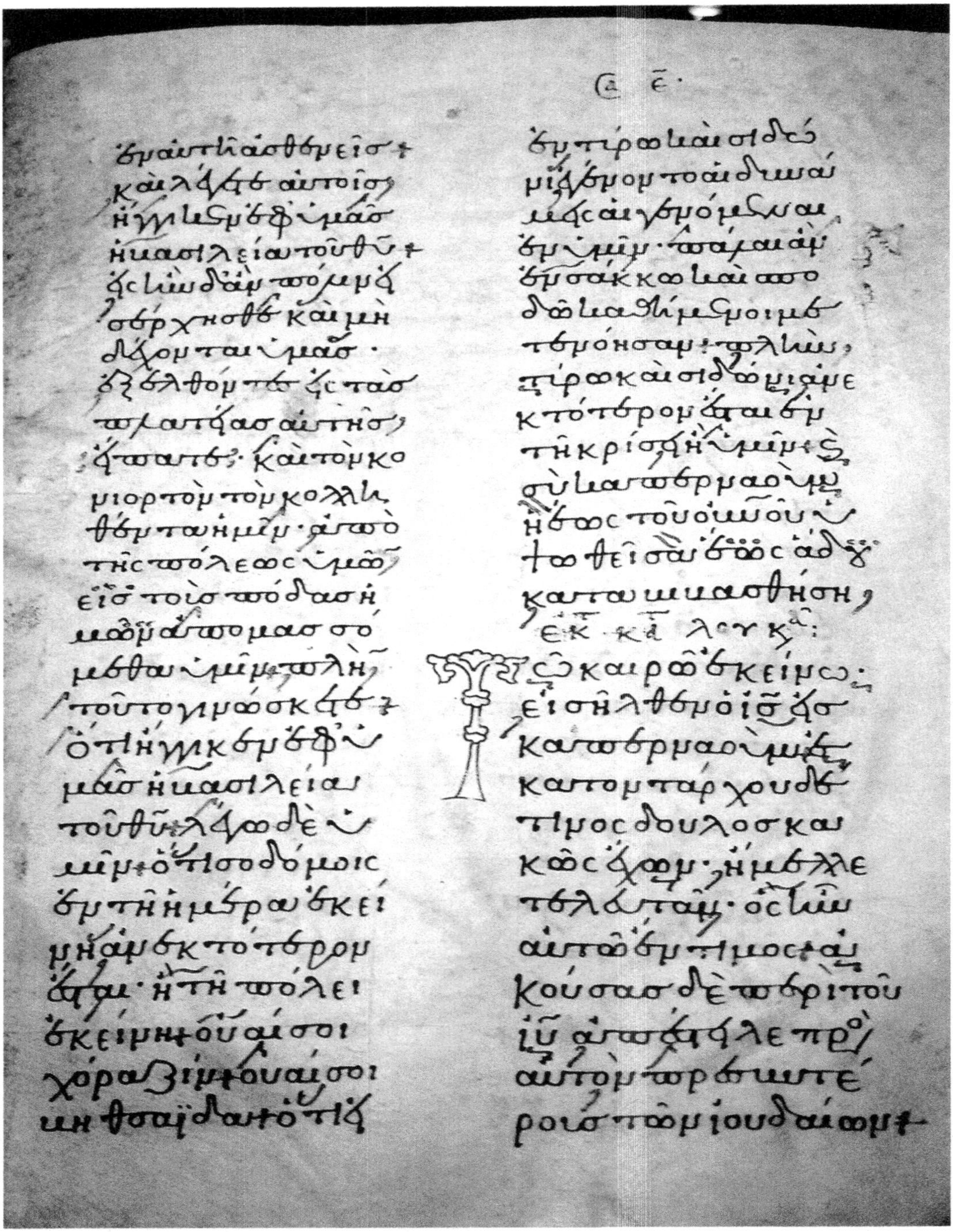

FIGURE 8. Gospel of Luke Lectionary. The text starts at Luke 10:5b–10, but then jumps several chapters backwards to 7:1–3 at the ornamental "T." At this jump in which the text sequence has been rearranged, a gloss is added, "in those days," to smooth the transition when reading publically in worship. This parchment manuscript illustrates the minuscule style, with small letters, separated words, and accents. Notice that the letters are *dropped* from a ruled line rather than written on top of a ruled line (as in modern, cursive, handwriting style).

LESSON 13

(δεκατρεῖς)

Imperfect Middle and Conditional Sentences

ὅλος, *whole*, *complete*, *all*, *entire*, **catholic** (general or universal in scope; literally, "according to the whole"), **holocaust** (great or total destruction, such as that of the Jews by the Nazis; literally, "to burn the whole"), **holograph** (a document written wholly in the handwriting of the person under whose name the work appears), **holistic** (emphasizing the importance of the whole and the interdependence of its parts)

οἰκία, *house*, *family*, *household*, **ecocide** (the destruction of an environment; literally, "house killer"), **ecology** (the science of the relationships between organisms and their environment), **economy** (the management of the resources of a community; literally, "household law"), **ecosystem** (an ecological community with its environment, considered as a unit), **ecumenical** (universal or worldwide in range)

ὀφθαλμός, *eye*, **Antigonus Monophthalmos** (Alexander the Great's general who ruled Asia Minor and was so named after he lost an eye in battle; literally, "the one-eyed"), **ophthalmology** (the branch of medicine dealing with the structure, functions, and diseases of the eye)

τόπος, *place*, **isotope** (any of two or more forms of an element having the same atomic number but different atomic weights; literally, "equal place"), **topic** (a subject of discussion or conversation; literally, "place"), **topography** (detailed description of an area; literally, "place writing"), **utopia** (an ideally perfect place; literally, "not a place")

φόβος, *fear*, **acrophobia** (an abnormal fear of being in high places), **claustrophobia** (a fear of confined spaces; literally, "fear of a closed space"), **hydrophobia** (the fear of water), **necrophobia** (a morbid fear of death or corpses; literally, "fear of the dead"), **ochlophobia** (an abnormal fear of crowds; literally, "crowd fear"), **phobia** (a strong fear or dislike)

ἀλλήλων, *of one another*, **parallel** (being equal distant apart; literally, "beside one another")

ἀκολουθέω, *I follow*, **acolyte** (an attendant or follower; literally, "follower"), **anacoluthon** (an abrupt change within a sentence to a second construction inconsistent with the first; literally, "not following")

ἀναβαίνω, *I go up*, **Anabasis** (a military advance, such as that of Cyrus the Younger into Asia Minor, as narrated by Xenophon; literally, "to go up"), **anabatic** (pertaining to rising wind currents; literally, "to go up"), cf. βαίνω (acrobat, diabetes)

ἄρχω, *I rule*, **anarchy** (the absence of political authority; literally, "without a ruler"), **Archelaus** (literally, "ruler of the people"), **ethnarch** (the ruler of a province or people; literally, "nation ruler"), **gynarchy** (government by women; literally, "female rule"), **matriarch** (a woman who rules a family or tribe; literally, "mother ruler"), **monarch** (a sole hereditary ruler; literally, "only ruler"), **oligarchy** (government by a few; literally, "few rulers"), **patriarch** (the male leader of a family or tribe; literally, "father ruler"), **tetrarch** (a governor of one of the four divisions of a country, especially in the Roman Empire; literally, "four rulers") ἄρχομαι, *I begin*, cf. ἀρχαῖος (archaeology, archaic, archaism), ἀρχή (archangel, archenemy, archetype)

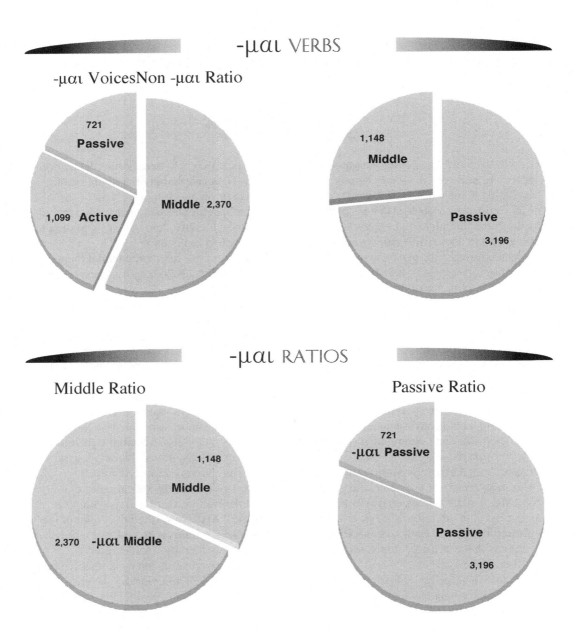

-μαι VERBS

-μαι VoicesNon -μαι Ratio

721 **Passive**

1,099 **Active**

Middle 2,370

1,148 **Middle**

Passive 3,196

-μαι RATIOS

Middle Ratio

1,148 **Middle**

2,370 **-μαι Middle**

Passive Ratio

721 **-μαι Passive**

Passive 3,196

(For the deponent debate, read the discussion in the index, "Deponents," *NTG*, 459–61.)

■■■ OBJECTIVE QUESTIONS ■■■

1. Give the imperfect middle indicative of φοβέομαι.

Number	Person	Form	Translation
singular	1st		
	2nd		
	3rd		
plural	1st		
	2nd		
	3rd		

2. The *possessive* pronoun is uncommon in the New Testament, because the preferred construction for indicating possession was to use the *personal* pronoun in the _____ case. Possessive pronouns grammatically function as _____ showing (full or partial?) _____ concord. All first and second person plural forms have _____ breathing.

    2.1 Translate: αἱ καρδίαι ὑμῶν = _____

    2.2 Translate: αἱ καρδίαι ὑμέτεραι = _____

3. What is the difference between first and second *personal* pronouns and first and second *possessive* pronouns in terms of gender?

    _____

4. Greek *possessive* pronouns have no _____ person forms. Instead, the reflexive pronoun _____ is used with possessive force.

5. First person *reflexive* pronouns in the singular look like the third personal pronoun prefixed with the letters _____, while second person looks like the third personal pronoun prefixed with _____. Moving from first to second to third person forms, all the plurals are all the _____ within each gender. Plural forms of the reflexive pronoun look like the third personal pronoun prefixed with _____ and _____ breathing.

    5.1 Translate: ἀπὸ τῶν ἑαυτῶν = _____

5.2 Translate: ἐν τῷ σεαυτῷ = _____

6. Reciprocal pronouns are always _____ in number, with just three forms _____, _____, and _____.

  6.1 Translate: ἀπ' ἀλλήλων = _____

  6.2 Translate: εἰς ἀλλήλους = _____

7. Complete the following chart on classifying conditional sentences by the mood of the protasis, which indicates the assumption by the speaker on the logic of the "if" statement.

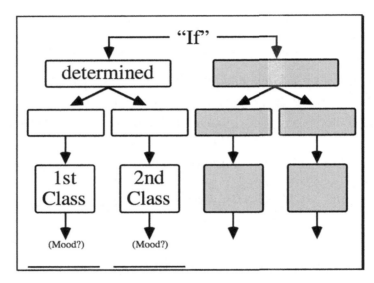

▰▰▰▰▰▰ TRANSLATION ▰▰▰▰▰▰

8. Translate the following, using the translation aids provided below:

....

○   Translation Aids   ○

διαλογίζομαι, *I discuss, argue*
Πέτρος, *Peter* (nominative)
Μάρθα, *Martha*
Μωϋσῆς, *Moses*
διὰ τί, *why? for what reason?*
ἀπέναντι, *before* (adv. prep.)

συνέδριον, τό, *Sanhedrin*
ψευδομαρτυρίαν, *false*
  testimony
κατά, with ablative (*NTG*, 100)
ἀληθής, *true*

....

8.1   ἐν τῷ σῷ ἀγρῷ [Matt. 13:27]

_____

8.2   ἐφοβούμην γάρ σε

_____

8.3   τὰς ἐντολὰς τὰς ἐμὰς [John 14:15]

_____

8.4   ἐπίστευον καὶ ἐβαπτίζοντο

_____

8.5   καὶ ἠκολούθει αὐτῷ ἐν τῇ ὁδῷ. [Mark 10:52]

_____

8.6   καὶ διελογίζοντο πρὸς ἀλλήλους

_____

8.7   ἀκολουθοῦσιν αὐτῷ οἱ μαθηταὶ αὐτοῦ. [Mark 6:1]

_____

8.8   Πέτρος δὲ καὶ Ἰωάννης ἀνέβαινον εἰς τὸ ἱερὸν

_____

8.9   ἀλλ᾽ ἦν ἔτι ἐν τῷ τόπῳ ὅπου ἦν ἡ Μάρθα [John 11:30, adapted]

_____

8.10   εἰ γὰρ ἐπιστεύετε Μωϋσεῖ, ἐπιστεύετε ἂν ἐμοί·

_____

       The protasis is in the _____ mood. This is a _____ class
       conditional sentence. The condition is assumed to be _____.

8.11   εἰ ἀλήθειαν λέγω, διὰ τί ὑμεῖς οὐ πιστεύετέ μοι;
       [John 8:46]

_____

The protasis is in the _____ mood. This is a _____ class conditional sentence. The condition is assumed to be _____.

8.12   ὁ ὄχλος ἤρχετο πρὸς αὐτόν, καὶ ἐδίδασκεν αὐτούς

_____

8.13   οὐκ ἔστιν φόβος θεοῦ ἀπέναντι τῶν ὀφθαλμῶν αὐτῶν [Rom. 3:18]

_____

8.14   τὸ συνέδριον ὅλον ἐζήτουν ψευδομαρτυρίαν κατὰ τοῦ Ἰησοῦ

_____

8.15   Σὺ περὶ σεαυτοῦ μαρτυρεῖς· ἡ μαρτυρία σου οὐκ ἔστιν ἀληθής. [John 8:13]

_____

LESSON 14

(δεκατέσσαρες)

Third Declension—Stop and Sibilant Stems

Vocabulary 14

γυνή, *woman*, **androgynous** (having both male and female characteristics; literally, "male-female"), **gynarchy** (government by women; literally, "female rule"), **gynecocracy** (political ascendancy of women; literally, "female power"), **gynecology** (the medical science of female physiology), **gynophore** (the stalk of a pistil, the seed-bearing organ of a flower); **misogyny** (hatred of women; literally, "women-hate")

σάρξ, *flesh*, **sarcasm** (a sharp, mocking remark intended to wound another; literally, "to tear flesh"), **sarcoma** (a malignant tumor usually in connective tissue), **sarcophagus** (a stone coffin; literally, "to eat flesh" because limestone coffins accelerated disintegration)

πούς, *foot*, **octopus** (a marine creature having eight legs; literally, "eight feet"), **platypus** (a semiaquatic mammal with webbed feet; literally, "flat feet"), **podiatry** (the study and treatment of foot ailments; literally, "foot healing"), **podium** (an elevated platform for a speaker; cf. podion which is the diminutive form of pouj), **tripod** (a three-legged stand; literally, "three feet")

χάρις, *grace*, *favor*, **Charissa** (literally, "grace"), **Eucharist** (Christian communion; literally, "thanksgiving" or "good favor")

αἷμα, *blood*, **anemia** (or anaemia; a deficiency of oxygen-carrying material in the blood; literally, "without blood"), **anemic** (or anaemic; listless, weak, or pallid; literally, "without blood"), **hematology** (the science of studying blood), **hemoglobin** (the oxygen-carrying substance in blood; literally, "a blood drop"), **hemophilia** (a disorder characterized by excessive bleeding; literally, "blood lover"), **hemorrhage** (a profuse discharge of blood; literally, "a blood flow"), **leukemia** (cancer of the white blood cells; literally, "white blood")

γράμμα, *letter*, **cardiogram** (the curve traced by a cardiograph to diagnose heart defects), **grammar** (the systematic study of a language), **grammatical** (relating to rules of a language; literally, "of letters"), **pentagram** (a five-pointed star usually used in magic), **telegram** (a communication transmitted by telegraph; literally, "end letter"), **Tetragrammaton** (the four Hebrew letters often transliterated as YHWH and used as a proper name for God; literally, "four letters")

ὄνομα, *name*, **acronym** (a word formed from the initial letters of words; literally, "high name"), **antonym** (a word having a meaning opposite to that of another word; literally, "name against"), **binomial** (a mathematical expression formed by two terms connected with a plus or minus sign; literally, "two names"), **homonym** (one of two or more words which have the same sound but different meanings; literally, "similar name"), **Jerome** (Hieronymos]Ιερώνυμος]; the biblical scholar, fourth to fifth centuries; literally, "sacred name"), **onomasticon** (a vocabulary of proper names), **onomatopoeia** (formation of words by making their sounds; literally, "making a name"), **patronymic** (a name received from a paternal ancestor, e.g. "Stevenson"; literally, "father's name"), polynomial (a mathematical expression consisting of two or more terms; literally, "many names"), **pseudonym** (a fictitious name assumed by an author; literally, "false name"), **synonym** (a word having the same meaning as that of another in the same language; literally, "name together"), cf. Latin *nomen, nominis* (cognomen, nomenclature, nominate, nominative, nominal, noun, pronoun, renown, denomination, ignominy)

πνεῦμα, *spirit, wind*, **pneumatic** (a device empowered by compressed air), **pneumatology** (the Christian doctrine of the Holy Spirit), **pneumonia** (infection or inflammation of the lungs)

ῥῆμα, *word*, cf. ῥητορική (rhetoric)

σπέρμα, *seed*, **sperm** (male reproductive cells; literally, "seed"), **spermatozoa** (the fertilizing gametes of a male animal; literally, "a seed animal"), **spermicide** (an agent that kills sperm; literally, "seed killer")

στόμα, *mouth*, **Chrysostom** (gifted orator of the fourth century; literally, "golden mouth"), **stoma** (a minute opening on the surface of a leaf; literally, "mouth"), **stomach** (principle organ of digestion in mammals)

σῶμα, *body*, **chromosome** (the part of a cell responsible for hereditary characteristics; literally, "body color"), **psychosomatic** (a physical disorder originating in or aggravated by the mind; literally, "mind-body")

ἄρχων, *ruler*, **anarchy** (the absence of political authority; literally, "without a ruler"), **Archelaus** (literally, "ruler of the people"), **ethnarch** (the ruler of a province or people; literally, "nation ruler"), **gynarchy** (government by women; literally, "female rule"), **matriarch** (a woman who rules a family, clan, or tribe; literally, "mother ruler"), **monarch** (a sole hereditary ruler; literally, "only ruler"), **oligarchy** (government by a few; literally, "few rulers"), **patriarch** (the male leader of a family or tribe; literally, "father ruler"), **tetrarch** (a governor of one of the four divisions of a country, especially in the Roman Empire; literally, "four rulers")

λέων, *lion*, cf. Latin *leo, leonis* (Leo, Leonard, leopard, lion)

ὀδούς, *tooth*, **odontology** (the study of the teeth), **orthodontist** (a dentist who corrects tooth irregularities; literally, "a tooth straightener"), **periodontal** (occurring around a tooth or affecting the gums; literally, "around the tooth")

νύξ, *night*, **nyctalopia** (night blindness; literally, "night blindness"), **nyctatropism** (the tendency of the leaves of some plants to change their position at night; literally, "turns at night"), cf. Latin *nox, noctis* (equinox, noctiluca, noctuid, nocturnal, nocturne)

οὖς, *ear*, **otology** (the scientific study of the ear), **otoscope** (an instrument used to view the ear)

ὕδωρ, *water*, **dehydrate** (to lose water or moisture), **hydrant** (a large discharge pipe for providing water), **hydraulic** (operated by water or fluid), **hydroelectric** (generating electricity by moving water), **hydrogen** (a gaseous element which produces water when burned; literally, "water producing"), **hydrolysis** (decomposition of a chemical compound by reaction with water; literally, "loosing by water"), **hydrophobia** (the fear of water), **hydroplane** (to skim on the surface of water), **hydrothermal** (pertaining to hot water; literally, "hot water")

φῶς, *light*, **aphotic zone** (the part of the ocean in total darkness; literally, "the zone without light"), **disphotic zone** (the part of the ocean with reduced light; literally, "the zone with little light"), **phosphorus** (a highly reactive element which burns easily; literally, "light carrier"), **phot** (a unit of illumination), **photograph** (an image or picture recorded a light-sensitive surface; literally, "light writing"), **photosynthesis** (the process in which plant cells convert chemicals and light into energy; literally, "to place light together")

γένος, *race*, **androgenous** (pertaining to production of male offspring; literally, "male offspring"), **eugenics** (the study of hereditary improvement by genetic control; literally, "good offspring"), **genocide** (the systematic killing of a whole race; literally, "to kill a race"), **homogenous** (of the same or similar nature or kind; literally, "same kind"), cf. Latin *genus*, *generis* (degenerate, gender, general, generic, generous, genitive, genuine, genus)

ἔθνος, *nation*, *gentile*, **ethnarch** (the ruler of a province or people; literally, "nation ruler"), **ethnic** (pertaining to a cultural, racial or national group), **ethnicity** (the condition of belonging to a cultural group), **ethnocen-trism** (belief in the superiority of one's own ethnic group), **ethnology** (anthropological study of culture)

ἔτος, *year*, **Etesian Winds** (the prevailing northerly summer winds of the Mediterranean; literally, "the yearly winds")

μέρος, *part*, **isomer** (any of two or more chemical compounds whose molecules contain the same atoms but in different arrangements; literally, "equal parts"), **pentamerous** (having five similar parts; literally, "five parts"), **polymer** (a substance consisting of giant molecules formed from smaller molecules of the same substance; literally, "many parts")

ὄρος, *mountain*, **ore** (a mined mineral or metal), **orogenesis** (the formation of a mountain; literally, "mountain beginning"),

orogenic belt (a belt of mountain building), **orogeny** (an episode in mountain formation), **orography** (the study of the physical geography of mountains and mountain ranges), **orology** (the study of mountains)

πλῆθος, *crowd*, **plethora** (an overabundance or excess; literally, "fullness"), **plethoric** (excessive in quantity)

σκότος, *darkness*, **scotobiotic** (capable of living in darkness; literally, "dark life"), **scotoma** (an area of diminished vision within a visual field), **scotopia** (ability to see in dim light; literally, "darkness vision"), **scotoscope** (a device used to enhance night vision; literally, "darkness vision")

τέλος, *end*, **telegram** (communication transmitted by telegraph; literally, "end letter"), **telegraph** (device transmitting messages by wire; literally, "end writing"), **teleology** (philosophical study of design or purpose), **telephone** (device transmitting sounds from one location to another; literally, "end sound"), **telescope** (device used to see distant objects; literally, "to see the end"), **telic** (directed toward a goal or purpose)

NOUN DECLENSIONS

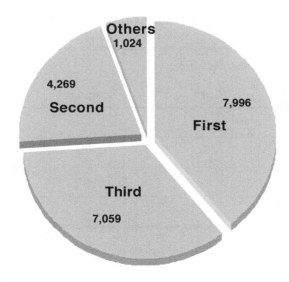

Others 1,024

4,269 Second

7,996 First

Third 7,059

ASSIGNMENT
1

Vocabulary #1: δεκατέσσαρες through σῶμα.

▰ OBJECTIVE QUESTIONS ▰

1. Third declension is known as the _____ declension and has no
    _____ vowel. Endings are added directly to the noun
    _____. Consonants collide, creating reactions, especially in the
    _____ singular and the _____ plural because of the letter
    _____ common to these inflections.

2. Check the case represented by the *third* declension ending -ος as used in a
    dictionary's second entry:

    ☐ nominative   ☐ genitive   ☐ vocative

3. In the third declension inflection, only *two* sets of endings are needed
    because the masculine and _____ gender have the same endings.
    Regardless of gender, all the interiors are all the _____. When
    a pattern shows *no ending*, stems still will change because the exposed
    consonant of the noun stem may _____, which may generate
    further volatilization.

4. Provide the two basic ending patterns for third declension:

	Masculine/Feminine		Neuter	
	Singular	Plural	Singular	Plural
N				
G				
D				
A				

5. Understanding sigma volatilization patterns is imperative for some very common third declension reaction patterns. These patterns relate specifically to volatilization with what type consonants?

☐ stops   ☐ liquids   ☐ nasals

Fill in the following chart:

Formation	Volatilization Pattern		
	volatilizing consonant	simple sibilant	resultant sibilant
labials		+ σ	= ψ
palatals		+ σ	= ξ
dentals		+ σ	= σ

6. The real trick to third declension nouns is to *nail down the nominative and accusative singular forms*. The plurals are quite predictable and stable, for even the dative plural always shows a characteristic iota ending, no matter what the consonant winds up being (e.g., -ψι, -ξι, -σι). The neuter plural, nominative and accusative, always is _____. Masculine accusative singular endings will vary between either _____ or _____. An odd ending is ἔθνος, whose accusative is like the _____ case, and the genitive form is _____. The accusative singular of σάρξ is _____; χάρις is _____; σῶμα is _____; ἄρχων is _____.

TRANSLATION

7. Translate the following, using the translation aids provided below:

○ *Translation Aids* ○

τις, *a certain* (indefinite pronoun)
Λυδία, *Lydia*

μισθός, ὁ, *wage*
ὀφείλημα, -τος, τό *debt*
παραλαμβάνω, *I bring along*

7.1   καί τις γυνὴ ὀνόματι Λυδία, . . ., ἤκουεν [Acts 16:14]

7.2   οὐκ ἐξ αἱμάτων οὐδὲ ἐκ θελήματος σαρκὸς [John 1:13]

_____

7.3   ὅ ἐστιν Χριστὸς ἐν ὑμῖν, ἡ ἐλπὶς τῆς δόξης [Col. 1:27]

_____

7.4   ὁ μισθὸς οὐ λογίζεται κατὰ χάριν ἀλλὰ κατὰ
      ὀφείλημα [Rom. 4:4]

_____

7.5   ἐν τῇ σαρκί μου ὑπὲρ τοῦ σώματος αὐτοῦ, ὅ ἐστιν
      ἡ ἐκκλησία [Col. 1:24]

_____

7.6   τότε πορεύεται καὶ παραλαμβάνει μεθ᾽ ἑαυτοῦ
      ἑπτὰ ἕτερα πνεύματα [Matt.. 12:45]

_____

ASSIGNMENT
2

Vocabulary #2: ἄρχων through τέλος.

OBJECTIVE QUESTIONS

8. Give the correct Greek article in concord with the following noun
   inflections:

8.1 _____ ἐλπίς	8.5 _____ σαρκί	8.9 _____ ἄρχοντα
8.2 _____ χάριν	8.6 _____ ἐθνῶν	8.10 _____ σάρκας
8.3 _____ ὅρος	8.7 _____ χάριτες	8.11 _____ πνεύματι
8.4 _____ σώματος	8.8 _____ ἄρχοντες	8.12 _____ ἔθνεσιν

9. Locate the first/second declension nouns in the right column, then match to the correct case, gender, and number of third declension nouns in the left column:

____ 9.1 χάριν   a. λόγους _____

____ 9.2 σαρκός   b. δώρου   _____

____ 9.3 σῶμα   c. καρδίαν _____

____ 9.4 ἄρχοντας d. δῶρον   _____

____ 9.5 ἔθνους   e. γραφῆς _____

TRANSLATION

10. Translate the following, using the translation aids provided below:

○ *Translation Aids* ○

Ἀβραάμ, *Abraham* (genitive)
καλύπτω, *I cover*
μετάνοια, ἡ, *repentance*
βαπτίσει, *he will baptize*, future tense, with future suffix -σ ; stem βαπτιδ- drops the -δ before the -σ.

κατακυριεύω, *I have power over*
ἐφ᾽ ὅσον μὲν, *in as much as* (treat as a unit)
πάθημα, -τος, τό, *suffering, passion*
ἐνεργέω, *I am at work in, am operative*

10.1 υἱοὶ γένους Ἀβραὰμ [Acts 13:26]

_____

10.2 τέλος γὰρ νόμου Χριστὸς

_____

10.3 Καὶ ἀναβαίνει εἰς τὸ ὄρος [Mark 3:13]

_____

10.4 οὐκ ἐσμὲν νυκτὸς οὐδὲ σκότους

_____

10.5 ἀγάπη καλύπτει πλῆθος ἁμαρτιῶν [1 Pet. 4:8]

_____

10.6 ἀπὸ τῆς δόξης τοῦ φωτὸς ἐκείνου

_____

10.7 οἱ ἄρχοντες τῶν ἐθνῶν κατακυριεύουσιν αὐτῶν [Matt. 20:25]

_____

10.8 ὑμῖν δὲ λέγω τοῖς ἔθνεσιν· ἐφ᾽ ὅσον μὲν οὖν εἰμι ἐγὼ ἐθνῶν ἀπόστολος

_____

_____

10.9 ἐγὼ μὲν ὑμᾶς βαπτίζω ἐν ὕδατι εἰς μετάνοιαν· . . . αὐτὸς ὑμᾶς βαπτίσει ἐν πνεύματι ἁγίῳ [Matt. 3:11]

_____

_____

10.10 ὅτε γὰρ ἦμεν ἐν τῇ σαρκί, τὰ παθήματα τῶν ἁμαρτιῶν τὰ διὰ τοῦ νόμου ἐνηργεῖτο ἐν τοῖς μέλεσιν ἡμῶν

_____

_____

LESSON 15
(δεκαπέντε)

Third Declension—Liquid and Vowel Stems

Vocabulary 15

αἰών, *age, eternity,* **eon** (an extremely long period of time)

μάρτυς, *witness,* **martyr** (a person whose testimony is sealed by their death), **martyrdom** (the death of a martyr), cf. μαρτυρέω

πῦρ, *fire,* **pyre** (a pile of wood for burning a corpse in a funeral rite), **pyretic** (characterized or affected by fever), **Pyrex** (heat-resistant glassware for cooking), **pyrogenous** (produced by or producing heat; literally, "fire producing"), **pyromania** (a compulsion to start destructive fires; literally, "fire madness"), **pyrotechnic** (pertaining to fireworks; literally, "fire art" or "fire skill")

σωτήρ, *savior,* **soteriology** (the theological study of salvation)

χείρ, *hand,* **chirography** (penmanship; literally, "hand writing"), **chiromancy** (palm-reading; literally, "hand divination"), **chiropractic** (therapy by manipulating the spinal column or joints; literally, "hand done")

Ἕλλην, *Greek, gentile,* **hellenism** (the spread of Greek culture in the ancient world), **Hellenist** (a person who adopted the Greek language and culture), **Panhellenic** (pertaining to the unifying of the Greek peoples or pertaining to Greek-letter fraternities and sororities; literally, "all the Greeks)

ἀήρ, *air,* **aerial** (pertaining to the air), **aerobic** (living or occurring only in the presence of oxygen), **aerodynamics** (the branch of mechanics dealing with the forces exerted by air; literally, "air power"), **aeronautics** (the science of aircraft design and operation; literally, "air-sailing"), **aeroplane** (the British variation of airplane), **aerosol** (the suspension of colloidal particles in a gas; literally, "an air solution"), **aerospace** (the earth's atmosphere), cf. Latin *aer, aeris*

ἀστήρ, *star,* **aster** (a daisy-like flower; literally, "star"), **asterisk** (a star-shaped symbol [*]; literally, "a little star"), **asteroid** (a small celestial body in an orbit), **astrology** (the study of the stars for influence on human affairs), **astronaut** (a navigator of a spacecraft; literally, "a star sailor"), **astronomy** (the scientific study of the universe beyond the earth), **disaster** (a misfortune causing widespread destruction; originally, the evil influence of a celestial body)

εἰκών, *likeness, image,* **icon** (an image or representation), **iconoclast** (one who attacks traditional ideas; literally, "an image breaker")

ἡγεμών, *governor, ruler,* **hegemony** (the predominant influence of one state over another; literally, "leadership"), cf. ἡγέομαι (eisegesis, exegesis)

ποιμήν, *shepherd,* **poimenic** (pastoral in nature; literally, "shepherdly"; cf. Latin *pastor, pastoris* ["shepherd"])

ἀνήρ, *man, husband,* **Alexander** (literally, "defending men"), **Andrew** (literally, "manly"), **androgen** (a male sex hormone), **androgenous** (pertaining to production of male offspring; literally, "male offspring"), **androgynous** (having both male and female characteristics; literally, "male-female"), **android** (possessing human features), **Neandrathal** (a prehistoric man; literally, "new man"), **philander** (to engage in casual love affairs; literally, "a loving man"), **polyandry** (having more than one husband; literally, "many husbands")

μήτηρ, *mother*, **metropolis** (a major city; literally, "mother city"), cf. Latin *mater*, *matris* (maternal, matriarchy, matrimony, matricide, matriculate, matron)

πατήρ, *father*, **patriarch** (the male leader of a family or tribe; literally, "father ruler"), **patriot** (a person who loves and supports his country; literally, "of one's fathers"), **patristic** (pertaining to the fathers of the early church), **patronymic** (a name received from a paternal ancestor, e.g. "Stevenson"; literally, "father's name"), cf. Latin *pater*, *patris* (paternal, paternity, patrician, patrimony, patron)

πόλις, *town*, **acropolis** (the elevated part of an ancient Greek city such as in Athens; literally, "the high city"), **decapolis** (the district of first-century Palestine comprised of ten hellenistic cities; literally, "ten cities"), **Hierapolis** (an ancient city of Asia Minor; literally, "sacred city"), **Indianapolis** (literally, "city of Indiana"), **megalopolis** (a vast, populous urban area; literally, "a great city"), **metropolis** (a major city; literally, "mother city"), **necropolis** (a cemetery, especially a large one of an ancient city; literally, "the city of the dead"), **Tripoli** (literally, "three cities"); cf. πολιτή (cosmopolitan, politics)

κρίσις, *judgment*, **crisis** (a decisive situation or turning point), **criterion** (a standard on which a judgment is based), **critic** (one who forms and expresses judgments), **critical** (characterized by careful or severe judgment), **critique** (a critical review of a work), **diacritical** (marking a distinction; literally, "to distinguish" or "to judge through"), **endocrine** (secreting internally; literally, "to separate inside"), **hypocrite** (a person who professes and acts in a contradictory manner; literally, "an actor" or "one under examination")

δύναμις, *power*, **aerodynamics** (the branch of mechanics dealing with the forces exerted by air; literally, "air power"), **dynamic** (pertaining to energy or force), **dynamo** (a generator), **dynasty** (a family or group that maintains power for several generations), **dynamite** (a powerful explosive), **thermodynamics** (the branch of physics dealing with the transformation of heat into mechanical energy; literally, "heat power")

ἀνάστασις, *resurrection*, cf. ἀνά, + ἵστημι

ἰχθύς, *fish*, ΙΧΘΥΣ (a Greek acronym for Ἰησοῦς Χριστός, Θεοῦ Υἱός, Σωτήρ ("Jesus Christ, God's Son, Savior"), which also spelled "fish"), **ichthyology** (the study of fish)

ἀρχιερεύς, *chief priest*, cf. ἀρχή + ἱερεύς

βασιλεύς, *king*, **Basil** (a Greek church father of the fourth century; literally, "kingly"), **basilica** (a type of a Roman building used as a court or place of assembly later used as churches; literally, "kingly")

γραμματεύς, *scribe*, **grammatical** (relating to rules of a language; literally, "of letters"), **Tetragrammaton** (the four Hebrew letters usually transliterated as YHWH which are used as a proper name for God; literally, "four letters"), cf. γράμμα (cardiogram, grammar, pentagram, telegram)

ἱερεύς, *priest*, **hierophant** (an interpreter of sacred mysteries; literally, "a revealer of sacred things"), **Hierapolis** (an ancient city of Asia Minor; literally, "sacred city"), **hierarchy** (a body of persons organized according to rank of authority; literally, "priestly rule"), **hieroglyphics** (a pictorial system of writing in ancient Egypt; literally, "sacred carvings"), **Jerome** (or Hieronymos [Ἱερώνυμος]; the biblical scholar of the fourth to fifth centuries; literally, "sacred name"), cf. ἱερόν

νοῦς, *mind, thought*, **noetic** (pertaining to or apprehended by the intellect), **paranoia** (a mental disorder characterized by delusions of persecution; literally, "beyond the mind"), cf. μετάνοια ("repentance"; literally, "a mind change")

OBJECTIVE QUESTIONS

1. Some rho stem third declension nouns suppress a short vowel between two single consonants for pronunciation, known as _____. The paradigm _____ is an example.

2. The vowels _____ and _____ on third declension nouns function as semivowels, that is, with _____ effect. The paradigm _____ is a semivowel stem whose _____ and _____ plurals are the same, i.e., the form _____. The genitive singular is Attic and has the form _____.

3. Another semivowel stem is the paradigm _____, ending with the diphthong _____, all of which such nouns are masculine. Plural forms of the _____ and _____ cases are the same, having the form _____. The genitive singular is Attic and has the form _____.

4. Match the inflected noun with the correct article form:

   _____ πατέρα   _____ πίστεως   _____ πίστει   _____ ἱερεῖς

5. Locate the first/second declension nouns in the right column, then match to the correct case, gender, and number of third declension nouns in the left column:

   _____ 5.1 πίστεως   a. λόγους _____

   _____ 5.2 πίστεις   b. λόγοις _____

   _____ 5.3 ἱερεῖς   c. καρδίας* _____

   _____ 5.4 πατράσι   d. καρδίαι _____

   *Assume singular (see Table 5.2, *NTG*, 59).

6. Adverb comparative and superlative in the neuter use the adjective ending pattern _____. Another pattern uses the comparative -τερω and the superlative _____. Thus, ἄνω as comparative is _____, meaning _____. The superlative is _____, meaning, _____.

7. A relative pronoun looks like an inflectional ending, but has _____ breathing and an accent. The nominative masculine singular Greek article

has the form _____, that is, without accent. In contrast, the nominative neuter singular relative pronoun has the form _____, with accent. Relative pronouns show concord in _____ and _____, but not in _____, determined by function in the relative clause.

═══════════════ TRANSLATION ═══════════════

8. Translate the following, using the translation aids provided below:

○   *Translation Aids*   ○

τε καί, *both . . . and* (#8.3)   Γνωρίζω, *I make known*
ἰσχυρός, *strong mighty*   Δαυίδ, *David*
    (adjective)   διαφέρω, *I differ*
ἱκανός, *worthy* (adjective)   ἀποκαλύπτω, *I reveal*
πολύς, *large, great* (adjective)   αὐτῷ, the antecedent is neuter
ὑπακούω, *I am obedient, obey*   (#8.13)

8.1   ἀπὸ πόλεως εἰς πόλιν [Matt. 23:34]

8.2   καὶ νῦν ὃν ἔχεις οὐκ ἔστιν σου ἀνήρ

8.3   ἐβαπτίζοντο ἄνδρες τε καὶ γυναῖκες [Acts 8:12]

8.4   τὸ δὲ ῥῆμα κυρίου μένει εἰς τὸν αἰῶνα.

8.5   ἰσχυρότερός μού ἐστιν, οὗ οὐκ εἰμὶ ἱκανὸς [Matt. 3:11]

8.6   ὃς γὰρ οὐκ ἔστιν καθ' ἡμῶν, ὑπὲρ ἡμῶν ἐστιν.

8.7   πολύς τε ὄχλος τῶν ἱερέων ὑπήκουον τῇ πίστει [Acts 6:7]

_____

8.8   Γνωρίζω δὲ ὑμῖν τὸ εὐαγγέλιον δι' οὗ καὶ σῴζεσθε

_____

8.9   σωτὴρ ὅς ἐστιν Χριστὸς κύριος ἐν πόλει Δαυίδ [Luke 2:11]

_____

8.10 τῆς δόξης τοῦ Χριστοῦ, ὅς ἐστιν εἰκὼν τοῦ θεοῦ

_____

8.11 οὐ πιστεύεις ὅτι ἐγὼ ἐν τῷ πατρὶ καὶ ὁ πατὴρ ἐν ἐμοί ἐστιν; [John 14:10]

_____

8.12 καὶ ἄλλη δόξα ἀστέρων· ἀστὴρ γὰρ ἀστέρος διαφέρει ἐν δόξῃ

_____

8.13 δικαιοσύνη γὰρ θεοῦ ἐν αὐτῷ ἀποκαλύπτεται ἐκ πίστεως εἰς πίστιν [Rom. 1:17]

_____

9. Diagram the following taken from the exercises above, referring to Tables 11.17 and 11.22 on relative pronouns (*NTG*, 127, 132).

9.1 καὶ νῦν ὃν ἔχεις οὐκ ἔστιν σου ἀνήρ

9.2 ἰσχυρότερός μού ἐστιν, οὗ οὐκ εἰμὶ ἱκανὸς

9.3 ὃς γὰρ οὐκ ἔστιν καθ᾽ ἡμῶν, ὑπὲρ ἡμῶν ἐστιν.

9.4 Γνωρίζω δὲ ὑμῖν τὸ εὐαγγέλιον δι᾽ οὗ καὶ σώζεσθε

LESSON 16
(δεκαέξ)
Adjectives and Comparisons—Again

αἰώνιος, *eternal*, *unending*, **eon** (an extremely long period of time), cf. αἰών

ἀκαθαρτός, *unclean*, **catharsis** (a process of purging)

ἁμαρτωλός, *sinful*, *sinner*, cf. ἁμαρτία (hamartiology)

ἔρημος, *lonely*, *deserted*, **eremite** (a religious recluse), **hermit** (a person who has withdrawn from society), **hermitage** (secluded retreat; Andrew Jackson's home)

χρυσοῦς, *golden*, **chrysanthemum** (a gold-color flower; literally, "gold flower"), **chryselephantine** (made of gold and ivory; literally, "gold and ivory"), **chrysolite** (a yellow or greenish gem; literally, "gold stone"), **Chrysostom** (the eloquent preacher of the fourth century; literally, "golden-mouthed")

ἀσθενής, *sick*, *weak*, **asthenia** (lack or loss of bodily strength), **asthenic** (a slender, lightly muscled human physique), **asthenopia** (eyestrain resulting in dim vision; literally, "weak sight"), **asthenosphere** (the less rigid layer of the earth's mantle), **neurasthenia** (fatigue once thought to result from nervous system exhaustion)

πλήρης, *full*, **pleroma** (in Valentinian Gnosticism, the *pleroma* was the fullness of the spiritual world as pairs of aeons; literally, "fullness"), cf. πληρόω

συγγενής, *relative*, cf. σύν + γενός

ὑγιής, *healthy*, **hygiene** (the science of health and prevention of disease), **hygienic** (tending to promote or preserve health)

ἄφρων, *foolish*, cf. ἀ + φρωνέω (literally, "not thinking")

ταχύς, *quick*, **tachometer** (an instrument that measures rotational speed; literally, "speed measure"), **tachy-cardia** (excessively rapid heartbeat; literally, "swift heart"), **tachygraphy** (rapid writing or shorthand; literally, "fast writing"), **tachypnea** (excessively rapid respiration; literally, "fast breathing")

πᾶς, *every*, *all*, *whole*, **Pan-American** (of North, South, and Central America collectively; literally, "all the Americas"), **pandemonium** (the abode of all demons in John Milton's *Paradise Lost*; literally, "all the demons"), **Pandora** (Greek mythology's first mortal woman who opened a box releasing all evil into the world; literally, "all giving"), **Panhellenic** (about the unifying of the Greek peoples or pertaining to Greek-letter fraternities and sororities; literally, "all the Greeks), **panorama** (an open view in all directions; literally "seeing all"), **pantheism** (belief that God is the sum of all things; literally, "all is God"), **pantheon** (a temple for all the gods; literally, "all the gods")

μέλας, *black*, **melancholy** (sadness, depression; literally, "black bile"), **melanin** (a dark pigment in skin or hair), **melanoma** (dark-pigmented malignant tumor)

μέγας, *large*, *great*, **megahertz** (one million cycles per second, especially in radio frequency; literally, "many cycles"), **megalith** (a very large stone; literally, "large stone"), **megalomania** (mental disorder characterized by delusions of grandeur, power, and wealth; literally, "madness of greatness"), **megalopolis** (a region made up of several large cities; literally, "large city"), **megaphone** (a device used to amplify the voice; literally, "loud sound"), **omega** (the last letter of the Greek alphabet; literally, "the great O") πολύς, *much*, *many*, **polyandry** (having more than one husband; literally, "many husbands"), **polygamy** (being married to more than one person at the same time; literally, "many marriages"), **polyglot** (a speech or writing in several languages; literally, "many tongues"), **polygon** (a multi-sided figure; literally, "many angles"), **polymath** (a person learned in many fields;

literally, "much learning"), **polynomial** (a mathematical expression consisting of two or more terms; literally, "many names"), **polytheism** (the belief in many gods; literally, "many gods")

πλείων, *more than* (also πλέον), **pleonasm** (speech redundancy), **pleonastic** (excessive amount of words)

TRANSLATION

1. Translate the following, using the translation aids provided below:

○   *Translation Aids* ○

κρατέω, *I hold, seize* (translate as a command)

πρῶτος, *first*

εὐδοκία, good will, pleasure, favor

Ἰουδαίας, *Judea* (ablative)

Ἰερουσαλήμ, *Jerusalem* (ablative)

1.1   ἀληθὴς εἶ

_____

1.2   Πάντες ζητοῦσίν σε

_____

1.3   ῥήματα ζωῆς αἰωνίου ἔχεις

_____

1.4   ἔρχομαι ταχύ· κράτει ὃ ἔχεις

_____

1.5   ἔλεγον· πνεῦμα ἀκάθαρτον ἔχει

_____

1.6   πόλις ἐστὶν τοῦ μεγάλου βασιλέως

_____

1.7   γυνὴ ἥτις ἦν ἐν τῇ πόλει ἁμαρτωλός

_____

1.8   αὕτη ἐστὶν ἡ μεγάλη καὶ πρώτη ἐντολή

_____

1.10   τὰ ἔργα σου τὰ ἔσχατα πλείονα τῶν πρώτων

_____

1.11   ἐπ' ἐρήμοις τόποις ἦν· καὶ ἤρχοντο πρὸς αὐτὸν

_____

1.12   οὗτοι οἱ ἄνθρωποι δοῦλοι τοῦ θεοῦ τοῦ ὑψίστου
        εἰσίν

_____

1.13   Ὁ πιστὸς ἐν ἐλαχίστῳ καὶ ἐν πολλῷ πιστός ἐστιν

_____

1.14   Οὐκ εἰσὶν ἡμῖν πλεῖον ἢ ἄρτοι πέντε καὶ ἰχθύες
        δύο

_____

1.15   ὁ δὲ μικρότερος ἐν τῇ βασιλείᾳ τῶν οὐρανῶν
        μείζων αὐτοῦ

_____

1.16   ἦν ἀνὴρ ἀγαθὸς καὶ πλήρης πνεύματος ἁγίου καὶ
        πίστεως

_____

1.17   δόξα ἐν ὑψίστοις θεῷ καὶ ἐπὶ γῆς εἰρήνη ἐν
        ἀνθρώποις εὐδοκίας

_____

1.18 ὄχλος πολὺς μαθητῶν αὐτοῦ, καὶ πλῆθος πολὺ τοῦ
λαοῦ ἀπὸ πάσης τῆς Ἰουδαίας καὶ Ἰερουσαλὴμ
ἤρχοντο πρὸς αὐτὸν

_____

_____

_____

LESSON 17

(ἑπτά καὶ δέκα)

Numerals

εἷς, μία, ἕν, *one*, **henotheism** (belief in one god without denying the existence of others; literally, "one god"), **hyphen** (a punctuation mark used to connect the parts of a compound word; literally, "under one")

δύο, *two*, **duet** (a musical composition for two people), **duo** (a pair or a couple), **dyad** (two units regarded as a pair), **dyothelitism** (the theological doctrine that in Christ there were two wills, both human and divine; literally, "two wills"), cf. Latin *duo*

τρεῖς, *three*, **triad** (a group of three), **triangle** (a figure with three sides and three angles; literally, "three angles"), **trigonometry** (the mathematical study of triangles; literally, "the measurement of triangles"), **trio** (a musical composition for three), **tripod** (a three-legged stand; literally, "three-feet"), cf. Latin *tres, tria* (trident, triumvirate, trivia)

τέσσαρες, *four*, **Diatessaron** (Tatian's harmony of the four gospels; literally, "through four"), **tetragon** (a four-sided polygon; literally, "four angles"), **Tetragrammaton** (the four Hebrew letters usually transliterated as YHWH which are used as a proper name for God; literally, "four letters"), **tetrahedron** (a solid figure with four triangular faces; literally, "four bases"), **tetrarch** (a governor of one of the four divisions of a country, especially in the Roman Empire; literally, "four rulers")

πέντε, *five*, **pentagon** (a figure with five sides and five angles; literally, "five angles"), **pentagram** (a five pointed star usually used in magic), **pentamerous** (having five similar parts; literally, "five parts"), **pentameter** (a line of verse containing five metrical feet), **Pentateuch** (the first five books of the Bible; literally, "five books"), **pentathlon** (an athletic competition consisting of five events)

ἕξ, *six*, **hexagon** (a figure with six sides and six angles; literally, "six angles"), **hexameter** (a line of verse containing six metrical feet), **Hexapla** (Origen's compilation of the Old Testament which consisted of six Hebrew and Greek texts written side by side), **Hexateuch** (designation for the first six books of the Bible; literally, "six books"), cf. Latin *sex* (sextet, sextant)

ἑπτά, *seven*, **heptagon** (a figure with seven sides and seven angles; literally, "seven angles"), **heptameter** (a unit of verse consisting of seven feet), **heptarchy** (rule of seven people), **heptathlon** (an athletic competition consisting of seven events), cf. Latin *septem* (September, septuagenarian, Septuagesima, Septuagint)

ὀκτώ, *eight*, **octagon** (figure with eight sides and eight angles; literally, "eight angles"), **octopus** (marine creature having eight legs; literally, "eight feet"), cf. Latin *octo* (octave, octavo, octet, October, octogenarian)

ἐννέα, *nine*, **ennead** (a group or set of nine)

δέκα, *ten*, **decalogue** (the Ten Commandments; literally, "the ten words"), **decapolis** (the district near Galilee comprised of ten hellenistic cities; literally, "ten cities"), **decade** (a period of ten years), **decathlon** (an athletic contest consisting of ten events), cf. Latin *decem* (December, decemvir, decimal, decimeter) ἕνδεκα, *eleven*, **hendecasyllabic** (a verse containing eleven syllables; literally, "eleven syllables")

δώδεκα, *twelve*, **dodecagon** (a polygon with twelve sides; literally, "twelve angles"), **dodecahedron** (a polyhedron with twelve faces; literally, "twelve bases"), **dodecaphonic** (pertaining to twelve-tone music; literally, "twelve sounds")

εἴκοσι, *twenty*, **icosahedron** (a polyhedron having twenty faces; literally, "twenty bases")

πεντήκοντα, *fifty*, **Pentecost** (a Jewish or Christian festival celebrated fifty days after Passover; literally, "the fiftieth")

ἑκατόν, *one hundred*, **hecatomb** (a sacrifice of a hundred oxen to the gods of ancient Greece and Rome), **hectometer** (metric unit of a hundred meters)

χίλιοι, *one thousand*, **chiliasm** (the doctrine stating that Christ will rule for a thousand years), **kilometer** (a distance of a thousand meters; literally, "thousand meters"), **kilogram** (a weight of a thousand grams; literally, "thousand grams"), **kiloliter** (a unit of volume equal to a thousand liters; literally, "thousand liters"), **kilowatt** (a unit of power equal to a thousand watts; literally, "thousand watts")

μύριοι, *ten thousand*, **myriad** (a very large, indefinite number)

πρῶτος, *first*, **protagonist** (the main character in a drama or novel; literally, "the first actor"), **protein** (a food substance essential for tissue growth; literally, "primary"), **proton** (a positively charged subatomic particle; literally, "first"), **protoplasm** (a colloidal substance essential to living matter; literally, "primary form"), **prototype** (the first example of an object; literally, "first model"), **protozoa** (a one-celled, primitive form of animal life; literally, "first life")

δεύτερος, *second*, **deuteragonist** (in classical Greek drama, the character of second importance; literally, "second actor"), **deuteranopia** (red-green color-blindness; literally, "without seeing the second"; so called because green is considered the second of the primary colors), **deuterium** (a heavy isotope of hydrogen, having an atomic weight of 2), **deuterocanonical** (the designation for the Apocrypha by the Council of Trent in 1548; literally, "canonized second"), **Deuteronomy** (the Old Testament book which contains the second giving of the Mosaic law; literally, "second law")

ἅπαξ, *once*, **hapax legomenon** (a word which only occurs one time in the Greek New Testament; literally, "spoken once")

OBJECTIVE QUESTIONS

1. The *interrogative* pronoun is translated _____, _____, or _____. The *indefinite* pronoun is not specific, and is translated _____, _____, or _____. The only difference between the interrogative pronoun and the indefinite pronoun is the _____. Both follow the inflection of the _____ declension.

2. The interrogative pronoun in the neuter singular form τί at the front of a clause can be used adverbially to mean _____.

3. The *indefinite relative* pronoun often is _____ of the relative clause, so is usually _____ case. The three genders yield just six typical forms:

Gender	Singular	Plural
3.1 masculine =	_____	_____
3.2 feminine =	_____	_____
3.3 neuter =	_____	_____

    The meaning of the indefinite relative pronoun generally is _____, _____, or _____.

4. The negative pronoun combines the negative _____ and the conjunction _____ with these declined forms of the numeral one: _____, _____, and _____.

5. A nominative that has no inherent grammatical relationship to the rest of the sentence is called a _____ _____.

6. The key to identification of a subjective or an objective genitive is a _____ of _____, which inherently carries a verbal idea. Translate and identify the genitive in the following as an objective or subjective gentive:

    6.1 φόβος θεοῦ [Rom. 3:18]

    _____

    ☐ subjective genitive   ☐ objective genitive

6.2   διὰ τῆς ἀγάπης **τοῦ πνεύματος** [Rom. 15:30]

_____

☐ subjective genitive   ☐ objective genitive

6.3   τὴν ὑπομονὴν **τοῦ Χριστοῦ** [2 Thess. 3:5]

_____

☐ subjective genitive   ☐ objective genitive

6.4   τὸ μαρτύριον **τοῦ Χριστοῦ** [1 Cor. 1:6]

_____

☐ subjective genitive   ☐ objective genitive

7. The accusative is more than just direct object. As the adverbial of
_____, the accusative adds extent in _____ or in
_____ to the verbal idea. As adverbial of _____, the
accusative adds purpose, result, or _____ to the verbal action.
Translate the following (check your work with Matt. 4:8):

7.1   παραλαμβάνει αὐτὸν ὁ διάβολος **εἰς ὄρος**

_____

7.2   Circle the kind of adverbial accusative the form ὄρος is:

     MEASURE   MANNER

8. The Greek article can be found by itself standing for a _____
pronoun. Sometimes the article can be used as a demonstrative pronoun
with the meaning _____ or _____ (sg.), or
_____ or _____ (pl.). When clarifying the conjunction
καί, the article functions according to the rule known as the _____
_____ Rule (_NTG_, 190, note 5). Translate the following (check
your work with 1 Pet. 5:14):

8.1   Εἰρήνη ὑμῖν πᾶσιν **τοῖς** ἐν Χριστῷ

_____

8.2   Circle the pronoun role of the article above: PERSONAL RELATIVE

9. A rhetorical question expecting a "no" answer will use the negative _____ and the _____ mood. An expected "yes" answer will be signaled by the use of the negative _____. Translate the following (check work with John 4:12):

9.1 μὴ σὺ μείζων εἶ τοῦ πατρὸς ἡμῶν Ἰακώβ;

_____

9.2 What answer is expected *by the Samaritan woman*? (circle):

YES   NO

10. The conjunction καί may be translated variously depending on context, such as _____, _____, or _____.

11. Nominative absolutes will diagram with _____ when found as _____ construction. A nominative in apposition diagrams with a separate line and an _____ mark pointing to the construction.

12. Recognizing number units is seeing the inflection patterns by category:

Category	Greek Inflection Pattern
Teens	
Twenties	
Ten Intervals	
One hundred & units	
Hundred intervals*	
Thousand intervals*	

*With inflection for the three genders understood.

TRANSLATION

13. Translate the following, using the translation aids provided below:

○ *Translation Aids* ○

ὡσεί, *about*   χοϊκός, *of the dust*
δηνάριον, τό, *denarius*   δοκέω, *I think, seem*
μεστός, *full*   τέλη, from τέλος, *end, goal,* but
Ἰερουσαλήμ, *Jerusalem*   here, *revenue, tax*
ἐλευθέρος, *free* (adjective)   κῆνσος, *tax*

13.1   ψυχαὶ ὡσεὶ τρισχίλιαι [Acts 2:41]

_____

13.2   ἄνθρωπός τις εἶχεν δύο υἱούς

_____

13.3   ὥρας ἕκτης . . . ἕως ὥρας ἐνάτης

_____

13.4   Τί με λέγεις ἀγαθόν; οὐδεὶς ἀγαθὸς

_____

13.5   καὶ ἦν ἐν τῇ ἐρήμῳ τεσσεράκοντα ἡμέρας [Mark 1:13]

_____

13.6   δηνάρια πεντακόσια, ὁ δὲ ἕτερος πεντήκοντα

_____

13.7   ὁ τέταρτος ἄγγελος . . . τὸ τρίτον τῶν ἀστέρων
        [Rev. 8:12]

_____

13.8   μεστὸν ἰχθύων μεγάλων ἑκατὸν πεντήκοντα τριῶν

_____

13.9 ἡ δὲ ἄνω Ἰερουσαλὴμ ἐλευθέρα ἐστίν, ἥτις ἐστὶν μήτηρ ἡμῶν [2 Cor. 12:8]

13.10 ὁ θεὸς φῶς ἐστιν καὶ σκοτία ἐν αὐτῷ οὐκ ἔστιν οὐδεμία.

13.11 ὁ πρῶτος ἄνθρωπος ἐκ γῆς χοϊκός, ὁ δεύτερος ἄνθρωπος ἐξ οὐρανοῦ. [1 Cor. 15:47]

13.12 τί σοι δοκεῖ, Σίμων; οἱ βασιλεῖς τῆς γῆς ἀπὸ τίνων λαμβάνουσιν τέλη ἢ κῆνσον;

---

14.   Diagram (from sentence 13.4):

14.1 Τί με λέγεις ἀγαθόν; οὐδεὶς ἀγαθὸς

CROSSWORD PUZZLE

This exercise reviews vocabulary 1–17 for fun in preparation for a vocabulary exam. A few words from later vocabulary are indicated. Some blocks do not spell a word. At times, the end of one word begins another word in the same row or column. (V = Vocabulary.)

ACROSS

1. I am
4. together with
7. I confess
12. race
13. in
14. one (num., nom. m. sg.)
15. hour
16. I love
17. therefore
18. blood
19. rel. pron. (acc. f. pl.)
20. yes, truly
23. against
24. with
26. rel. pron. (acc. m. sg.)
27. I lead, bring, go
28. rel. pron. (gen. m. pl.)
29. healthy
31. hour
32. except
33. hair
34. need (see lexicon)
36. rel. pron. (acc. m. sg.)
37. rel. pron. (gen. f. pl.)
38. def. article (nom. n. sg.)
39. how? (3 letters)
40. lion
43. rel. pron. (nom. m. sg.)
44. for
45. I honor
46. Jesus
48. dead
50. not (before rough breathing)
53. tribulation
55. beside
56. but (mild adver.)
58. man (2nd declen.)
60. and (particle)
61. light
62. under
64. but (strong adver.)
66. but (mild adver.)
68. 2nd per. poss. pron. (nom. m. sg.)
69. I loose
70. one (num., nom. f. sg.)
71. 1st per. poss. pron. (nom. f. sg.)
73. word
75. wherefore (V20)
76. fig tree
77. here (V19)
78. 2nd per. poss. pron. (gen. f. sg.)
79. I am (pres. ind. 3pp)
80. 2nd per. poss. pron. (acc. f. sg.)

DOWN

1. 1st per. pron. (nom. m. sg.)
2. temple
3. coin
5. great
6. up
7. I see
8. people
9. I beget
10. if
11. as (compar. particle)
18. age (gen. m. pl.)
19. man (3rd declen.)
21. field
22. John
23. vineyard
24. flesh
25. night
26. house
30. 2nd per. pronoun (acc. sg.)
35. all (alternate of πᾶς, V21)
38. def. article (nom. n. sg.)
41. indef. rel. pronoun
42. and
44. earth
45. def. art. (gen. m. sg.)
46. fish
47. highest
49. I preach
51. eye
52. water
54. strong
57. upon
58. good
59. no one (nom. m. sg.)
61. I love
63. much
65. rel. pron. (dat. f. pl.)
67. 1st per. poss. pron. (nom. m. pl.)
71. into
72. earth (acc. f. sg.)
74. earth (nom. f. sg.)

CROSSWORD PUZZLE

(ἑπτά καὶ δέκα)

Vocabulary

1	2	3			4	5	6		7			8		9	10	11
12						13								14		
15					16							17				
			18								19			20	21	22
23						24		25		26				27		
			28					29				30		31		
32					33					34			35		36	
			37						38				39			
40					41		42		43			44				
				45							46				47	
48		49							50							
						51		52			53		54			
55								56	57							
				58						59					60	
61													62	63		
				64			65			66	67		68			
69						70				71						72
			73		74				75				76			
77				78				79						80		

Crossword Puzzle Answers

ε	ι	μ	ι		α	μ	α		ο	μ	ο	λ	ο	γ	ε	ω
γ	ε	ν	ο	ς		ε	ν		ρ			α		ε	ι	ς
ω	ρ	α			α	γ	α	π	α	ω		ο	υ	ν		
	ο		α	ι	μ	α			ω		α	ς		ν	α	ι
α	ν	τ	ι			σ	υ	ν		ο	ν			α	γ	ω
μ			ω	ν		α		υ	γ	ι	η	ς		ω	ρ	α
π	λ	η	ν		θ	ρ	ι	ξ		κ	ρ	ε	α		ο	ν
ε		ω	ν		ξ			τ	ο			π	ω	ς	ν	
λ	ε	ω	ν		τ		κ		ο	ς		γ	α	ρ		η
ω			τ	ι	μ	α	ω			ι	η	σ	ο	υ	ς	
ν	ε	κ	ρ	ο	ς		ι		ο	υ	χ			ψ		
	η		υ		ο		υ			θ	λ	ι	ψ	ι	ς	
π	α	ρ	α		φ		δ	ε		υ		σ		σ		
	υ		α	ν	θ	ρ	ω	π	ο	ς		χ		τ	ε	
φ	ω	σ		γ		α		ρ	ι	υ		υ	π	ο		
ι		σ		α	λ	λ	α		δ	ε		σ	ο	ς		
λ	υ	ω		θ		μ	ι	α		ε	μ	η		λ		γ
ε			λ	ο	γ	ο	ς		δ	ι	ο		σ	υ	κ	η
ω	δ	ε		ς	η	ς		ε	ι	ς	ι	ν		ς	η	ν

LESSON 18

(δεκαοκτώ)

Future and Liquid Future

αἴρω, *I take up, take away*, **aorta** (the main artery of the heart which carries blood to the body; literally, "that which raises"), **dieresis** (or diaeresis; a mark [¨] placed over a pair of vowels indicating the two sounds are separate; literally, "to take apart")

κρίνω, *I judge, decide*, **crisis** (a decisive situation or turning point), **criterion** (a standard on which a judgment is based), **critic** (one who forms and expresses judgments), **critical** (characterized by careful or severe judgment), **critique** (a critical review of a work), **diacritical** (marking a distinction; literally, "to distinguish" or "to judge through"), **endocrine** (secreting internally; literally, "to separate inside"), **hypocrite** (a person who professes and acts in a contradictory manner; literally, "an actor" or "one under examination")

ἀγγέλλω, *I tell, announce*, **angel** (a heavenly messenger), **evangelist** (a messenger of good news, particularly the Christian gospel)

βάλλω, *I throw*, **ballistics** (the study of projectiles), **diabolical** (devilish or satanic; cf. diaboloj; literally, "to cast against"), **emblem** (an object which functions as a symbol; literally, "to insert" or "to throw in"), **embolism** (the obstruction of a blood vessel by a clot or air bubble; literally, "insertion" or "thrown in"), **hyperbole** (an exaggeration; literally, "over throw"), **parable** (a simple story to illustrate a lesson or moral; literally, "to compare" or "to throw alongside"), **symbol** (something that represents something else; literally, "to throw together"), **metabolism** (physical, chemical processes involved in a living organism; literally, "thrown across")

πράσσω, *I do, practice*, **praxis** (a practical application or exercise for learning), cf. Latin *practico* (practical, practice)

δοξάζω, *I glorify, honor*, **doxology** (a liturgical formula of praise to God; literally, "to speak glory", **heterodox** (not in agreement with accepted belief; literally, "other opinion"), **orthodox** (in agreement with accepted belief; literally, "correct opinion"), **paradox** (a seemingly contradictory statement that still may be true; literally, "against opinion")

θέλω, *I wish, desire*, **dyothelitism** (the theological doctrine that in Christ there were two wills, both human and divine; literally, "two wills"), **monothelitism** (the theological doctrine that in Christ there was only one will though two natures; literally, "only one will")

καταβαίνω, *I go down*, Cf. βαίνω (acrobat, Anabasis, anabatic, diabetes)

πίνω, *I drink*, **symposium** (a meeting or conference for discussion of some topic; literally, "to drink together"), cf. Latin *poto* (potion)

πίπτω, *I fall*, **peripeteia** (a sudden change of events as in a literary work; literally, "to fall around"), **symptom** (an indication of a condition or event; literally, "to fall together")

φέρω, *I bring, carry*, **Christopher** (literally, "Christ bearer"), **euphoria** (a feeling of well-being; literally, "to carry good"), **metaphor** (a figure of speech; literally, "to carry across"), **periphery** (the outermost region within a precise boundary; literally, "to carry around"), **phosphorus** (a highly reactive element which burns easily; literally, "light carrier"), **semaphore** (a device which uses flags, lights, or arms to signal; literally, "signal carrier"), cf. Latin *fero*

(fertile, circumference, confer, defer, differ, infer, offer, prefer, proffer, refer, suffer, transfer)

φεύγω, *I flee*, cf. Latin *fugio* (centrifugal, fugitive, refuge, subterfuge, Tempus Fugit)

INDICATIVE TENSES

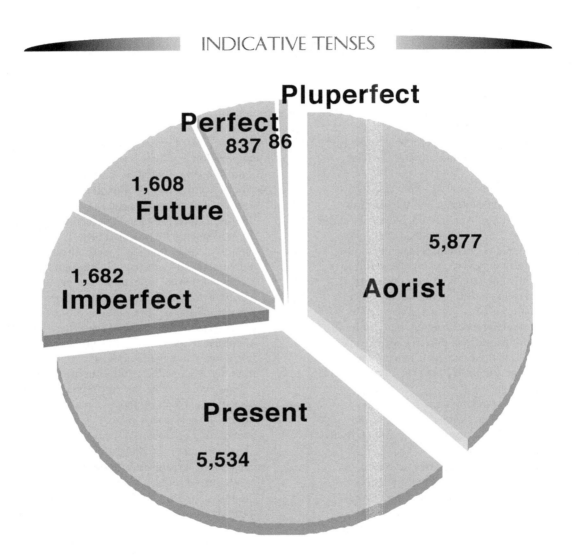

Pluperfect

Perfect
837 86

1,608
Future

1,682
Imperfect

5,877
Aorist

Present

5,534

OBJECTIVE QUESTIONS

1. The future tense is a primary tense taking _____ endings. However, in this lesson, we learn only active and middle voices because

   _____.

2. The tense formative is a suffix, _____, added to the tense stem. With stop consonants, volatilization occurs on the pattern of _____ declension nouns. Labials will wind up as _____, palatals as _____, and dentals as _____. These resultant letters then also are signals of the future tense. "_____" stems react according to these patterns also, because the actual verb stem ends in one of these stop consonants.

3. Liquid verbs are a special class of verbs whose stems end in either _____, _____, _____, or _____. These verbs form the future using the future tense suffix _____. The letter _____ drops, creating a reaction exactly as seen in _____ verbs. The resultant signal is a _____ accent.

4. Contract verbs _____ the contract vowel before the future tense suffix.

5. Identify the component parts of the future active indicative:

$$\lambda\upsilon\text{-}\sigma\text{-}\omega$$

6. Three common verbs with deponent futures are:

Present	Deponent Future	Translation
6.1 γινώσκω =	_____	_____
6.2 λαμβάνω =	_____	_____
6.3 ὁράω =	_____	_____

7. The *correlative* pronoun meaning "so much," "so great," "so many" has the prefix _____ on front of the inflections _____, _____, and

_____. The correlative pronoun οἷος means _____, and ὅσος means _____. Both have _____ breathing.

8. The *interrogative* pronoun ποῖος means _____, and is called the _____ interrogative. The pronoun πόσος means _____ and is the _____ interrogative.

9. Give the lexical form, identify the stem type (regular, stop, hidden, liquid, deponent, irregular, contract), then translate the following future tense verbs:

Future	Lexical	Stem Type	Translation
9.1 λαλήσει	_____	_____	_____
9.2 πέμψουσιν	_____	_____	_____
9.3 διδάξει	_____	_____	_____
9.4 κρινεῖ	_____	_____	_____
9.5 ἐλεύσομαι	_____	_____	_____
9.6 ἐρῶ	_____	_____	_____
9.7 ὄψεται	_____	_____	_____
9.8 δοξάσει	_____	_____	_____
9.9 λήμψεται*	_____	_____	_____
9.10 αγγελεῖ	_____	_____	_____

*The stem is λαβ- (cf. second aorist form, ἔλαβον). Going into the present tense, the stem is modified two ways. First, -αν is added, making λαβαν-. Then, an "epenthetic nasal" μ is added before the labial β for pronunciation purposes, creating the present tense form, λαμβάνω. The future form shows the epenthetic nasal *and* vowel gradation (α to η), thus, λημβ-. From here, add your future tense suffix, so what type reaction is involved at this point? In terms of translation, remember, this is a so-called *"deponent future"* (i.e., use *active* voice).

▰ TRANSLATION ▰

10. Translate the following, using the translation aids provided below:

O *Translation Aids* O

ὅσα, from ὅσος, correlative
  pronoun
λίθος, ὁ, *stone*
ἐλεύσομαι, see Table 18.6,
  NTG, 200
ἐρῶ, see Table 18.6, *NTG*, 200
ποία, from ποῖος, interrogative
  pronoun
ὄψεται, see Table 18.6, *NTG*,
  200

λήμψεται, from λαμβάνω
ἀναγγελεῖ, compound form of
  ἀγγέλλω, nearly
  synonymous, but perhaps
  some emphasis on more
  detail in reporting
ἐρεῖ, see Table 18.6, *NTG*, 200
ποίῳ, from ποῖος, interrogative
  pronoun

10.1   ὅσα ἀκούσει λαλήσει [John 16:13]

_____

10.2   γνώσῃ δὲ μετὰ ταῦτα

_____

10.3   πάντες πιστεύσουσιν εἰς αὐτόν [John 11:48]

_____

10.4   ἀκουσόμεθά σου περὶ τούτου καὶ πάλιν

_____

10.5   καὶ ἔσομαι αὐτῶν θεός, καὶ αὐτοὶ ἔσονταί μου
       λαός

_____

10.6   καλέσεις τὸ ὄνομα αὐτοῦ Ἰησοῦν, αὐτὸς γὰρ σώσει
       τὸν λαὸν αὐτοῦ ἀπὸ τῶν ἁμαρτιῶν αὐτῶν

_____

10.7 οἱ λίθοι κράξουσιν [John 16:13]

_____

10.8 δῶρα πέμψουσιν ἀλλήλοις

_____

10.9 ἐκεῖνος ὑμᾶς διδάξει πάντα

_____

10.10 πῶς κρινεῖ ὁ θεὸς τὸν κόσμον;

_____

10.11 ἐλεύσομαι δὲ ταχέως πρὸς ὑμᾶς

_____

10.12 καὶ ἐρῶ ὑμῖν ἐν ποίᾳ ἐξουσίᾳ ταῦτα ποιῶ

_____

10.13 καὶ ὄψεται πᾶσα σὰρξ τὸ σωτήριον τοῦ θεοῦ

_____

10.14 ἐκεῖνος ἐμὲ δοξάσει, ὅτι ἐκ τοῦ ἐμοῦ λήμψεται καὶ
      ἀναγγελεῖ ὑμῖν

_____

_____

10.15 Ἀλλὰ ἐρεῖ τις· πῶς ἐγείρονται οἱ νεκροί; ποίῳ δὲ
      σώματι ἔρχονται; [1 Cor. 15:35]

_____

_____

LESSON 19

(ἐννέα καὶ δέκα)

First Aorist and Liquid Aorist

Vocabulary 19

ἀρχή, *beginning*, **archangel** (a celestial being above the rank of an angel; literally, "chief angel"), **archenemy** (the primary opponent; literally, "chief enemy"), **archetype** (an original model upon which subsequent things are patterned; literally, "chief model"), cf. ἄρχαιος (archaeology, archaic, archaism)

δαιμόνιον, *demon*, **demon** (an evil being), **demoniac** (possessed by a demon), **demonic** (pertaining to evil powers), **demonology** (the study of demons), **pandemonium** (the abode of all demons in John Milton's *Paradise Lost*; literally, "all the demons")

διδάσκαλος, *teacher*, **Didache** (literally, "the teaching"), **didactics** (art or science of teaching), **didactic** (intended to instruct)

θρόνος, *throne*, **throne** (a ruler's royal chair)

καρπός, *fruit*, **carpology** (the area of botany concerned with fruit and seeds), **homocarpous** (having all the fruits of a flowerhead alike), **macrocarpous** (having large fruit), **parthenocarpy** (production of fruit without fertilization; literally, "virgin fruit"), **Polycarp** (literally, "much fruit")

κεφαλή, *head*, **acephalous** (headless or lacking a clearly defined head; literally, "without a head"), **brachycephalic** (a having a short, almost round head; literally, "short headed"), **cephalic** (of the head or skull), **encephalitis** (inflammation of the brain), **enkephalins** (chemicals in the brain), **macrocephalous** (having a large head)

σάββατον, *sabbath*, **Sabbath** (the seventh day of the week), **sabbatical** (a period of rest or study usually after an interval of time)

σημεῖον, *sign*, *miracle*, **semantics** (the study of words and nonverbal symbols), **semaphore** (a device which uses flags, lights, or arms to signal; literally, "signal carrier"), **semiology** (the science dealing with signs or sign language)

συναγωγή, *synagogue*, **synagogue** (a building for Jewish gatherings; literally, "assembly" or "to lead together"; cf. su,n + a;gw)

μέσος, *middle*, **mesosphere** (the layer of air between the stratosphere and the thermosphere; also the layer of the earth between the athenosphere and the earth's core), **Mesopotamia** (literally, "between the rivers"), **Mesozoic** (the third era of geologic time; literally, "middle of life")

πρεσβύτερος, *elder*, **presbyter** (an elder in the church), **Presbyterian** (the denomination of churches governed by a group of elders)

δοκέω, *I think*, *seem*, **Docetism** (the heresy that Christ only seemed to have a body), **dogma** (a system of doctrines), **dogmatic** (stating an opinion positively or arrogantly)

ἁμαρτάνω, *I sin*, **hamartiology** (the theological study of the doctrine of sin)

ὑπάγω, *I go away*, cf. ἄγω, **demagogue** (a person who stirs up people to gain power; literally, "a people leader"), **pedagogue** (a school teacher or educator; literally, "child leader"), **stratagem** (a military maneuver designed to surprise an enemy; literally, "to lead an army"), **synagogue** (a building for Jewish gatherings; literally, "assembly" or "to lead together"; cf. σύν + ἄγω), cf. Latin *ago* (agenda, agent, agile, agitate)

INDICATIVE TENSES

OBJECTIVE QUESTIONS

1. The third principal part involves only _____ and _____
    voices because _____.

2. The tense formative is a suffix, _____, added to the tense stem. With stop
    consonants, volatilization occurs on the pattern of _____
    declension nouns. Labials will wind up as _____, palatals as _____, and
    dentals as _____. "_____" stems react according to these patterns
    also, because the actual verb stem ends in one of these stop consonants.

3. Liquid verbs are a special class of verbs whose stems end in either _____,
    _____, _____, or _____. In forming a liquid aorist, the letter _____ drops,
    leaving behind only the letter _____ of the aorist tense suffix. Sometimes
    this liquid aorist then is called an "_____" aorist because of this
    lost letter. On occasion, the liquid aorist also reacts by _____ the
    stem vowel.

4. Contract verbs _____ the contract vowel before the aorist tense
    suffix.

5. Identify the component parts of the first aorist active indicative:

$$\acute{\epsilon}\text{-}\lambda\upsilon\text{-}\sigma\alpha\text{-}\nu$$

6. If a verb exists in the third principal part only in middle forms, this verb is
    called a _____ _____. Though the form is middle, the
    translation is _____ voice.

7. While we may call the verbal aspect of the aorist _____ with the
    idea of a point in time, a more accurate description is _____, that
    is, not defining anything particular about the activity described.

8. The typical use of the aorist is simply to give a summary report of a past
    action, called the _____ aorist. If the emphasis is upon the

beginning of the action, this use is called the _____ aorist. If the emphasis is upon the *conclusion* of the action, this use is called the _____ aorist.

9. A convention of letter writing in the first century was to refer to a letter's composition using the aorist tense, which is called the _____ aorist. This aorist properly is translated with _____ tense.

▬▬ TRANSLATION ▬▬

10. Translate the following, using the translation aids provided below:

○   *Translation Aids* ○

ἔγραψα (#10.10), how would this translate if taken as an "epistolary aorist"?
ἀπήγγειλαν, compound form of ἀγγέλλω, nearly

synonymous, including ideas such as *I tell*, *report*, *inform*, *acknowledge*, etc.
εὐαγγελίζω, *I bring the good news, preach good news*

10.1   οὐκ ἔστιν ὧδε

_____

10.2   ἐποίησεν καρπὸν

_____

10.3   ἐπερωτῶσιν αὐτὸν

_____

10.4   σάββατον οὐ τηρεῖ

_____

10.5   Κύριε, ποῦ ὑπάγεις;

_____

10.6   οἱ δὲ λοιποὶ ἔλεγον

_____

10.7   ἐθεώρουν τὰ σημεῖα ἃ ἐποίει

_____

10.8   τί ὑμῖν δοκεῖ περὶ τοῦ χριστοῦ;

_____

10.9   ἀπ' ἀρχῆς ὁ διάβολος ἁμαρτάνει

_____

10.10   ἐγὼ Παῦλος ἔγραψα τῇ ἐμῇ χειρί

_____

10.11   ἀπήγγειλαν ταῦτα πάντα τοῖς ἕνδεκα

_____

10.12   τὸ τοῦ θεοῦ εὐαγγέλιον εὐηγγελισάμην ὑμῖν

_____

10.13   ἐκηρύξαμεν εἰς ὑμᾶς τὸ εὐαγγέλιον τοῦ θεοῦ

_____

10.14   καὶ ἐπηρώτησεν αὐτὸν ὁ Πιλᾶτος, Σὺ εἶ ὁ
βασιλεὺς τῶν Ἰουδαίων;

_____

10.15   καὶ ἠγάπησαν οἱ ἄνθρωποι μᾶλλον τὸ σκότος ἢ τὸ
φῶς, ἦν γὰρ αὐτῶν πονηρὰ τὰ ἔργα

_____

_____

10.16   εἰ ἐμὲ ἐδίωξαν, καὶ ὑμᾶς διώξουσιν· εἰ τὸν λόγον
μου ἐτήρησαν, καὶ τὸν ὑμέτερον τηρήσουσιν

_____

_____

FIGURE 10. Trajan Aureus. Gold coin of Trajan, whose rule from AD 98–117 represents the height of the Roman empire's expansion and might. He is depicted wearing the iconic laurel wreath of victory. The inscription reads IMP = Imperator, CAES = Caesar, NERVA = Nerva, TRAIAN = Trajan, AVG = Augustus, GERM = Germanicus (Pergamon Museum, Berlin).

FIGURE 9. Augustus Cameo. This three-layered sardonyx cameo of Augustus held in the British Museum in London depicts Augustus wearing the Aegis (shield) of Minerva and a sword belt (14–20 BC). The gem-bedecked headband evokes the Greek laurel wreath of victory, and became iconic on imperial coins.

Octavian's defeat of Antony ended two centuries of civil wars. He unified the Roman world, resurrected the Roman Republic as a successful provincial system, and reorganized the army into a system of military careers with personal loyalty to the emperor. Renamed Augustus by the Roman senate, his life's work lasted a thousand years. What Alexander did for the Greek world, Augustus did for the Roman world. These two cultures fused together as the Greco-Roman world.

Part of the impact of this Roman world on New Testament Greek is the presence of "Latinisms," which are Latin loanwords that transferred over directly from Latin into Hellenistic Greek. The Gospel of Mark is notable for its Latinisms. The following are examples:

census	κῆνσος	"poll tax"	Mark 12:14
centurio	κεντυρίων	"centurion"	Mark 15:39, 44, 45
denarius	δηνάριον	Roman coin	Mark 12:15
flagellum	φραγελλόω	"to flog"	Mark 15:15
legio	λεγιών	"legion"	Mark 5:9, 15
modius	μόδιος	"peck measure"	Mark 4:21
praetorium	πραιτώριον	"governor's residence"	Mark 15:16
quadrans	κοδράντης	Roman coin	Mark 12:42
sextarius	ξέστης	quart, "pitcher"	Mark 7:4
speculator	σπεκουλάτωρ	"executioner"	Mark 6:27

LESSON 20

(εἴκοσι)

Second Aorist and Indirect Discourse

δεξιός, *right* (direction), cf. Latin *dexter*, *dextra*, *dextrum* (ambidextrous, dexterity, dexterous)

παιδίον, *child*, **pedagogue** (a school teacher or educator; literally, "child leader"), **pediatrics** (the medical treatment of infants and children; literally, "child healing")

σοφία, *wisdom*, **philosophy** (pursuit of wisdom by intellectual means; literally, "the love of wisdom"), **Sophia** (literally, "wise"), **sophism** (a plausible but fallacious argument), **sophist** (a member of a philosophical school in ancient Greece), **sophisticated** (refinement or complexity), **sophomore** (a second-year student; literally, "a wise fool"), **sophomoric** (immature and overconfident; literally, "foolishly wise")

χρόνος, *time*, **anachronism** (a chronological disorder of events; literally, "backward in time"), **chronic** (prolonged or occurring for a long time), **chronicle** (an extended account of historical events), **chronograph** (an instrument that records time intervals; literally, "time writing"), **chronology** (the determination of dates and the sequence of events), **synchronize** (to occur at the same time; literally, "timed together")

εὐαγγελίζω, *I bring good news*, **evangelism** (the process of proclaiming the gospel), **evangelist** (a proclaimer of the gospel), **evangelize** (to proclaim the gospel)

λείπω, *I leave*, **eclipse** (the partial or complete obscuring of a celestial body; literally, "to leave out"), **ellipsis** (the omission of a word necessary for syntax but not necessary for understanding; literally, "to lack within")

εἶδον (ὁράω), *I saw*, **idea** (a mental image; literally, "something seen")

ἔφαγον (ἐσθίω), *I ate*, **anthropophagus** (a cannibal or an eater of human flesh; literally, "human eater"), **esophagus** (the tube for the passage of food to the stomach), **sarcophagus** (a stone coffin; literally, "to eat flesh" because a limestone coffin accelerates disintegration)

OBJECTIVE QUESTIONS

1. The third principal part has two forms, a first aorist that is _____
    (regular or irregular?) in formation, comparable to forming the past tense in
    English with the suffix _____. The second aorist on the other hand is
    _____ in formation and must be memorized as vocabulary, similar
    in English to the past tense of "I go" as _____.

2. Second aorist and _____ look exactly the same, except for the
    stem alone, and does *not* have the first aorist suffix _____.

3. Some second aorist verbs can be found with first aorist endings, but minus
    the letter _____. The most common verbs that do this in the New Testament
    are the second aorist verbs _____ and _____.

4. Identify the component parts of the *second* aorist active indicative:

$$\overset{\displaystyle\downarrow\qquad\qquad\downarrow}{\underset{\displaystyle\nearrow\qquad\qquad\qquad\nwarrow}{ἐ-λιπ-ο-ν}}$$

5. The second aorist middle indicative is regular in the endings, except for the
    second singular, which for the verb λείπω is the form _____. The
    actual pronominal suffix for this ending is _____. The sigma becomes an
    "_____" sigma when the thematic vowel is added. The sigma
    drops, leaving the vowel combination _____, which contracts to the form
    _____.

6. In reporting indirect discourse what does the Greek structure always do?
    _____. However, English
    convention is to modify the verbs of the original statement into
    _____ tenses. Thus, generally, a Greek present in indirect
    discourse will convert to English _____. A Greek past in indirect
    discourse will convert to English _____.

7. Second Aorist *Active*. Indicate the second aorist stem (*without* augmentation), secondary *active* ending, and final form in the required person and number.

Verb	2Aor Stem	Per/Num	Act. Suffix	2Aor Form
γινώσκω		1st sing.		
ὁράω		2nd sing.		
λέγω		3rd sing.		
λαμβάνω		1st plu.		
ἐσθίω		2nd plu.		
ἔχω		3rd plu.		
ἄγω		2nd plu.		
ἔρχομαι		3rd plu.		
φέρω		3rd sing.		

8. Second Aorist *Middle*. Indicate the second aorist stem (*without* augmentation), secondary *middle* ending, and final form in the required person and number.

Verb	2Aor Stem	Per/Num	Mid. Suffix	2Aor Form
βάλλω		1st sing.		
λείπω		2nd sing.		
πίπτω		3rd sing.		
πίνω		1st plu.		
εὑρίσκω		2nd plu.		
φεύγω		3rd plu.		
γίνομαι		3rd sing.		

▬ TRANSLATION ▬

9. Translate the following, using the translation aids provided below:

O Translation Aids O

Τρόφιμος, *Trophimus*
ἀπολείπω, *I leave behind*
Μιλήτος, *Miletus*
εἰσπορεύομαι, *I come in, go in, enter in*
φάντασμά, τό, *ghost*

ἔξω, *outside* (adverbial preposition, vocabulary, Lesson 9)
Ἠσαΐας, *Isaiah*
Ναζαρέτ, *Nazareth*
Γαλιλαία, *Galilee*

9.1　ἀνθρώπους πείθομεν

9.2　ἔπεισαν τοὺς ὄχλους

9.3　ἡμεῖς ὑμᾶς εὐαγγελιζόμεθα

9.4　εὐηγγελισάμεθα ὑμῖν

9.5　Εἰ δέ τις ὑμῶν λείπεται σοφίας

9.6　Τρόφιμον δὲ ἀπέλιπον ἐν Μιλήτῳ

9.7　εἰσπορεύεται ὅπου ἦν τὸ παιδίον

9.8　ἔδοξαν ὅτι φάντασμά ἐστιν

9.9 εἶπεν γὰρ ὅτι θεοῦ εἰμι υἱός

_____

9.10 Εὐθέως ἐγενόμην ἐν πνεύματι

_____

9.11 ἤγγιζεν ὁ χρόνος τῆς ἐπαγγελίας

_____

9.12 ἦλθον πρὸς τὸν Ἰωάννην καὶ εἶπαν αὐτῷ

_____

9.13 Ἤκουσεν Ἰησοῦς ὅτι ἐξέβαλον αὐτὸν ἔξω

_____

9.14 ἡμεῖς δὲ οὐ τὸ πνεῦμα τοῦ κόσμου ἐλάβομεν

_____

9.15 ταῦτα εἶπεν Ἠσαΐας ὅτι εἶδεν τὴν δόξαν αὐτοῦ

_____

9.16 ἦλθαν οὖν καὶ εἶδαν ποῦ μένει καὶ παρ' αὐτῷ
ἔμειναν

_____

9.17 ἐπίστευσα, διὸ ἐλάλησα, καὶ ἡμεῖς πιστεύομεν, διὸ
καὶ λαλοῦμεν

_____

_____

9.18 Καὶ ἐγένετο[1] ἐν ἐκείναις ταῖς ἡμέραις ἦλθεν
Ἰησοῦς ἀπὸ Ναζαρὲτ τῆς Γαλιλαίας

_____

_____

---

[1]Often, in this third singular form, this verb means "it happened" or "it came about." What is the lexical form?

10. Diagram sentence four:

10.1 ῎Ηκουσεν ᾿Ιησοῦς ὅτι ἐξέβαλον αὐτὸν ἔξω

LESSON 21

(εἷς καὶ εἴκοσι)

Passive System—Aorist and Future

γενεά, *generation*, **genealogy** (the recorded history of one's ancestors)

θηρίον, *beast*, **theriomorphic** (having the form of a beast)

σωτηρία, *salvation*, **soteriology** (the theological doctrine of salvation)

τιμή, *honor*, *price*, **Timothy** (cf. Τιμόθεος; literally, "honor of God")

φυλακή, *guard*, *prison*, *watch*, **phylactery** (a small box which contained portions of the Hebrew Scriptures for Jewish men), **phylaxis** (inhibiting of infection by the body), **prophylactic** (protective or preventative; literally, "guarding beforehand"), **prophylaxis** (protective treatment against disease; literally, "guarding beforehand")

ὅμοιος, *like*, **homeostasis** (physiological equilibrium within an organism; literally, "standing constant"), **homoeoteleuton** (an incorrect copy of an original text caused by the similar ending of lines; literally, "similar endings"), **homoiotherm** (a warm-blooded animal; literally, "constant warmth"), **Homoiousion** (an Arian teaching of the fourth century that Jesus the Son and God the Father were of similar but different substance; literally, "similar essence")

τυφλός, *blind*, **typhlology** (the scientific study of blindness)

δέω, *I bind*, **anadem** (a wreath or garland for the head; literally, "to bind up"), **asyndeton** (the omission of conjunctions in constructions which normally would need them; literally, "without being bound together"), **diadem** (a royal crown or headband; literally, "to bind across")

θαυμάζω, *I marvel*, *wonder*, **thaumaturge** (a performer of miracles or magic feats; literally, "miracle worker")

θεραπεύω, *I heal*, **chemotherapy** (treatment of disease with chemicals), **therapeutic** (having healing powers), **therapy** (treatment of an illness or disability)

καθίζω, *I seat*, *sit*, cf. καθέδρα ("a bishop's chair"; cathedra, cathedral)

κρατέω, *I grasp*, *seize*, **aristocracy** (government by the nobility; literally, "the best in power"), **democracy** (government by the people; literally, "people in power"), **plutocrat** (a person with political influence or control because of wealth; literally, "power in wealth")

OBJECTIVE QUESTIONS

1. Fill in the following theta volatilization chart for stops:

Formation	Stops	Suffix	Result
labials		+ θ =	
palatals		+ θ =	
dentals		+ θ =	

2. Fill in the following theta volatilization chart for liquids:

Liquid	Suffix	Result
λ	+ θ =	
ρ	+ θ =	
μ	+ θ =	
ν	+ θ =	

3. Identify the component parts of the aorist passive indicative:

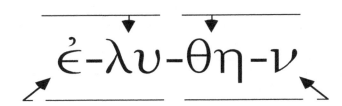

$$ἐ-λυ-θη-ν$$

4. Describe the three basic distinctions representing the difference between the aorist and future passive; that is, the future:

    4.1   Prefix: _____

    4.2   Voice suffix   _____

    4.3   Endings   _____

5. Complete the following paradigms for first aorist passive indicative and first future passive indicative of πέμπω:

Number	Person	Aorist Passive	Future Passive
singular	1st		
	2nd		
	3rd		
plural	1st		
	2nd		
	3rd		

6. The second passive is quite similar to the first passive system, with the main distinction being the dropping of the letter _____ from the aorist passive suffix _____ or the future passive suffix _____.

7. When endings of the second future passive are compared with those of a contract future middle, they are exactly the same.

    ☐ True   ☐ False

    Why/Why not? _____

8. Describe the following forms with the appropriate deponent terminology:

	Tense	Deponent Terminology

    8.1 ἠρχόμην   = _____ _____

    8.2 ἐβουλήθην   = _____ _____

    8.3 ὄψομαι   = _____ _____

    8.4 ἔρχομαι   = _____ _____

    8.5 ἐλογισάμην = _____ _____

9. Complete the following:

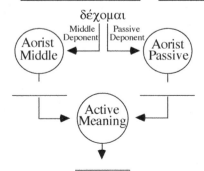

10. Translate the following; for the interior cases (Genitive, Dative), use any legitimate option (Genitive or Ablative; Dative, Locative, or Instrumental):

		Translation	Case	Gender	Number
10.1	ἰσχυροί	_____	_____	_____	_____
10.2	ἄπαντας	_____	_____	_____	_____
10.3	θηρίον	_____	_____	_____	_____
10.4	σωτηρίας	_____	_____	_____	_____
10.5	χρείαν	_____	_____	_____	_____
10.6	ναῷ	_____	_____	_____	_____
10.7	θηρίου	_____	_____	_____	_____
10.8	τιμαῖς	_____	_____	_____	_____
10.9	φυλακῇ	_____	_____	_____	_____
10.10	τυφλούς	_____	_____	_____	_____

11. Translate the following and specify the tense and voice, person and number:

		Translation	Tense	Voice	P/N
11.1	ἐσπείραμεν	_____	_____	_____	_____
11.2	ἐκάθισαν	_____	_____	_____	_____
11.3	ἐδίωξας	_____	_____	_____	_____
11.4	ἀπολύσω	_____	_____	_____	_____
11.5	ἀπήγγειλαν	_____	_____	_____	_____
11.6	δήσουσιν	_____	_____	_____	_____
11.7	ἐθαύμαζεν	_____	_____	_____	_____
11.8	ἐθαύμασεν	_____	_____	_____	_____
11.9	προσέφερον	_____	_____	_____	_____
11.10	προσήνεγκαν	_____	_____	_____	_____
11.11	παρελάβετε	_____	_____	_____	_____
11.12	ἐθεραπεύοντο	_____	_____	_____	_____
11.13	κατοικεῖς	_____	_____	_____	_____
11.14	ἐκράτησαν	_____	_____	_____	_____
11.15	φανεροῦται	_____	_____	_____	_____

TRANSLATION

12. Translate the following, using the translation aids provided below:

○   *Translation Aids* ○

Ἠλίας, *Elijah*
πόλεμος, *war, battle*
πάρδαλις, -εως, ἡ, *leopard*

παῖς, παῖδος, ὁ, ἡ, *child, boy,
    girl*
πληγή, *wound*
ὀπίσω, *after* (adverbial prep.)

12.1 σωθήσομαι

_____

12.2 ἤχθη ὁ Παῦλος

_____

12.3 ἐπέμφθη Ἠλίας

_____

12.4 ἐπείσθησαν δὲ αὐτῷ[1]

_____

12.5 τῇ γὰρ ἐλπίδι ἐσώθημεν

_____

12.6 ἐγενήθησαν ἰσχυροὶ ἐν πολέμῳ

_____

12.7 ἠκολούθησεν[2] αὐτῷ ὄχλος πολύς

_____

12.8 ἐν ἁμαρτίαις σὺ ἐγεννήθης ὅλος

_____

---

[1]Take this dative case as instrumental in function ("by").
[2]Do not be fooled—this verb is not what you think. Study lexical form carefully.

12.9   καὶ τὸ θηρίον ὃ εἶδον ἦν ὅμοιον παρδάλει

12.10   ἐγενήθητε ἐγγὺς ἐν³ τῷ αἵματι τοῦ Χριστοῦ

12.11   οἱ⁴ δὲ εἶπαν⁵ ὅτι Ὁ κύριος αὐτοῦ χρείαν ἔχει

12.12   τὸ βάπτισμα ὃ ἐγὼ βαπτίζομαι βαπτισθήσεσθε

12.13   τοῦτο ἤδη τρίτον ἐφανερώθη Ἰησοῦς τοῖς μαθηταῖς

12.14   ἄρα γε ἀπὸ τῶν καρπῶν αὐτῶν ἐπιγνώσεσθε αὐτούς

12.15   ἐκράτησεν τὸν Ἰωάννην καὶ ἔδησεν αὐτὸν ἐν φυλακῇ

12.16   καὶ ἐξῆλθεν ἀπ' αὐτοῦ τὸ δαιμόνιον καὶ ἐθεραπεύθη ὁ παῖς ἀπὸ τῆς ὥρας ἐκείνης

12.17   καὶ ἡ πληγὴ τοῦ θανάτου⁶ αὐτοῦ ἐθεραπεύθη. καὶ ἐθαυμάσθη ὅλη ἡ γῆ ὀπίσω τοῦ θηρίου

---

³Take this preposition as instrumental ("by").
⁴The Greek article here is being used for a personal pronoun. See *NTG*, 188-89.
⁵Notice that this verb has the alternate ending pattern. See Table 20.3 in *NTG*, 224.
⁶Take this genitive descriptively; i.e., make an adjective ("___ ly") to πληγή.

LESSON 22

(δύο καὶ εἴκοσι)

Perfect Active and Future Perfect

Vocabulary 22

ἄξιος, *worthy*, **axiology** (the study of the nature of values and value judgments; literally, "the study of worth"), **axiom** (a self-evident or universally recognized truth; literally, "a worthy statement")

ἅπτομαι, *I touch*, **haptometer** (an instrument for measuring the sense of touch), **periapt** (a charm worn as protection against misfortune; literally, "fastened around"), **synapse** (the point of contact where nerve impulses are transmitted from one neuron to another; literally, "to touch together")

δικαιόω, *I justify*, **syndicate** (a combination control of a business; literally, "together equals"), **theodicy** (a vindication of divine justice; literally, "justice of the gods")

εὐχαριστέω, *I give thanks*, **Eucharist** (Christian communion; literally, "thanksgiving" or "good favor")

φωνέω, *I call*, **euphony** (a pleasant combination of agreeable sounds; literally, "good sound"), **megaphone** (a device used to amplify the voice; literally, "loud sound"), **phoneme** (the smallest unit of speech), **phonetics** (the linguistical study of sounds), **phonics** (the study of sound and speech), **symphony** (a harmonious combination of musical sounds; literally, "to sound together"), **telephone** (a device that transmits sounds from one location to another; literally, "end sound"), **xylophone** (a wooden musical percussion instrument; literally, "wood sound")

INDICATIVE TENSES

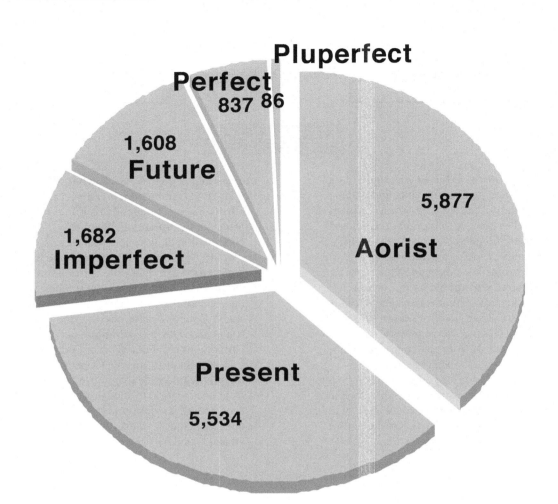

OBJECTIVE QUESTIONS

1. The fourth principal part involves only the _____ voice, because
   _____.

2. Show the reduplication pattern of the following:

Verb	Reduplication Type	Result
2.1 δικαιόω =	_____	_____
2.2 ἑτοιμάζω =	_____	_____
2.3 φωνέω =	_____	_____
2.4 σταυρόω =	_____	_____
2.5 ἀκούω =	_____	_____
2.6 γίνομαι =	_____	_____
2.7 ἔρχομαι =	_____	_____

3. Identify the component parts of the perfect active indicative:

$$λε\text{-}λυ\text{-}κα\text{-}σι$$

4. The *future perfect* active, though part of the perfect active system, is not
   covered in this lesson because the New Testament has only _____
   occurrences, with all but one as _____, a form not yet covered.

5. In Greek the perfect tense aspect is focused on the _____
   _____ of a completed action. The helping verb used is
   _____ or _____.

6. Complete the following paradigms for the perfect active indicative of
   θαυμάζω and of ἐρωτάω:

Number	Person	θαυμάζω	ἐρωτάω
singular	1st		
	2nd		
	3rd		
plural	1st		
	2nd		
	3rd		

7. Translate the following; for the interior cases (Genitive, Dative), use any legitimate option (Genitive or Ablative; Dative, Locative, or Instrumental):

	Translation	Case	Gender	Number
7.1 θύραν	_____	_____	_____	_____
7.2 ἐπιθυμίᾳ	_____	_____	_____	_____

8. Translate the following and specify the tense and voice, person and number:

	Translation	Tense	Voice	P/N
8.1 ἥψατο	_____	_____	_____	_____
8.2 ἔπαθον	_____	_____	_____	_____
8.3 ἡτοίμασας	_____	_____	_____	_____
8.4 ἔκλαιεν	_____	_____	_____	_____

TRANSLATION

9. Translate the following, using the translation aids provided below:

....

○ *Translation Aids* ○

Going out on a limb here: you should be just fine. Hope you agree!

Review vocabulary and "Variations," *NTG*, 244 if a form is unyielding.

....

9.1   οὐκ εἰμὶ ἱκανὸς

_____

9.2   τὴν πίστιν τετήρηκα

9.3   ὃ γέγραφα, γέγραφα

9.4   ὑμεῖς ἐμὲ πεφιλήκατε

9.5   Εὐχαριστῶ τῷ θεῷ μου

9.6   ὁ Ἰησοῦς ἐφώνησεν αὐτοὺς

9.7   πολλὰ γὰρ ἔπαθον σήμερον

9.8   ἡμεῖς ἠγαπήκαμεν τὸν θεὸν

9.9   ὁ πονηρὸς οὐχ ἅπτεται αὐτοῦ

9.10   ἐγώ εἰμι ἡ θύρα τῶν προβάτων

9.11   οὐ δικαιοῦται ἄνθρωπος ἐξ ἔργων νόμου

9.12   καὶ ἔκλαιον[1] πολύ, ὅτι οὐδεὶς ἄξιος εὑρέθη

9.13   ὁ κόσμος παράγεται καὶ ἡ ἐπιθυμία αὐτοῦ

---

[1]Translate as first person singular.

9.14   οἴδαμεν ὅτι ἀπὸ θεοῦ ἐλήλυθας διδάσκαλος

_____

9.15   μεμαρτύρηκα ὅτι οὗτός ἐστιν ὁ υἱὸς τοῦ θεοῦ

_____

9.16   ὃ ἑωράκαμεν καὶ ἀκηκόαμεν, ἀπαγγέλλομεν καὶ ὑμῖν

_____

9.17   καὶ ἡμεῖς πεπιστεύκαμεν καὶ ἐγνώκαμεν ὅτι σὺ εἶ ὁ ἅγιος τοῦ θεοῦ

_____

_____

LESSON 23

(εἴκοσι τρεῖς)

Perfect Middle Indicative

Vocabulary 23

διάβολος, Devil (adj.: slanderous, falsely accusing), **diabolical** (devilish, satanic; literally, "to cast against")

λίθος, *stone*, **lithification** (the formation of sedimentary rock from silt), **lithium** (a soft, silvery metallic element), **lithography** (a printing process which uses a flat surface; literally, "stone writing"), **litholysis** (treatment for kidney stones; literally, "to break up stones"), **lithophyte** (a plant that grows on a rocky surface; literally, "stone plant"), **lithosphere** (the outer rigid shell of the earth's crust), **monolith** (a single large block of stone), **neolithic** (the last period of the stone age; literally, "the new stone age"), **paleolithic** (the earliest stone age period; literally, "the old stone age")

μαρτυρία, testimony, witness, cf. μάρτυς (martyr, martyrdom)

μνημεῖον, *tomb*, *monument*, **amnesia** (partial or total lost of memory; literally, "without memory"), **amnesty** (a general pardon for offenders by a government; literally, "not remembered"), **anamnesis** (a recollection or a complete case history of a patient; literally, "to recall again"), **mnemonic** (something which aids memory)

ὀλίγος, *little*, *few*, **oligarchy** (a government controlled by a few people; literally, "the rule of a few")

ἀσθενέω, *I am weak*, **asthenia** (lack or loss of bodily strength), **asthenic** (a slender, lightly muscled human physique), **asthenopia** (eyestrain resulting in dim vision; literally, "weak sight"), **asthenosphere** (the less rigid layer of the earth's mantle), **neurasthenia** (fatigue once thought to result from nervous system exhaustion)

βλασφημέω, *I blaspheme*, **blaspheme** (to speak of something sacred in an irreverent manner), **blasphemous** (impiously irreverent), **blasphemy** (a profane act or utterance against something sacred)

διακονέω, *I serve*, **deacon** (a layman who assists the clergy), **diaconal** (pertaining to deacons or the diaconate), **diaconate** (the rank or office of a deacon)

ἐπιστρέφω, *I turn to*, *return*, cf. στρέφω (apostrophe, catastrophe, strophe)

μισέω, *I hate*, **misanthrope** (a person who hates or mistrusts people; literally, "to hate persons"), **misogamy** (hatred of marriage; literally, "marriage-hate"), **misogyny** (hatred of women; literally, "hates women"), **misology** (hatred of reason or enlightenment), **misoneism** (hatred of change; literally, "hate the new")

πλανάω, *I deceive*, *lead astray*, **planet** (a nonluminous celestial body in an orbit; literally, "a wanderer")

ὑποστρέφω, *I return*, cf. στρέφω (apostrophe, catastrophe, strophe)

NON -μαι RATIO

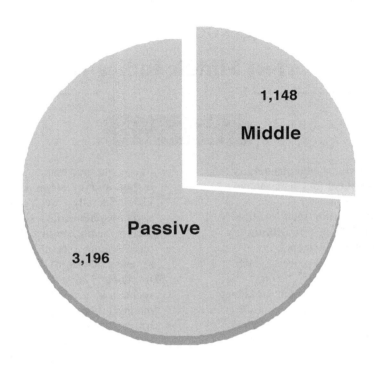

1,148

Middle

Passive

3,196

-μαι RATIO

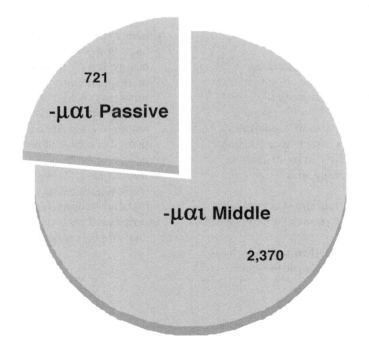

721

-μαι Passive

-μαι Middle

2,370

OBJECTIVE QUESTIONS

1. The fifth principal part involves only the _____ and
    _____ voices. The reduplication is the same pattern as for the
    _____ principal part, but no _____ _____ is
    added to the tense stem, and no _____ _____ is used
    before the pronominal suffix.

2. Identify the component parts of the perfect middle indicative:

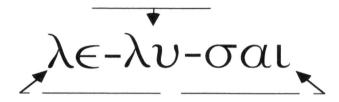

3. Create the perfect form for the following verbs in the given person and
    number. Show consonants colliding, volatilization result, and the final
    perfect middle form (use Table 25.3; be sure to distinguish reactions with σ
    from those with σθ):

Verb/Person		Cons.	Result	Perfect Middle Form
3.1 δέχομαι	=	_____	_____	_____
3.2 ἄγῃ	=	_____	_____	_____
3.3 γράφεται	=	_____	_____	_____
3.4 πειθόμεθα	=	_____	_____	_____
3.5 αἵρεσθε	=	_____	_____	_____
3.6 ὑποστρεφῃ*	=	_____	_____	_____
3.7 ἀγγέλλεσθε	=	_____	_____	_____
3.8 θλίβομαι	=	_____	_____	_____

    * The epsilon of the stem vowel is an alpha in the fifth principal part. Do not forget
    that this verb is a compound verb as you study reduplication of the stem.

4. Other verbs insert a letter before the perfect middle ending. For example,
    γινώσκω becomes _____, inserting the letter _____. The verb
    βάλλω inserts the letter _____.

5. One peculiarity of formation of consonant stems is with the _____ person plural. Instead of forming regularly with the ending _____, consonant stems are formed _____.

6. Fill in the following for the perfect middle indicative:

Number	Person	θλίβω	διώκω
singular	1st		
	2nd		
	3rd		
plural	1st		
	2nd		
	3rd		

7. Translate the following; for the interior cases (Genitive, Dative), use any legitimate option (Genitive or Ablative; Dative, Locative, or Instrumental):

	Translation	Case	Gender	Number
7.1 διαβόλου				
7.2 περιτομῆς				
7.3 οργῇ				
7.4 μαρτυρίαι				
7.5 λίθων				
7.6 μνημεῖα				

8. Translate the following and specify the tense and voice, person and number:

	Translation	Tense	Voice	P/N
8.1 ἐπιστρέψει				
8.2 ἐπερίσσευσεν				
8.3 διηκόνουν				
8.4 ὑπέστρεψαν				
8.5 μεμισήκασιν				

8.6 οἰκοδομεῖσθε _____ _____ _____ _____

8.7 παρεγενόμην _____ _____ _____ _____

TRANSLATION

9. Translate the following, using the translation aids provided below:

O   *Translation Aids* O

Λάζαρος, *Lazarus*   προσκυλίω, *I roll against*
εἶχον, from ἔχω   ἰχθύδιον, *little fish*

9.1 Λάζαρος ἠσθένει

_____

9.2 ὥσπερ γέγραπται

_____

9.3 εἶχον ἰχθύδια ὀλίγα

_____

9.4 οὗτος ἔγνωσται ὑπ' αὐτοῦ

_____

9.5 Μὴ καὶ ὑμεῖς πεπλάνησθε;[1]

_____

9.6 οἶδα καὶ πέπεισμαι ἐν κυρίῳ Ἰησοῦ

_____

9.7 οὐ μετενόησαν ἐκ τῶν ἔργων αὐτῶν

_____

9.8 ὁ ἄρχων τοῦ κόσμου τούτου κέκριται

_____

---

[1]Review "Expected Answers," *NTG*, 191.

9.9   ἡ ὁδὸς τῆς ἀληθείας βλασφημηθήσεται

9.10   σὺ τετήρηκας τὸν καλὸν οἶνον ἕως ἄρτι

9.11   προσεκύλισεν λίθον ἐπὶ τὴν θύραν τοῦ μνημείου

9.12   ὅτι[2] οὐ πεπίστευκεν εἰς τὴν μαρτυρίαν ἣν
μεμαρτύρηκεν ὁ θεὸς περὶ τοῦ υἱοῦ αὐτοῦ

---

[2]Translate as causal.

LESSON 24

(εἴκοσι τέσσαρες)

Pluperfect Indicative

βιβλίον, *book*, **Bible** (the sacred book of Christianity), **bibliography** (a list of books), **bibliolatry** (excessive adherence to the Bible; literally, "Bible worship"), **bibliomania** (an excessive desire for books; literally, "book madness"), **bibliophile** (one who loves and collects books; literally, "book lover"), **bibliotheca** (a library or book collection; literally, "book case")

δυνατός, *powerful*, *able*, **aerodynamics** (the branch of mechanics dealing with the forces exerted by air; literally, "air power"), **dynamic** (pertaining to energy or force), **dynamo** (a generator), **dynasty** (a family or group that maintains power for several generations), **dynamite** (a powerful explosive), **thermodynamics** (the branch of physics dealing with the transformation of heat into mechanical energy; literally, "heat power")

ὑποτάσσω, I *put in subjection*, **hypotaxis** (the subordinate relationship of clauses with connectives)

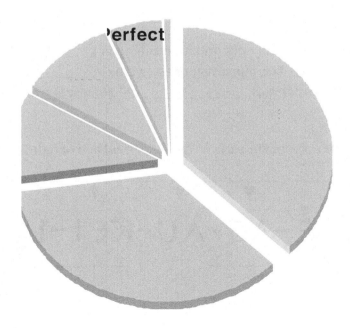

Perfect

OBJECTIVE QUESTIONS

1. The pluperfect active is derived from the _____ principal part, and the pluperfect middle/passive is derived from the _____ principal part. The difference between the perfect tense and the pluperfect is that the pluperfect is a _____ (primary or secondary?) tense.

2. The active voice suffix for the pluperfect is _____ instead of the perfect's _____. Dropping the _____ of the tense suffix makes a second pluperfect, with the resultant suffix being just _____.

3. Pluperfect uses _____ (primary or secondary?) endings, which are:

Number	Person	Active	Mid/Pass.
singular	1st		
	2nd		
	3rd		
plural	1st		
	2nd		
	3rd		

4. One perfect verb with only present meaning is _____, translated _____. The pluperfect of this verb is _____, but this pluperfect translates as _____ (what tense?) with the meaning _____.

5. Identify the component parts of the pluperfect active indicative:

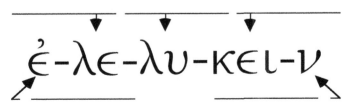

6. Identify the perfect aspect in the following:

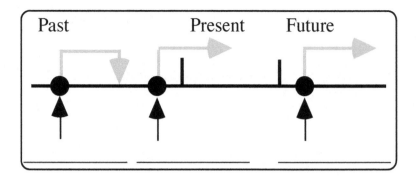

Past   Present   Future

_____   _____   _____

7. The second class conditional sentence assumes the condition _____ (is or is not?) fulfilled. Present time conditions for second class conditional sentences use the _____ tense. Past time conditions use either the _____ or the _____ tense. Remember that the key to the class conditional sentence is the _____ of the _____, not the type of _____ used.

8. Translate the following; for the interior cases (Genitive, Dative), use any legitimate option (Genitive or Ablative; Dative, Locative, or Instrumental):

		Translation	Case	Gender	Number
8.1	διαθήκης	_____	_____	_____	_____
8.2	πτωχοῖς	_____	_____	_____	_____
8.3	ἐπιθυμίας	_____	_____	_____	_____
8.4	ἔνατος	_____	_____	_____	_____

9. Translate the following and specify the tense and voice, person and number:

		Translation	Tense	Voice	P/N
9.1	ὤφειλεν	_____	_____	_____	_____
9.2	ὑπέταξας	_____	_____	_____	_____

TRANSLATION

10. Translate the following, using the translation aids provided below:

○ *Translation Aids* ○

ἠνοίχθη, from ἀνοίγω
εἰρήκει, associated with λέγω
ἦσαν, from εἰμί

ἄν, untranslatable particle of
contingency

10.1   καὶ ἄλλο βιβλίον ἠνοίχθη

10.2   εὗρον καθὼς εἰρήκει αὐτοῖς

10.3   ἐπὶ τὴν ὥραν τῆς προσευχῆς τὴν ἐνάτην

10.4   εἰ ἐμὲ ᾔδειτε, καὶ τὸν πατέρα μου ἂν ᾔδειτε[1]

10.5   ἕκαστος δὲ πειράζεται ὑπὸ τῆς ἰδίας ἐπιθυμίας

10.6   καὶ σκοτία ἤδη ἐγεγόνει καὶ οὔπω ἐληλύθει πρὸς
       αὐτοὺς ὁ Ἰησοῦς

10.7   ἐξ ἡμῶν ἐξῆλθαν[2], ἀλλ' οὐκ ἦσαν ἐξ ἡμῶν· εἰ γὰρ
       ἐξ ἡμῶν ἦσαν, μεμενήκεισαν ἂν μεθ' ἡμῶν[3]

---

[1] What class conditional sentence is this?
[2] Notice that this verb has the alternate ending pattern. See Table 20.3, *NTG*, 224.
[3] What class conditional sentence is this?

10.8   εἰ τὰ ἔργα μὴ ἐποίησα ἐν αὐτοῖς ἃ οὐδεὶς ἄλλος
       ἐποίησεν, ἁμαρτίαν οὐκ εἴχοσαν·⁴ νῦν δὲ καὶ⁵
       ἑωράκασιν καὶ μεμισήκασιν καὶ⁶ ἐμὲ καὶ τὸν
       πατέρα μου.

_____

_____

_____

---

⁴An unusual imperfect form, from the verb ἔχω. The old stem is σεχ- (*NTG*, 23). An initial σ
before a vowel or semivowel often dropped. Rough breathing was used as a result. For ἔχω, this σ
of the verb stem dropped in going to the present stem, but no rough breathing was used (σέχ- →
ἔχω). In the imperfect, the syllabic augment volatilized as ἐσεχ- → ἐεχ- → εἰχ- (see *NTG*, 150 n.
2). The form above, εἴχοσαν, is one of only two New Testament occurrences of ἔχω taking the
third plural option -σαν instead of -ν. In the future tense, the σ on the front of the tense stem was
dropped, and rough breathing was used; the stop consonant on the end of the stem volatilized with
the tense suffix (σέχ- → ἕξω). Second aorist and first perfect *retain* the σ of σεχ- but then *dropping* the ε stem vowel (ἔσχον and ἔσχηκα, with the perfect inserting η before the perfect suffix)!

⁵This construction is a καὶ . . . καί combination ("both . . . and").

⁶This construction is another καὶ . . . καί combination ("both . . . and").

FIGURE 11. Artemision Bronze. The seven-foot tall Artemision Bronze displayed in the National Archeological Museum of Athens was found in the 1920s off Cape Artemision in north Euboea. The god (likely Zeus) is cast in heroic style (nude) in extended stride throwing a great thunderbolt (or trident, if Poseidon). One of the most famous pieces of the early Classical Period, the bronze is a rare, original example of the Severe Style, whose hallmark was extraordinary detail combined with anatomical precision. The statue probably was a votive for a Zeus temple created by one of the unknown masters of this style about 460 BC. In his Areopagus sermon, Paul reminded the Athenians that the God who made heaven and earth, "does not live in shrines made by human hands" (Acts 17:29), echoing Stephen's words to the Sanhedrin, "Yet the Most High does not dwell in houses made with human hands" (Acts 7:48).

LESSON 25

(εἴκοσι πέντε)

Infinitives

διακονία, *service*, *ministry*, **deacon** (a layman who assists the clergy), **diaconal** (pertaining to deacons or the diaconate), **diaconate** (the rank or office of a deacon)

ἥλιος, *sun*, **aphelion** (the orbital point farthest from the sun; literally, "away from the sun"), **heliocentric** (having the sun as the center), **Helios** (the Greek sun god who drove his chariot daily across the sky), **heliotrope** (a plant which turns toward the sun; literally, "sun turn"), **Helium** (a gaseous element initially discovered from the solar spectrum), **perihelion** (the orbital point nearest the sun; literally, "near the sun")

οἶνος, *wine*, **wine** (the fermented juice of grapes), cf. Latin *vinum*, *vini* (vine, vinegar, viniculture, vintage, vinyl)

φυλή, *tribe*, **phyle** (a large citizen's group based on kinship in an ancient Greek city-state; literally, "tribe"), **phylogeny** (the origin and evolution of a group or race of animal or plants; literally, "the beginning of a tribe"), **phylum** (a main division of the animal or plant kingdom; literally, "a tribe")

ἀγοράζω, *I buy*, **agora** (a marketplace in ancient Greece)

δύναμαι, *I am able*, **aerodynamics** (the branch of mechanics dealing with the forces exerted by air; literally, "air power"), **dynamic** (pertaining to energy or force), **dynamo** (a generator), **dynasty** (a family or group that maintains power for several generations; literally, "standing in power"), **dynamite** (a powerful explosive), **thermodynamics** (the branch of physics dealing with the transformation of heat into mechanical energy; literally, "heat power")

καθαρίζω, *I cleanse*, **catharsis** (a process of purging)

φαίνω, *I shine*, *appear*, **diaphanous** (being transparently thin; literally, "appears through"), **Epiphany** (the festival commemorating the manifestation of Christ to the magi; literally, "manifest" or "appears to"), **fantasy** (creative imagination; literally, "an appearance"), **phantasm** (an imaginary image which seems to appear; literally, "an appearance"), **phantom** (something which apparently is seen but has no physical reality; literally, "an appearance"), **phenomenon** (an occurrence that is perceptible by the senses; literally, "something which appears"), **theophany** (a divine manifestation; literally, "the appearance of a god")

φυλάσσω, *I guard*, *keep*, **phylactery** (a small box which contained portions of the Hebrew Scriptures for Jewish men), **phylaxis** (inhibiting of infection by the body), **prophylactic** (protective or preventative; literally, "guarding beforehand"), **prophylaxis** (protective treatment against disease; literally, "guarding beforehand")

VERBAL FORMS

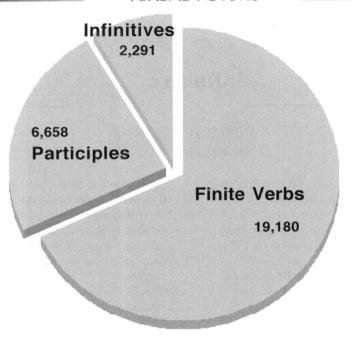

Infinitives
2,291

6,658
Participles

Finite Verbs
19,180

INFINITIVE TENSES

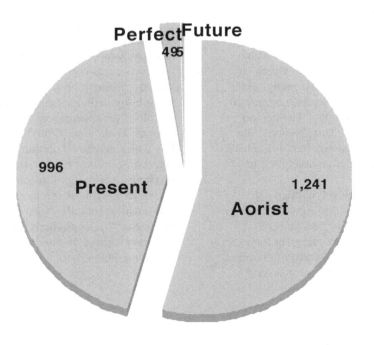

Perfect Future
495

996
Present

1,241
Aorist

ASSIGNMENT

Vocabulary: all verb forms.

OBJECTIVE QUESTIONS

1. Infinitives are hybrids, verbal structures with _____ function. Fill in the following description of infinitive heritage:

2. Of the infinitive endings, _____ and _____ are always active, _____ is always middle/passive, and _____ varies.

3. An infinitive does not have person and number, that is, is not limited by a _____. However, the _____ (what case?) of general reference has this function.

4. Infinitives have case function without case _____. They appear as if indeclinable _____ nouns found in construction with _____ and _____. Constructions with _____ are specialized and must be learned for each particular form.

5. As a verbal noun, the infinitive has three main uses, which are: _____, _____, and _____.

6. The infinitive as direct object has three main uses, which are: _____, _____, and _____.

7. As an infinitive, εἰμί has just two forms, the present tense form
_____ and the future tense form _____.

================ TRANSLATION ================

8. Translate the following, using the translation aids provided below:

○   *Translation Aids* ○

δουλεύω, *I serve*   Βεελζεβούλ, *Beelzebub*
κέρδος, ὁ, *gain*

8.1   ἐζήτουν αὐτὸν κρατῆσαι

_____

Identify the infinitive use: _____

8.2   καλόν ἐστιν ἡμᾶς ὧδε εἶναι

_____

Identify the infinitive use: _____

8.3   οὐκ ἔχομεν ἐξουσίαν μὴ ἐργάζεσθαι;

_____

Identify the infinitive use: _____

What answer is expected? (See *NTG*, 191):   _____

8.4   Οὐδεὶς δύναται δυσὶ κυρίοις δουλεύειν

_____

Identify the infinitive use: _____

8.5   πολλὰ ἔχω περὶ ὑμῶν λαλεῖν καὶ κρίνειν

_____

Identify the infinitive use: _____

8.6   λέγει αὐτοῖς· ὑμεῖς δὲ τίνα με λέγετε εἶναι;

_____

     Identify the infinitive use: _____

8.7   λέγετε ἐν Βεελζεβοὺλ ἐκβάλλειν με τὰ δαιμόνια

_____

     If the preposition ἐν is taken as *instrumental*, what is the translation?

     Identify the infinitive use: _____

     Identify the use of με: _____

8.8   Ἐμοὶ γὰρ τὸ ζῆν Χριστὸς καὶ τὸ ἀποθανεῖν κέρδος

_____

     Identify the infinitive use: _____

8.9   οὐδεὶς ἄξιος εὑρέθη ἀνοῖξαι τὸ βιβλίον οὔτε
     βλέπειν αὐτό

_____

     Identify the infinitive use: _____

8.10   Τοῦτο οὖν λέγω καὶ μαρτύρομαι ἐν κυρίῳ, μηκέτι
     ὑμᾶς περιπατεῖν, καθὼς καὶ τὰ ἔθνη περιπατεῖ

_____

_____

     Identify the infinitive use: _____

9.   Diagram the following four sentences on the next page.

9.1 καλόν ἐστιν ἡμᾶς ὧδε εἶναι

9.2 ἐζήτουν αὐτὸν κρατῆσαι

9.3 Οὐδεὶς δύναται δυσὶ κυρίοις δουλεύειν

9.4 οὐκ ἔχομεν ἐξουσίαν μὴ ἐργάζεσθαι;

ASSIGNMENT
2

Vocabulary: all other words (conjunctions, nouns, adjectives, etc.).

OBJECTIVE QUESTIONS

10. Translate the following:

10.1 τὸ ἀρνίον ἀρνοῦνται = _____

10.2 καθαρίζετε τὸ ποτήριον = _____

10.3 φαίνει ὁ ἥλιος = _____

10.4 δεῖ φυλάσσειν = _____

10.5 ἔξεστιν ἀγοράσαι = _____

10.6 αἱ φυλαὶ τῆς γῆς = _____

10.7 τὸν μόνον ἀληθινὸν θεόν = _____

10.8 τὴν ὑπομονὴν Ἰώβ = _____

10.9 ἐποίησεν τὸ ὕδωρ οἶνον = _____

11. The adverbial use of the infinitive means the infinitive modifies the
_____ _____ or adds a verbal idea to this element.

12. Identify the adverbial use of the following constructions and translate:

Construction	Use	Translation
12.1 ἐν τῷ ἀγοράζειν =	_____	_____
12.2 πρὸ τοῦ ἀρνήσασθαι =	_____	_____
12.3 πρὸς τό φαίνειν =	_____	_____
12.4 μετὰ τό καθαρίζειν =	_____	_____
12.5 τοῦ ἀρνεῖσθαι =	_____	_____

TRANSLATION

13. Translate the following, using the translation aids provided below:

○   *Translation Aids*   ○

εἴρηκα, associated with λέγω   σατανᾶς, ὁ, *Satan, the*
φιλία, ἡ, *friendship*   *Adversary*
προάγω, *I go before*   ἄφεσις, -εως, ἡ, *forgiveness*
Γαλιλαία, *Galilee*   τοῖς ἀνθρώποις, use "by"
θεάομαι, *I see, observe*   (#13.11)

13.1   καὶ νῦν εἴρηκα ὑμῖν πρὶν γενέσθαι

_____

13.2   οὐκ ἔχετε διὰ τὸ μὴ αἰτεῖσθαι ὑμᾶς

_____

13.3   Ἐγένετο δὲ ἐν τῷ εἶναι αὐτοὺς ἐκεῖ

_____

13.4   ἡ φιλία τοῦ κόσμου¹ ἔχθρα τοῦ θεοῦ ἐστιν

_____

13.5   λέγει αὐτῷ· ναὶ κύριε, σὺ οἶδας ὅτι φιλῶ σε

_____

13.6   εἰ ἄλλοις οὐκ εἰμὶ ἀπόστολος, ἀλλά γε ὑμῖν εἰμι

_____

13.7   ὁμοίως καὶ ὁ δεύτερος καὶ ὁ τρίτος ἕως τῶν ἑπτά²

_____

13.8   μὴ γὰρ οἰκίας οὐκ ἔχετε εἰς τὸ ἐσθίειν καὶ πίνειν;

_____

---

¹Translate τοῦ κόσμου and the following τοῦ θεοῦ using "with" phrases.
²Here ἑπτά is used as an ordinal number, not cardinal. The actual ordinal form is ἕβδομος.

13.9   μετὰ τὸ ἐγερθῆναί με προάξω ὑμᾶς εἰς τὴν
        Γαλιλαίαν

13.10   οἶδεν γὰρ ὁ πατὴρ ὑμῶν ὧν χρείαν ἔχετε πρὸ τοῦ
        ὑμᾶς αἰτῆσαι αὐτόν

13.11   πάντα δὲ τὰ ἔργα αὐτῶν ποιοῦσιν πρὸς τὸ
        θεαθῆναι τοῖς ἀνθρώποις

13.12   Οἶδά σου τὰ ἔργα καὶ τὴν ἀγάπην καὶ τὴν πίστιν
        καὶ τὴν διακονίαν καὶ τὴν ὑπομονήν σου

3.13   ἐγὼ ἀποστέλλω σε ἀνοῖξαι ὀφθαλμοὺς αὐτῶν,
        τοῦ ἐπιστρέψαι ἀπὸ σκότους εἰς φῶς καὶ τῆς
        ἐξουσίας τοῦ σατανᾶ ἐπὶ τὸν θεόν, τοῦ λαβεῖν
        αὐτοὺς ἄφεσιν ἁμαρτιῶν

---

14.   Diagram the following three sentences:

14.1   ἐγὼ ἀποστέλλω σε ἀνοῖξαι ὀφθαλμοὺς αὐτῶν

14.2	οὐκ ἔχετε διὰ τὸ μὴ αἰτεῖσθαι ὑμᾶς
14.3	μετὰ τὸ ἐγερθῆναί με προάξω ὑμᾶς εἰς τὴν Γαλιλαίαν

LESSON 26

(εἴκοσι ἕξ)

Present Active Participle

φίλος, *loving*, **bibliophile** (one who loves and collects books; literally, "book lover"), **hemophilia** (a disorder characterized by excessive bleeding; literally, "blood lover"), **Philadelphia** (literally, "brotherly love"), **philander** (to engage in casual love affairs; literally, "a loving man"), **philanthropy** (a desire to help humankind; literally, "human lover"), **philharmonic** (devoted to or appreciating music; literally, "harmony loving"), **philhellene** (one who loves Greece or the Greeks; literally, "Greek lover"), **Philip** (literally, "lover of horses"), **philodendron** (a tropical American vine; literally, "loves trees"), **philosophy** (pursuit of wisdom by intellectual means; literally, "the love of wisdom"), **Theophilus** (literally, "loved of God")

γνῶσις, *wisdom*, **agnostic** (someone who believes whether God exists cannot be known), **diagnosis** (a critical analysis of the nature of something; literally, "to know through"), **gnomic** (characterized by brief statements of truth), **Gnosticism** (the early Christian sect which centered on spiritual knowledge), **physiognomy** (the face or countenance as an index to character), **prognosis** (a prediction or a forecast; literally, "to know beforehand")

παρακλησις, *exhortation, consolation*, **Paraclete** (a theological designation for the Holy Spirit)

παρρησία, boldness, confidence, cf. παρά, + ῥέω (diarrhea, hemorrhage)

γαμέω, *I marry*, **bigamy** (being married to two persons; literally, "two marriages), **gamete** (a sex cell which combines with another sex cell to produce a new organism), **misogamy** (hatred of marriage; literally, "marriage-hate"), **monogamy** (being married to only one person; literally, "only marriage"), **polygamy** (being married to more than one person at the same time; literally, "many marriages")

ἐλεάω (also ἐλεέω), *I have mercy*, **alms** (money or goods given to the poor in charity), **eleemosynary** (dependent upon charity or alms)

ἐνδύω, *I put on, clothe*, **endue** (to provide)

ἡγέομαι, *I am chief, think, regard*, **eisegesis** (reading a meaning into a text; literally, "to lead into"), **exegesis** (a critical analysis of a text to obtain meaning; literally, "to lead out"), **hegemony** (the predominant influence of one state over another; literally, "leadership")

σκανδαλίζω, *I cause to stumble*, **scandal** (a disgraceful circumstance), **scandalize** (to shock disgracefully)

VERBAL FORMS

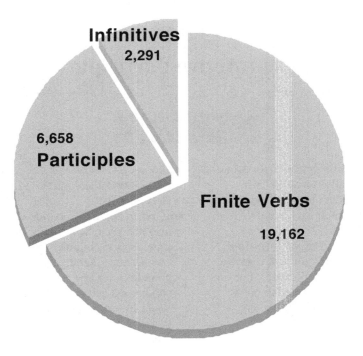

Infinitives
2,291

6,658
Participles

Finite Verbs
19,162

PARTICIPLE TENSES

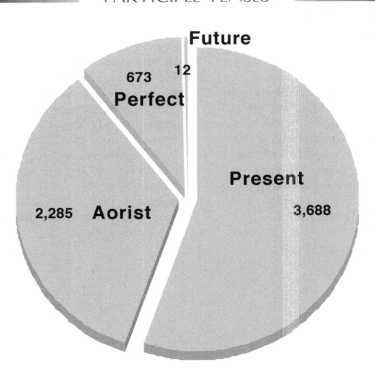

Future

673   12
Perfect

Present
3,688

2,285   **Aorist**

ASSIGNMENT

1

Vocabulary: all verb forms.

OBJECTIVE QUESTIONS

1. Participles are hybrids, verbal structures with _____ function. Fill in the following description of participle heritage:

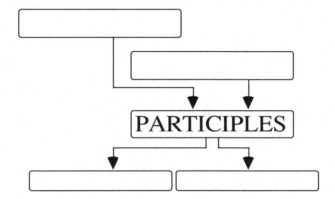

2. Complete the following on participle heritage:

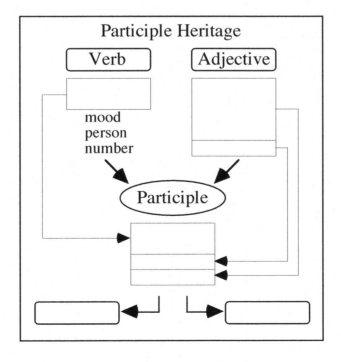

3. The active participial suffix is _____. However, feminine stems have the resultant letters _____. Masculine and neuter use _____ declension endings in the present active. Masculine endings are like the noun _____. Feminine endings wind up like the _____ declension noun _____.

4. Identify the component parts of the present active participle:

$$λυ\text{-}ο\text{-}ντ\text{-}ες$$

5. Participles generally are constructed two main ways: (1) with the Greek _____, with _____ function, (2) *without* the Greek _____, with _____ function.

6. A participle's substantive association is clarified by _____. Translation of an articular participle can use a *relative clause*. A nominative case participle would be set up by "who" or "which." For a given gender and number, a pronoun could be used: "*he* who," "*those* who," or "*that* which." For genitive and dative cases, try a prepositional phrase: "of those who" or "to those who," etc. Give a relative clause that translates the following articular participles as substantival:

6.1 οἱ ἀκούοντες = _____

6.2 τοῦ λέγοντος = _____

6.3 τοῖς αἰτοῦσιν = _____

Give a relative clause that translates these attributive articular participles:

6.4 ἄνθρωποι οἱ ἀκούοντες = _____

6.5 τοῦ λόγου τοῦ λέγοντος = _____

6.6 τοῖς αἰτοῦσιν δούλοις = _____

7. Translate (or give a short phrase for) the following:

7.1   οἱ γαμοῦντες =   _____

7.2   τοῦ ἐλεῶντος θεοῦ =   _____

7.3   οὐκ ἐνεδύσατο ἱμάτιον =   _____

7.4   σκανδαλίζω =   _____

7.5   προσκαλεῖται τοὺς δώδεκα   _____

7.6   τὸν θεὸν ἐπικαλοῦμαι =   _____

7.7   ἡγοῦνται =   _____

7.8   παρήγγειλεν ἡμῖν =   _____

7.9   ἐπετίμησεν αὐτοῖς =   _____

TRANSLATION

8. Translate the following, using the translation aids provided below:

○ *Translation Aids* ○

οὖσιν, from εἰμί
Ῥώμη, *Rome*
πᾶς ὁ [participle] = "every one
    who . . .," a very common
    participle construction
τοιαῦτα, correlative pronoun

θνήσκω, *I die*
εἰσελεύσεται, from
    εἰσέρχομαι
εἰδώλον, τό, *idol*
δουλεύω, *I serve*

8.1   τοῖς οὖσιν ἐν Ῥώμῃ

_____

8.2   εἶπεν τῷ λέγοντι αὐτῷ

_____

8.3   ὑμῖν λέγω τοῖς ἀκούουσιν

8.4   πᾶς γὰρ ὁ αἰτῶν λαμβάνει

8.5   τὴν ἀλήθειαν τὴν μένουσαν ἐν ἡμῖν

8.6   ὁ κρίνων τοὺς τὰ τοιαῦτα πράσσοντας

8.7   δὲ φωνὴν οὐκ ἤκουσαν τοῦ λαλοῦντός μοι

8.8   σὺ εἶ ὁ χριστὸς ὁ υἱὸς τοῦ θεοῦ τοῦ ζῶντος

8.9   εἰς τὸ εἶναι αὐτὸν πατέρα πάντων τῶν
πιστευόντων

8.10   τεθνήκασιν γὰρ οἱ ζητοῦντες τὴν ψυχὴν τοῦ
παιδίου

8.11   Οὐ πᾶς ὁ λέγων μοι· κύριε κύριε, εἰσελεύσεται εἰς
τὴν βασιλείαν τῶν οὐρανῶν

8.12   ἐπεστρέψατε πρὸς τὸν θεὸν ἀπὸ τῶν εἰδώλων
δουλεύειν θεῷ ζῶντι καὶ ἀληθινῷ

ASSIGNMENT
2

Vocabulary: all other words (conjunctions, nouns, adjectives, etc.).

▰ OBJECTIVE QUESTIONS ▰

9. Adverbial Translation. The anarthrous participle, like the anarthrous adjective, basically is an _____ construction. This participle *could* function as an _____ adjective, usually keyed by concord So, the following translates:

$$θεῷ \ ζῶντι = \text{\underline{\hspace{4cm}}}$$

Usually, anarthrous participles are used _____. This requires relating the participle's time to the main verb. Circle the main verb in the following:

$$ἔρχομαι \ αὐτῷ \ λέγοντι$$

While such a participle can have at least nine uses, a short cut is to try an anarthrous participle as a *temporal* clause started by words such as _____, _____, or _____, for example. (Most often, a *present* participle when temporal is taken as *simultaneous* to the main verb.)

10. Give an English clause that would translate the suggested adverbial sense:

    10.1   as *temporal, simultaneous* to a *past* tense main verb:

    διδάσκοντι (subject: "he") = _____

    10.2   as a *purpose* clause:

    πειράζοντες αὐτὸν =   _____

    10.3   as a *causal* clause:

    οὔσης (hint: from εἰμί) =   _____

    10.4   as a *conditional* clause:

    ἁμαρτανόντων ἡμῶν =   _____

10.5   as a *concession* clause:

θέλων (subject: "he") =   _____

10.6   as a *means* clause:

τοῦτο γὰρ ποιῶν =   _____

10.7   as a *manner* clause:

ἐπορεύετο χαίρων =   _____

10.8   as a *complementary* participle (παύω = "I stop, cease"):

οὐ παύεται λαλῶν =   _____

10.9   as a *circumstantial* clause (coordinate with an indicative):

λέγοντες (subject: "they") =   _____

11.   Participle Concord. The following translate differently according to
      participle location. Translate each as simultaneous to the main verb:

      11.1   ἔρχομαι αὐτῷ λέγοντι ταῦτα

             _____

      11.2   ἔρχομαι αὐτῷ λέγων ταῦτα

             _____

12.   Periphrasis. A periphrastic construction redundantly uses *two* verbal forms
      when one indicative verb would do, that is, a form of a _____
      _____ and a _____. Translate the following periphrastic
      construction, then give the verb form in the indicative that could have been
      used:

      12.1   ἦν διδάσκων =   _____

      12.2   Indicative verb form? = _____

13.   Genitive Absolute. The genitive absolute is an abrupt shift of construction
      that is signaled by a participle in the _____ case. This often
      happens when the subject of the main verb changes from the subject of the
      opening participle. The substantive associated with such a participle will be
      in the _____ case. From a grammatical stand point, this clause is
      _____ (independent or dependent?) of/on the main verb. Check which of
      the following is a genitive absolute:

13.1 ☐ λέγοντος αὐτοῦ ἐξέρχονται

13.2 ☐ ἤκουσεν αὐτοῦ λέγοντος

14. Translate (or give a short phrase for) the following:

14.1 φίλοι μού ἐστε = _____

14.2 οὐ θέλω θυσίαν = _____

14.3 οὔπω ἐστὶν τὸ τέλος = _____

14.4 οἶδας πόθεν ἔρχεται = _____

14.5 τίνα μισθὸν ἔχετε; = _____

14.6 ἐν καθαρᾷ συνειδήσει = _____

14.7 εἴτε γνῶσις = _____

14.8 τὸ κρίμα τοῦ θεοῦ = _____

14.9 διὰ τῆς παρακλήσεως = _____

14.10 παρρησίᾳ λαλεῖ = _____

TRANSLATION

15. Translate the following, using the translation aids provided below:

○ Translation Aids ○

Φαρισαῖος, *Pharisee*
ἀποκτείνω, *I kill, murder*
ἀπειθέω, *I disobey, am
    disbelieving*
κακολογέω, *I speak evil of*
ἐνώπιον, *before, in the
    presence of* (vocabulary,
    Lesson 9)
ὄψιος, *late*

οὔσης, from εἰμί
Βηθανία, *Bethany*
παύω, *I stop, cease*
Ἑκουσίως, *freely, willingly*
ἐπίγνωσις, -εως, ἡ, *knowledge*
ἀπολείπω, *I leave behind,
    abandon, desert*
ποία, interrogative pronoun
    (qualitative)

["Translation Hints" also are provided at the end of the exercise, but do your best first to try to discover an adverbial use on your own that would work.]

15.1   ἐπορεύετο γὰρ τὴν ὁδὸν αὐτοῦ χαίρων

15.2   καὶ ἦν διδάσκων αὐτοὺς ἐν τοῖς σάββασιν[1]

15.3   προσῆλθον αὐτῷ Φαρισαῖοι πειράζοντες αὐτόν

15.4   καὶ θέλων αὐτὸν ἀποκτεῖναι ἐφοβήθη τὸν ὄχλον

15.5   ἠπείθουν κακολογοῦντες τὴν ὁδὸν ἐνώπιον τοῦ πλήθους

15.6   καὶ ἐν τῷ ἱερῷ περιπατοῦντος αὐτοῦ ἔρχονται πρὸς αὐτόν

15.7   ὀψίας ἤδη οὔσης τῆς ὥρας, ἐξῆλθεν εἰς Βηθανίαν μετὰ τῶν δώδεκα

15.8   τοῦτο γὰρ ποιῶν καὶ σεαυτὸν σώσεις καὶ τοὺς ἀκούοντάς σου

15.9   ὁ ἄνθρωπος οὗτος οὐ παύεται λαλῶν ῥήματα κατὰ τοῦ τόπου τοῦ ἁγίου καὶ τοῦ νόμου

---

[1]Oddly, the second declension σάββατον uses a *third* declension ending for the dative plural alone. The durative focus here seems iterative (that is, each Sabbath). Perhaps this habit of thought explains the *plural* form of the noun.

15.10 Τότε λέγει αὐτοῖς ὁ Ἰησοῦς, Πάντες ὑμεῖς σκανδαλισθήσεσθε ἐν² ἐμοὶ ἐν τῇ νυκτὶ ταύτῃ

_____

_____

15.11 Ἑκουσίως γὰρ ἁμαρτανόντων ἡμῶν μετὰ τὸ λαβεῖν τὴν ἐπίγνωσιν τῆς ἀληθείας, οὐκέτι περὶ ἁμαρτιῶν ἀπολείπεται θυσία

_____

_____

15.12 προσῆλθον αὐτῷ διδάσκοντι οἱ ἀρχιερεῖς καὶ οἱ πρεσβύτεροι τοῦ λαοῦ λέγοντες, Ἐν³ ποίᾳ ἐξουσίᾳ ταῦτα ποιεῖς;

_____

_____

O *Translation Hints* O

15.1	Try adverbial of manner	15.7	Try adverbial of cause
15.2	Periphrastic	15.8	Perhaps means
15.3	Try adverbial of purpose	15.9	Complementary
15.4	Try adverbial of concession	15.10	[straightforward]
15.5	Perhaps circumstantial	15.11	Try adverbial of condition
15.6	The genitives suggest what?	15.12	1) Temp., simul.; 2) Circumstan.

---

²Use "because of" (instrumental of cause).
³Use "by."

FIGURE 12. Eteocretan Inscription at Heraklion. One fascinating piece of the story of the Greek language is on the island of Crete. A half dozen or so inscriptions discovered in Dreros and Praisos in eastern Crete ranging in date from the sixth century to third century BC use Greek alphabets, but the words are not Greek. Minoan civilization a millennium earlier preserved its language in the Linear A form, but these inscriptions cannot be shown to be based on that history. Rather, they seem to represent a spoken language on Crete before Greeks were on the scene. Thus, the language is given the name, Eteocretan, which means "true Cretans." The inscription above in the Archeological Museum of Heraklion, Crete dates about the fourth century BC and is from Praisos. The inscription is written in standard Ionic alphabet, except for the archaic, Cretan-style lambda. The ship bound for Rome upon which Paul sailed passed on the leeward side of Crete tacking against strong prevailing winds. They stopped at Fair Havens to debate wintering there, but decided to try to make the better harbor at Phoenix, a fateful decision that put them in the path of a Euroquilo (hurricane) that drove them out to sea and eventual shipwreck on Malta (Acts 27:7–44). We encounter in the New Testament a proverbial saying about the residents of Crete, who claimed to have the burial place of Zeus on their island, which to Greeks simply made the Cretans perpetual liars, since the immortal gods do not die (Tit 1:12).

LESSON 27

(εἴκοσι ἑπτά)

Present Middle Participle

Vocabulary 27

καθαρός, *clean*, *pure*, **catharsis** (a process of purging)

πλούσιος, *rich*, **Pluto** (the Roman god of the dead and the underworld), **plutocracy** (government by the wealthy; literally, "wealthy power"), **plutocrat** (a person with political influence or control because of wealth; literally, "power in wealth")

πνευματικός, *spiritual*, cf. πνεῦμα

ἀδελφή, *sister*, cf. ἀδελφός (Philadelphia)

ἔλεος, *mercy*, *pity*, **alms** (money or goods given to the poor in charity), **eleemosynary** (dependent upon charity or alms)

πάσχα, *Passover*, **paschal lamb** (a lamb eaten at the feast of the Passover)

χώρα, *country* (district), **chorography** (the technique of mapping a region or district; literally, "region writing")

ἁγιάζω, *I sanctify*, **Hagiographa** (the third of three divisions of the Old Testament; literally, "the sacred writings"), **hagiography** (biography of saints; literally, "writing of the saints"), **hagiology** (literature dealing with the lives of saints), **hagioscope** (a small opening in an interior wall of a church to view inside; literally, "to see the sacred")

ἀποκαλύπτω, *I reveal*, **apocalypse** (a prophetic revelation; literally, "revelation"), **apocalyptic** (pertaining to a prophetic disclosure), **eucalyptus** (an Australian evergreen; literally, "well covered"; cf. εὐ + καλύπτω)

γνωρίζω, *I make known*, cf. γνῶσις

ἰάομαι, *I heal*, **geriatrics** (the medical study of old age; literally, "old age healing"), **pediatrics** (the medical treatment of infants and children; literally, "child healing"), **psychiatry** (the medical study and treatment of mental illness; literally, "soul healing")

νικάω, *I conquer*, **Berenice** (the Macedonian Greek form for "victory bringer"), **Eunice** (literally, "good victory"), **Nicodemus** (literally, "victory of the people"), **Nicholas** (literally, "victory of the people"), **Nike** (the Greek goddess of victory; literally, "victory")

προφητεύω, *I prophesy*, **prophet** (a person who speaks by divine inspiration; literally, "to speak before"; cf. πρό + φημί)

τελέω, *I complete*, *fulfill*, **telegram** (a communication transmitted by telegraph; literally, "end letter"), **telegraph** (a device which transmits messages by wire; literally, "end writing"), **teleology** (the philosophical study of design or purpose), **telephone** (a device that transmits sounds from one location to another; literally, "end sound"), **telescope** (a device used to see distant objects; literally, "to see the end"), **telic** (directed toward a goal or purpose)

φρονέω, *I think*, **phrenic** (pertaining to the mind), **phrenology** (a system of analyzing character and mental faculties based on the shape of the head), **schizophrenia** (a mental disorder characterized by split personality; literally, "split mind")

PARTICIPLE VOICES

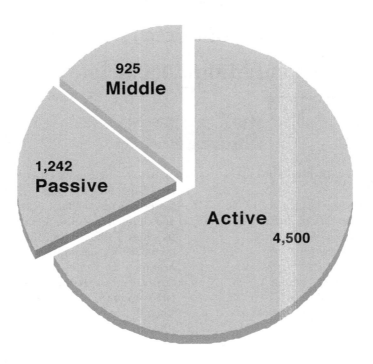

PARTICIPLE CASES

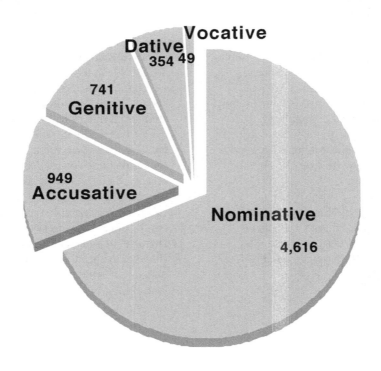

OBJECTIVE QUESTIONS

1. The middle participial suffix is _____. The thematic vowel is _____. The inflection follows exactly that of the adjective _____, except for accent.

2. Identify the component parts of the present middle participle:

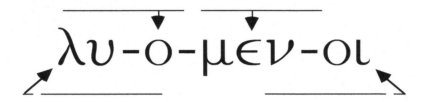

3. Verbs so-called "deponent" in indicative forms also are "deponent" in participial forms.

    ☐ True   ☐ False

4. Try your hand at identifying dative (locative, instrumental) uses with reference to Paul's comments to the church at Philippi.* As a reminder, some options are:

    Dative of: (1) advantage/disadvantage, (2) possession, (3) reference
    Locative of: (1) place, (2) point in time, (3) sphere
    Instrumental of: (1) original cause, (2) impersonal means, (3) manner as accompanying circumstance, (4) measure of time interval, (5) association

    *Remember, these identifications do have an element of subjectivity to them, so you will want to discuss them with your teacher. Sometimes, syntactical categories do not have a "right" or a "wrong" answer, but a more probable or less probable option.

    πᾶσιν τοῖς **ἁγίοις** ἐν **Χριστῷ** Ἰησοῦ τοῖς οὖσιν ἐν **Φιλίπποις** [Phil. 1:1]

    4.1 ἁγίοις = _____

    4.2 Χριστῷ = _____

    4.3 Φιλίπποις = _____

    Εὐχαριστῶ τῷ **θεῷ** μου ἐπὶ πάσῃ τῇ **μνείᾳ** ὑμῶν [Phil. 1:3]

    4.4 θεῷ = _____

4.5   μνείᾳ = _____

πάντοτε ἐν πάσῃ **δεήσει** μου ὑπὲρ πάντων ὑμῶν μετὰ χαρᾶς τὴν δέησιν ποιούμενος, ἐπὶ τῇ **κοινωνίᾳ** ὑμῶν [Phil. 1:4, 5]

4.6   δεήσει = _____

4.7   κοινωνίᾳ = _____

ὅτι παντὶ **τρόπῳ**, εἴτε προφάσει εἴτε **ἀληθείᾳ**, Χριστὸς καταγγέλλεται [Phil. 1:18]

4.8   τρόπῳ = _____

4.9   ἀληθείᾳ = _____

5. The periphrastic construction only rarely incorporates the middle or passive voice.

◻True   ◻False

6. Translate (or give a short phrase for) the following:

6.1   κώμη χήρας ἐν τῇ χώρᾳ = _____

6.2   ἐν τῷ σταυρῷ = _____

6.3   νικᾷ ἐν τῇ μαχαίρῃ = _____

6.4   ἡ ἑορτή τοῦ πάσχα = _____

6.5   γνωρίζω ταῖς ἀδελφαῖς = _____

6.6   ἄνθρωπος πλούσιος = _____

6.7   ὑμεῖς καθαροί ἐστε = _____

6.8   ὁ νόμος πνευματικός ἐστιν = _____

6.9   ἐκεῖθεν ἐξέρχεσθε = _____

6.10 κατὰ τὸ αὐτοῦ ἔλεος = _____

6.11 ἰαθήσεται = _____

6.12 ἐγνώρισα ὑμῖν = _____

6.13 κελεύεις με; = _____

TRANSLATION

7. Translate the following, using the translation aids provided below:

○ *Translation Aids* ○

θυσιαστήριον, τό, *altar*
κτῆμα, -τος, τό, *possession, property*
εὐφραίνω, *I make glad*
εἰ μή, *except* (#7.7)
Κρανίον, *Skull*
τόπος, *place* (Lesson 13)
ἀσέβεια, ἡ, *godlessness*

εἰ μή, *except* (#7.10)
ἀπολλυμένοις, from ἀπόλλυμι, a -μι verb, but like -ω verb as participle (minus thematic vowel); middle = *I perish*
μωρία, *foolishness*

7.1   τὰ τῆς σαρκὸς φρονοῦσιν

7.2   Ἰησοῦς εἶπεν, Τετέλεσται

7.3   τὸ θυσιαστήριον τὸ ἁγιάζον¹ τὸ δῶρον

7.4   νόμον οὖν καταργοῦμεν διὰ τῆς πίστεως;

7.5   ἀπῆλθεν λυπούμενος, ἦν γὰρ ἔχων κτήματα πολλά

7.6   τούτῳ δὲ ἦσαν θυγατέρες τέσσαρες παρθένοι προφητεύουσαι

---

¹This form is a participle, from ἁγιάζω.

7.7   εἰ γὰρ ἐγὼ λυπῶ ὑμᾶς, καὶ[2] τίς ὁ εὐφραίνων με εἰ
μὴ ὁ λυπούμενος ἐξ ἐμοῦ;

_____

_____

7.8   καὶ βαστάζων ἑαυτῷ τὸν σταυρὸν ἐξῆλθεν εἰς τὸν
λεγόμενον Κρανίου Τόπον

_____

_____

7.9   Ἀποκαλύπτεται γὰρ ὀργὴ θεοῦ ἀπ' οὐρανοῦ ἐπὶ[3]
πᾶσαν ἀσέβειαν καὶ ἀδικίαν ἀνθρώπων

_____

_____

7.10 Τίς [δέ] ἐστιν ὁ νικῶν τὸν κόσμον εἰ μὴ ὁ
πιστεύων ὅτι Ἰησοῦς ἐστιν ὁ υἱὸς τοῦ θεοῦ;

_____

_____

7.11 Ὁ λόγος γὰρ ὁ τοῦ σταυροῦ τοῖς μὲν
ἀπολλυμένοις μωρία ἐστίν, τοῖς δὲ σῳζομένοις
ἡμῖν δύναμις θεοῦ ἐστιν

_____

_____

---

[2] In this context, a loose conjunction joining clauses; just drop out of the translation.
[3] Translate as "against."

8.   Diagram the following five sentences.

8.1	σὺ εἶ ὁ υἱὸς τοῦ θεοῦ τοῦ ζῶντος

8.2	Ὁ λόγος γὰρ ὁ τοῦ σταυροῦ τοῖς μὲν ἀπολλυμένοις μωρία ἐστίν

8.3	ἀπῆλθεν λυπούμενος

8.4	ἦν διδάσκων αὐτοὺς ἐν τοῖς σάββασιν

8.5	προσῆλθον αὐτῷ διδάσκοντι οἱ ἀρχιερεῖς καὶ οἱ πρεσβύτεροι τοῦ λαοῦ λέγοντες, Ἐν ποίᾳ ἐξουσίᾳ ταῦτα ποιεῖς;

LESSON 28

(εἴκοσι ὀκτώ)

Aorist and Future Participles

Vocabulary 28

δένδρον, *tree*, **dendrite** (a mineral crystalizing within another in a tree-branching pattern; branches of a nerve cell transmitting impulses), **dendrology** (botanical study of trees), **philodendron** (a tropical American vine; literally, "loves trees"), **Rhododendron** (an evergreen shrub with pink or purple flowers; literally, "a rose tree")

νεφέλη, *cloud*, **nepheline** (a mineral used with ceramics and enamels; literally, "cloudy," because the material becomes cloudy when placed in nitric acid), **nephelometer** (a device used to measure particles in a liquid; literally, "cloud measurement"), **nephology** (the study of clouds), cf. Latin *nebula*, *nebulae* (nebula, nebulous)

πορνεία, *fornication*, **pornography** (sexually explicit writings or pictures; literally, "immoral writings")

PARTICIPLE TENSES

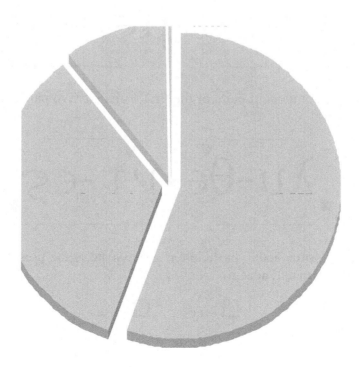

OBJECTIVE QUESTIONS

1. The first aorist active tense suffix is _____, and the participial suffix is
    _____. Feminine forms wind up as _____. The middle voice adds the voice
    suffix _____. The passive voice has the suffix _____. Feminine passive
    forms wind up as _____.

2. The aorist participle has an augment.

    ☐ True   ☐ False

3. Identify the component parts of the first aorist active participle:

    $$\lambda \upsilon - \sigma \alpha - \nu \tau - \epsilon \varsigma$$

4. Identify the component parts of the first aorist middle participle:

    $$\lambda \upsilon - \sigma \alpha - \mu \epsilon \nu - o \varsigma$$

5. Identify the component parts of the first aorist passive participle:

    $$\lambda \upsilon - \theta \epsilon - \nu \tau - \epsilon \varsigma$$

6. The second aorist active participle is a duplicate of the present participle,
    except for stem and accent.

    ☐ True   ☐ False

7. The second aorist passive participle drops the _____ of the passive suffix, and the endings are _____, _____, _____.

8. Future participles are rare, but simply add the tense suffix _____ to the tense stem. The active voice still would have the participial suffix _____, and the middle voice the _____ suffix. Future passive hypothetically would use the passive suffix _____, finished off with the voice indicator _____ and inflection.

9. Translate the following (ἐλεύσομαι is a principle part of ἔρχομαι):

   9.1 ἔρχεται μετὰ τῶν νεφελῶν = _____

   9.2 πᾶν δένδρον ἀγαθὸν = _____

   9.3 ἐκ τῆς πορνείας αὐτῆς = _____

   9.4 μήποτε ἐλεύσομαι = _____

▰▰▰ TRANSLATION ▰▰▰

10. Translate the following, using the translation aids provided below:

○ *Translation Aids* ○

ἐχάρησαν, from χαίρω
ὄπισθεν, *behind* (adv. prep.)
ἥψατο, from ἅπτω, *I light*;   middle, *I touch*

Βαρναβᾶς, *Barnabas*
Σαῦλος, *Saul*
ἐπιζητέω, *I seek, desire, want*

10.1 ἰδόντες δὲ τὸν ἀστέρα ἐχάρησαν

_____

10.2 πᾶν δένδρον ἀγαθὸν καρποὺς καλοὺς ποιεῖ

_____

10.3 οὐ θέλει μετανοῆσαι ἐκ τῆς πορνείας αὐτῆς

_____

10.4 Δικαιωθέντες οὖν ἐκ πίστεως εἰρήνην ἔχομεν

10.5 αὕτη ἐστὶν ἡ νίκη ἡ νικήσασα τὸν κόσμον, ἡ πίστις ἡμῶν

10.6 περὶ τοῦ υἱοῦ αὐτοῦ τοῦ γενομένου ἐκ σπέρματος Δαυὶδ

10.7 τοῦτο ἤδη τρίτον ἐφανερώθη Ἰησοῦς τοῖς μαθηταῖς ἐγερθεὶς ἐκ νεκρῶν

10.8 ἀκούσασα περὶ τοῦ Ἰησοῦ, ἐλθοῦσα ἐν τῷ ὄχλῳ ὄπισθεν ἥψατο τοῦ ἱματίου αὐτοῦ

10.9 οὗτος προσκαλεσάμενος Βαρναβᾶν καὶ Σαῦλον ἐπεζήτησεν ἀκοῦσαι τὸν λόγον τοῦ θεοῦ

LESSON 29

(εἴκοσι ἐννέα)

Perfect Participles

Vocabulary 29

ἀκοή, *hearing*, *report*, **acoumeter** (an instrument for measuring the power of the sense of hearing), **acoustical** (pertaining to sound or hearing), **acoustics** (pertaining to sound or hearing)

ἀσθένεια, *weakness*, **asthenia** (lack or loss of bodily strength), **asthenic** (a slender, lightly muscled human physique), **asthenopia** (eyestrain resulting in dim vision; literally, "weak sight"), **asthenosphere** (the less rigid layer of the earth's mantle), **neurasthenia** (fatigue once ... t from exhaustion of the nervous system)

ἐπιστολή, *letter*, **epistle** (a letter)

συνέδριον, *Sanhedrin*, **Sanhedrin** (Jewish legal council)

ἐκλεκτός, *chosen*, *elect*, **eclectic** (consisting of components selected from diverse sources)

μανθάνω, *I learn*, **mathematics** (the science of numbers and their relationships), **polymath** (a person learned in many fields; literally, "much learning")

FINITE VS. INFINITE

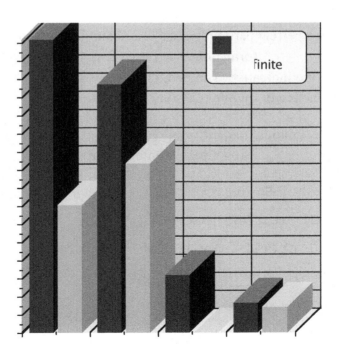

OBJECTIVE QUESTIONS

1. For masculine and neuter perfect active participles, identify the following components for λύω:

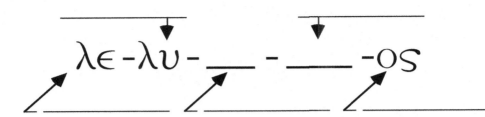

2. For λύω, the nominative masculine singular perfect active participle volatilizes to the form _____; nominative neuter singular winds up as _____.

3. The feminine perfect active participle has the inexplicable resultant form _____; the endings follow the "_____ pure" pattern of the first declension paradigm _____.

4. The perfect middle participle just uses the reduplicated perfect stem _____ and the middle voice suffix _____, with the endings like the adjective _____.

5. The future perfect participle always is found in the New Testament in a _____ formation. The future tense is given by the verb _____ in the future indicative. The perfect aspect is given by the _____ in either active or middle (passive) voice.

6. The perfect middle *indicative* of _____ stems is formed _____ using a perfect middle participle.

7. Translate the following (ἐλεύσομαι is a principle part of ἔρχομαι):

    7.1 διότι μαρτύρομαι ὑμῖν = _____

    7.2 δυσὶ κυρίοις δουλεύειν = _____

    7.3 εἰς τὸ συνέδριον αὐτῶν = _____

    7.4 οὐκ ἀδικῶ σε = _____

    7.5 τῇ ἀσθενείᾳ ἡμῶν = _____

7.6 οὐ καταλείπει = _____

7.7 ἀκοῇ ἀκούσετε = _____

7.8 ὀμνύουσιν = _____

7.9 ᾧ προσεῖχον πάντες = _____

TRANSLATION

8. Translate the following, using the translation aids provided below:

○ *Translation Aids* ○

καταλιπών, from καταλείπω
γράμματα, idiom for education
μεμαθηκώς, from μανθάνω
τίς, indefinite pronoun; the
    accent is due to the enclitic
    that follows
Φῆλιξ, *Felix*
δέσμιος, *prisoner*
Ἰουδαῖος, *Jew*

πρεσβύτης, *elderly man*
προβεβηκυῖα, from προβαίνω, *I*
    go on, am old
ἐπιγραφή, *superscription*
αἰτία, *reason, cause, charge*
ἐπιγράφω, *I write upon*
περιβάλλω, *I clothe, am clothed*
βάπτω, *I dip*

8.1 καταλιπών[1] αὐτοὺς ἀπῆλθεν

_____

8.2 πῶς οὗτος γράμματα οἶδεν[2] μὴ μεμαθηκώς;

_____

8.3 πολλοὶ γάρ εἰσιν κλητοί, ὀλίγοι δὲ ἐκλεκτοί

_____

8.4 ἀνήρ τίς ἐστιν καταλελειμμένος ὑπὸ Φήλικος
δέσμιος

_____

---

[1]Try a circumstantial participle; that is, just make the sense like an indicative verb joined to the next by καί.

[2]The expression γράμματα οἶδεν is an idiom, similar in idea to our colloquial "an educated man."

8.5   ἔλεγεν οὖν ὁ Ἰησοῦς πρὸς τοὺς πεπιστευκότας
αὐτῷ Ἰουδαίους

_____

8.6   καὶ αὐτὸς ἤμην . . . φυλάσσων τὰ ἱμάτια τῶν
ἀναιρούντων αὐτόν

_____

8.7   ἐγὼ γάρ εἰμι πρεσβύτης καὶ ἡ γυνή μου
προβεβηκυῖα[3] ἐν ταῖς ἡμέραις αὐτῆς

_____

_____

8.8   καὶ ἦν[4] ἡ ἐπιγραφὴ τῆς αἰτίας αὐτοῦ
ἐπιγεγραμμένη· ὁ βασιλεὺς τῶν Ἰουδαίων

_____

_____

8.9   καὶ περιβεβλημένος ἱμάτιον βεβαμμένον αἵματι,
καὶ κέκληται τὸ ὄνομα αὐτοῦ ὁ λόγος τοῦ θεοῦ

_____

_____

---

[3]The expression προβεβηκυῖα ἐν ταῖς ἡμέραις αὐτῆς is an idiom for being old.
[4]Periphrastic with ἐπιγεγραμμένη; also, translate the αὐτοῦ using "against."

LESSON 30

(τριάκοντα)

Subjunctive Mood

Vocabulary 30

λευκός, *white*, **leukemia** (cancer of tne wnite blood cells; literally, "white blood"), **leukocyte** (a white corpuscle in the blood)

παῖς, παιδός, *boy*, *girl*, *child*, *servant*, **pedagogue** (a school teacher or educator; literally, "child leader"), **pediatrics** (the medical treatment of infants and children; literally, "child healing")

παρουσια, presence, **parousia** (theological term for the second coming of Christ)

κοινωνία, *fellowship*, cf. κοινή (cenobite, Koine Greek)

θεάομαι, *I behold*, **theater** (a structure for observing dramatic performances)

πάρειμι, *I am present*, **parousia** (theological term for the second coming of Christ)

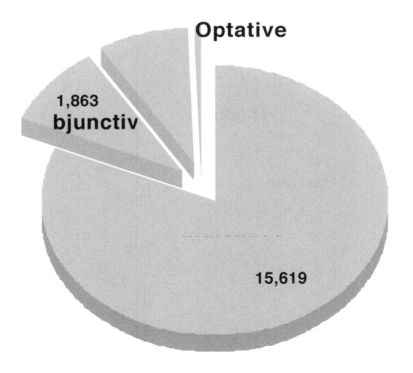

SUBJUNCTIVE TENSES

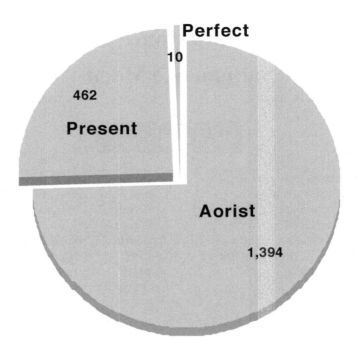

Perfect

10

462

Present

Aorist

1,394

SUBJUNCTIVE VOICES

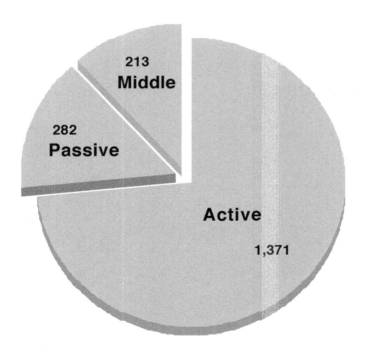

213
Middle

282
Passive

Active

1,371

OBJECTIVE QUESTIONS

1. The subjunctive is one of three moods of _____ outside the indicative and indicates _____ reality.

2. Indicate True or False:

    ____ 1. A definite time element is communicated with the subjunctive mood.

    ____ 2. The third class conditional sentence is one major use of the subjunctive mood.

    ____ 3. The difference in the translation of an aorist subjunctive and a present subjunctive always can be distinguished.

    ____ 4. The aorist subjunctive has an augment.

    ____ 5. The main indicator of the subjunctive mood is a lengthened thematic vowel.

    ____ 6. The epsilon contract verb gives the most trouble in distinguishing the indicative form from the subjunctive.

    ____ 7. The third class conditional sentence always is found with the conjunction ἐάν in the protasis.

3. The hortatory subjunctive key is _____ person plural, which, with the lengthened thematic vowel, would be the ending _____, translated as _____.

4. Prohibition with the subjunctive might mean do not _____ an action, if the context allows.

5. When one sees an interrogative adverb or pronoun with the subjunctive mood, the deliberative translation _____ _____ is used.

6. A dependent _____ clause is introduced by _____ or ὅπως and is followed by a verb in the subjunctive.

7. Complete the following chart on classifying conditional sentences by the mood of the protasis, which indicates the assumption about the "if" statement logic.

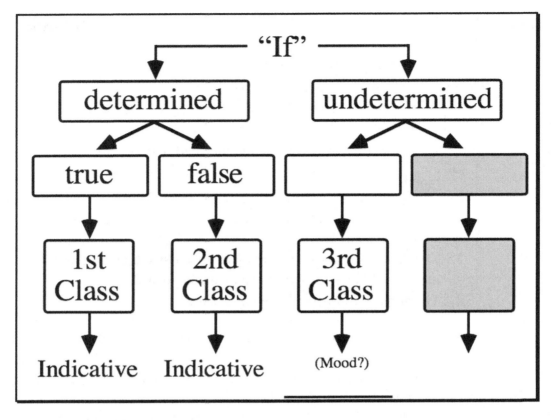

8. Translate the following:

    8.1 ὁ διδάσκαλος πάρεστιν = _____

    8.2 τότε ἥξει τὸ τέλος = _____

    8.3 τεθέαμαι τὸ πνεῦμα = _____

    8.4 ἱμάτια λευκά = _____

    8.5 εἰς μετάνοιάν σε ἄγει = _____

    8.6 ἰαθήσεται ὁ παῖς μου = _____

TRANSLATION

9. Translate the following, using the translation aids provided below:

○   *Translation Aids*   ○

Ἰουδαία, *Judea*
ὃς δ᾽ ἄν, idiom for *whoever*; see
    Depen. Clauses, "Relative
    Pronoun," *NTG*, 337

τελειόω, *I fulfill, finish, make
    complete*

9.1   μὴ πιστεύσητε

_____

9.2   ταῦτα γράφω ὑμῖν ἵνα μὴ ἁμάρτητε

_____

9.3   καὶ ὅταν ἀκούσωσιν εὐθὺς ἔρχεται ὁ Σατανᾶς

_____

9.4   Ἐὰν ἀγαπᾶτέ[1] με, τὰς ἐντολὰς τὰς ἐμὰς
      τηρήσετε

_____

9.5   λέγει τοῖς μαθηταῖς, ᾽Αγωμεν εἰς τὴν Ἰουδαίαν
      πάλιν

_____

9.6   ὃς δ᾽ ἄν τηρῇ αὐτοῦ τὸν λόγον, ἀληθῶς ἐν τούτῳ ἡ
      ἀγάπη τοῦ θεοῦ τετελείωται

_____

_____

---

[1]This could be indicative or subjunctive (see Table 30.4, *NTG*, 334). Which is it? How do
you know?

I JOHN

10. Translate 1 John 1:1–4 (be ready to answer all questions in footnotes in class):

1.1 Ὃ² ἦν³ ἀπ' ἀρχῆς, ὃ ἀκηκόαμεν⁴, ὃ ἑωράκαμεν⁵ τοῖς⁶

_____

ὀφθαλμοῖς ἡμῶν, ὃ ἐθεασάμεθα καὶ αἱ χεῖρες ἡμῶν

_____

ἐψηλάφησαν⁷ περὶ⁸ τοῦ λόγου τῆς ζωῆς—⁹ **1.2** καὶ ἡ ζωὴ

_____

ἐφανερώθη, καὶ ἑωράκαμεν καὶ μαρτυροῦμεν καὶ

_____

ἀπαγγέλλομεν ὑμῖν τὴν ζωὴν τὴν αἰώνιον ἥτις¹⁰ ἦν

_____

πρὸς¹¹ τὸν πατέρα καὶ ἐφανερώθη ἡμῖν— **1.3** ὃ

_____

---

²Relative pronoun; remember: "Relatives are rough!" What is the gender?

³From εἰμί. Be able to locate.

⁴From ἀκούω. Be able to locate.

⁵From ὁράω. Be able to locate.

⁶Take as instrumental: "with."

⁷From ψηλαφάω, "I grope about," "feel after" (like a person in the dark); the derivative idea, then, is "handle," "touch." Observe the augment, and also that the verb is an α contract.

⁸Used with the genitive case, so check options, _NTG_, 100.

⁹The dash in the text indicates broken grammatical construction ("anacoluthon"). The author interrupts the thought by inserting a parenthetical remark provoked by his mention of the idea of ζωή. He pursues reflection on this ζωή. Then, the author will return to his original thought, but have to repeat a verb or two in the process (notice just after the second dash, at the beginning of verse three). Exegetically, this parenthetical thought is significant, for the broken construction itself reveals how important is ζωή as a major theological idea for this author.

¹⁰Indefinite relative pronoun; remember: "Relatives are rough!" Note how the added τις then makes the relative pronoun indefinite. What is the gender? What is the antecedent?

¹¹What case is the preposition used with? Notice options, _NTG_, 101, are: "with," "with respect to," "for."

ἑωράκαμεν καὶ ἀκηκόαμεν, ἀπαγγέλλομεν καὶ ὑμῖν, ἵνα

καὶ ὑμεῖς κοινωνίαν ἔχητε μεθ᾽ ἡμῶν. καὶ ἡ κοινωνία

δὲ[12] ἡ ἡμετέρα[13] μετὰ τοῦ πατρὸς καὶ μετὰ τοῦ υἱοῦ

αὐτοῦ Ἰησοῦ Χριστοῦ. **1.4** καὶ ταῦτα γράφομεν ἡμεῖς,

ἵνα ἡ χαρὰ ἡμῶν ᾖ πεπληρωμένη.[14]

---

[12]A double conjunction (καὶ . . . δὲ). Treat καί as "and," then δέ as "indeed," "also," or "even."

[13]Remember: predicate constructions (i.e., they take the verb εἰμί) in Greek do not require an explicit form of εἰμί.

[14]For the form ᾖ, see *NTG*, Table 30.7. Perhaps two options for this construction: (1) the ᾖ πεπληρωμένη could be periphrastic; if so, what is the function of the participle? or (2) the participle πεπληρωμένη could function as a predicate adjective.

FIGURE 13. Hydra Amphora. On display in the Archeological Museum of Reggio Calabria, Italy, is this exquisite amphora produced around 550–540 BC, considered to belong to the Hyrda Group of Cambridge and representing a masterpiece of the style. A sequence of young horsemen feature in the central panel, perhaps depicting a horserace, overflown by birds (of prey?). The top panel is an intricate, beautifully performed floral chain around the neck. The bottom panel forms a border of carefully-executed, concentric rosettes, finished by a crown of rays at the foot. Greek artistry of such skill and craftsmanship matured half a millennium before the New Testament world came on the scene.

LESSON 31

(εἷς καὶ τριάκοντα)

Imperative Mood

ζῷον, *living creature*, **Mesozoic** (the third era of geologic time; literally, "middle of life"), **protozoa** (a one-celled, primitive form of animal life; literally, "first life"), **Zoe** (lit., "life"), **zoo** (a park where animals are kept), **zoology** (the scientific study of animals)

αὐξάνω, *I cause to grow*, **auxin** (a plant hormone which causes growth), cf. Latin *augeo* (augment, auxiliary)
γρηγορέω, *I watch*, **Gregory** (literally, "watchful")

MOODS

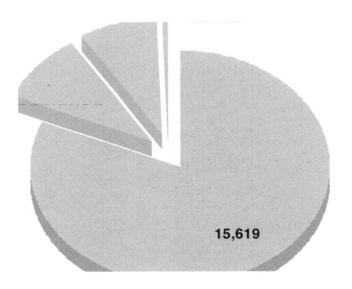

15,619

IMPERATIVE TENSES

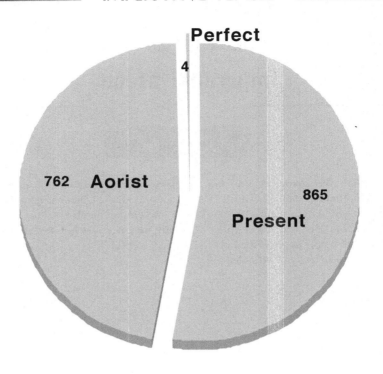

Perfect

4

762 Aorist

865

Present

IMPERATIVE VOICES

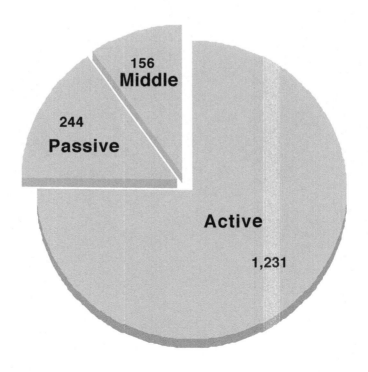

156 Middle

244 Passive

Active

1,231

OBJECTIVE QUESTIONS

1. The imperative is one of three moods of _____ outside the indicative and indicates _____ reality.

2. Indicate True or False:
   ____ 1. No time element is communicated with the imperative mood.
   ____ 2. The difference in the translation of an aorist imperative and a present imperative often cannot be distinguished.
   ____ 3. The aorist imperative has an augment.
   ____ 4. The main indicator of the imperative mood is a distinctive ending.
   ____ 5. The imperative has no first person forms.
   ____ 6. The Greek third person command has no exact equivalent in English.
   ____ 7. The second person plural of present imperative verbs are the same as the second person plural of present indicative verbs.

3. Prohibition with the imperative occurs in the _____ tense, whose _____ aspect might imply that the action already is in _____.

4. Instead of "let him" for third person imperative, we can use the format "he _____," which preserves the _____ nature of the Greek imperative.

5. The pronominal suffix endings for the imperative mood are:

Number	Person	Active	Mid./Pass.
singular	1st		
	2nd		
	3rd		
plural	1st		
	2nd		
	3rd		

6. Translate the following:
   6.1 ἐλευθέρα ἐστὶν ἀπὸ τοῦ νόμου = _____
   6.2 γρηγορῶμεν = _____

6.3   ἀνήχθημεν ἐν πλοίῳ = _____

6.4   τὰ τέσσαρα ζῷα = _____

6.5   Τὸ δὲ παιδίον ηὔξανεν = _____

6.6   ἰδοὺ μυστήριον ὑμῖν λέγω = _____

TRANSLATION

7.   Translate the following, using the translation aids provided below:

○   *Translation Aids* ○

ὦτα, nom. and acc. pl. of οὖς
ὄρος, -ους, τό, *mountain* (*NTG*,
    162, 14.8)
κρίνετε, indicative or
    imperative? Why?

ἔστω, from εἰμί
κόπτομαι, *I beat my breast*,
    idiom for a mourning
    custom; use *I mourn*

7.1   ὁ ἔχων ὦτα ἀκουέτω

_____

7.2   ἐλθέτω ἡ βασιλεία σου

_____

7.3   φευγέτωσαν εἰς τὰ ὄρη

_____

7.4   Μὴ κρίνετε, ἵνα μὴ κριθῆτε

_____

7.5   ἄλλους ἔσωσεν, σωσάτω ἑαυτόν

_____

7.6   ἔστω δὲ ὁ λόγος ὑμῶν ναὶ ναί, οὒ οὔ

_____

7.7   ἔκλαιον δὲ πάντες καὶ ἐκόπτοντο αὐτήν. ὁ δὲ
       εἶπεν, Μὴ κλαίετε

═══════════════ | JOHN ═══════════════

8. Translate 1 John 1:5–10 (be ready to answer questions in footnotes in class):

1.5 Καὶ ἔστιν αὕτη ἡ ἀγγελία ἣν ἀκηκόαμεν ἀπ᾽ αὐτοῦ

καὶ ἀναγγέλλομεν ὑμῖν, ὅτι ὁ θεὸς φῶς ἐστιν καὶ

σκοτία ἐν αὐτῷ οὐκ ἔστιν οὐδεμία.[1] **1.6** Ἐὰν εἴπωμεν[2]

ὅτι κοινωνίαν ἔχομεν μετ᾽ αὐτοῦ καὶ ἐν τῷ σκότει

περιπατῶμεν, ψευδόμεθα καὶ οὐ ποιοῦμεν τὴν ἀλήθειαν·

1.7 ἐὰν δὲ ἐν τῷ φωτὶ περιπατῶμεν[3] ὡς αὐτός ἐστιν ἐν

τῷ φωτί, κοινωνίαν ἔχομεν μετ᾽ ἀλλήλων καὶ τὸ αἷμα

Ἰησοῦ τοῦ υἱοῦ αὐτοῦ καθαρίζει ἡμᾶς ἀπὸ πάσης

---

[1] From οὐδείς, negative pronoun (*NTG*, 130–31).
[2] What class conditional sentence is this? (What is the mood of the protasis?)
[3] What class conditional sentence is this? (What is the mood of the protasis?)

ἁμαρτίας. **1.8** ἐὰν εἴπωμεν[4] ὅτι ἁμαρτίαν οὐκ ἔχομεν,

ἑαυτοὺς πλανῶμεν καὶ ἡ ἀλήθεια οὐκ ἔστιν ἐν ἡμῖν.

1.9 ἐὰν ὁμολογῶμεν[5] τὰς ἁμαρτίας ἡμῶν, πιστός ἐστιν

καὶ δίκαιος, ἵνα ἀφῇ[6] ἡμῖν τὰς[7] ἁμαρτίας καὶ καθαρίσῃ[8]

ἡμᾶς ἀπὸ πάσης ἀδικίας. **1.10** ἐὰν εἴπωμεν[9] ὅτι οὐχ

ἡμαρτήκαμεν ψεύστην ποιοῦμεν αὐτὸν καὶ ὁ λόγος

αὐτοῦ οὐκ ἔστιν ἐν ἡμῖν.

---

[4]What class conditional sentence is this? (What is the mood of the protasis?)

[5]What class conditional sentence is this? (What is the mood of the protasis?)

[6]From the -μι verb ἀφίημι, "I forgive," "release." Aorist, active, subjunctive (notice the ἵνα). The syntax of ἵνα ἀφῇ may be equivalent to an infinitive of result ("to ___"). The καθαρίσῃ should be treated similarly.

[7]The article used for the possessive pronoun; see *NTG*, 189.

[8]If the first construction is treated as an infinitive of result (ἵνα ἀφῇ), the following verb joined by καί should be treated similarly ("to ___").

[9]What class conditional sentence is this? (What is the mood of the protasis?)

LESSON 32

(δύο καὶ τριάκοντα)

Optative Mood

Vocabulary 32

κατηγορέω, *I accuse*, cf. κατά + ἀγορα
("against the assembly")

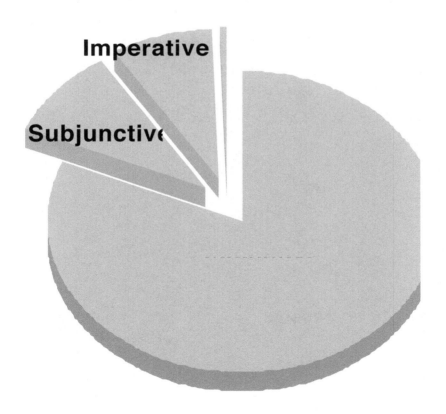

OPTATIVE TENSES

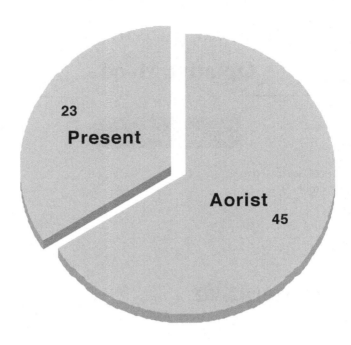

OPTATIVE VOICES

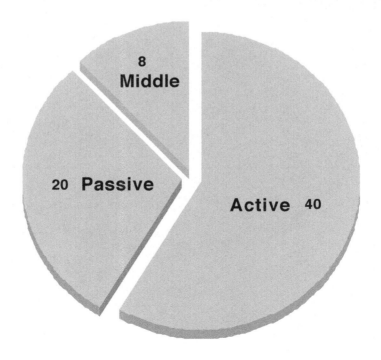

OBJECTIVE QUESTIONS

1. The optative is one of three moods of _____ outside the indicative and indicates _____ reality.

2. Indicate True or False:

    ____ 1. A time element is communicated with the optative mood.

    ____ 2. The difference in the translation of an aorist optative and a present optative can be distinguished easily.

    ____ 3. The aorist optative does not have an augment.

    ____ 4. The main indicator of the optative mood is the pronominal suffix ending.

    ____ 5. The optative generally uses secondary endings.

    ____ 6. The second aorist passive optative is quite common in the New Testament.

3. Optative mood endings *with* mood indicator are:

Number	Person	Active	Mid/Pass.
singular	1st		
	2nd		
	3rd		
plural	1st		
	2nd		
	3rd		

4. The one optative form of the verb εἰμί is _____, meaning _____.

5. Paul uses the optative expression ____ _____ regularly in his rhetoric, usually translated "_____."

6. While subjunctive treats the potentiality of an action as objectively possible, the optative treats the potentiality of an action as only _____ possible. So the optative is a diluted subjunctive, a move from _____ to _____.

7. Optative contingency commonly is generated by the words "if," "may," or
   "_____" in English translation.

8. The fourth class conditional sentence uses the _____ mood in the
   protasis, assuming that the condition is _____ but _____.
   Regularly, the conjunction used is _____. However, no New Testament
   example of a complete fourth class conditional sentence exists, for either the
   _____ or the _____ is left off.

9. Complete the following chart on classifying conditional sentences by the
   mood of the protasis, which indicates the assumption by the speaker on the
   logic of the "if" statement.

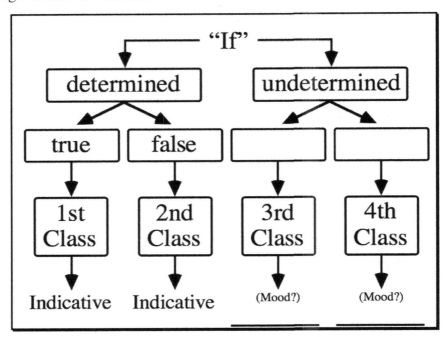

10. Translate the following:

   10.1 δέομαί σου = _____

   10.2 περιεβάλετέ με = _____

   10.3 κατηγοροῦμεν αὐτοῦ = _____

   10.4 ἔχομεν θυσιαστήριον = _____

   10.5 σκεύη ὀργῆς = _____

   10.6 οὐκ ἐδοκίμασαν τὸν θεὸν = _____

TRANSLATION

11. Translate the following, using the translation aids provided below:

○   *Translation Aids*   ○

ἔλεγον, first person singular   αὕτη, see *NTG*, 124, Table
Ἱεροσόλυμα, *Jerusalem*   11.12
διαλαλέω, *I discuss*   ψεύστης, *liar*
Ἐπηρώτων, see *NTG*, 140,
    Table 12.7

11.1   ὁ κόσμος ὅλος ἐν τῷ πονηρῷ κεῖται

_____

11.2   ἔλεγον εἰ βούλοιτο πορεύεσθαι εἰς Ἱεροσόλυμα

_____

11.3   καὶ διελάλουν πρὸς ἀλλήλους τί ἂν ποιήσαιεν τῷ
         Ἰησοῦ

_____

11.4   Ἐπηρώτων δὲ αὐτὸν οἱ μαθηταὶ αὐτοῦ τίς αὕτη
         εἴη ἡ παραβολή

_____

11.5   μὴ γένοιτο· γινέσθω δὲ ὁ θεὸς ἀληθής, πᾶς δὲ
         ἄνθρωπος ψεύστης

_____

_____

ι JOHN

12. Translate 1 John 2:1–6 (be ready to answer footnote questions in class):

2.1 Τεκνία μου, ταῦτα γράφω ὑμῖν ἵνα μὴ ἁμάρτητε.

καὶ ἐάν τις ἁμάρτῃ,[1] παράκλητον ἔχομεν πρὸς τὸν

πατέρα Ἰησοῦν Ἀριστὸν δίκαιον· **2.2** καὶ αὐτὸς ἱλασμός

ἐστιν περὶ τῶν ἁμαρτιῶν ἡμῶν, οὐ περὶ τῶν ἡμετέρων

δὲ μόνον ἀλλὰ καὶ περὶ ὅλου τοῦ κόσμου. **2.3** Καὶ ἐν

τούτῳ γινώσκομεν ὅτι ἐγνώκαμεν αὐτόν, ἐὰν τὰς

ἐντολὰς αὐτοῦ τηρῶμεν. **2.4** ὁ λέγων[2] ὅτι Ἔγνωκα

αὐτόν καὶ τὰς ἐντολὰς αὐτοῦ μὴ τηρῶν, ψεύστης ἐστίν

---

[1] What class conditional sentence is this? (What is the mood of the protasis?)
[2] The articular participle is "The one who says," and the ὅτι is "ὅτι recitative."

καὶ ἐν τούτῳ ἡ ἀλήθεια οὐκ ἔστιν· **2.5** ὃς δ' ἂν[3] τηρῇ

αὐτοῦ τὸν λόγον, ἀληθῶς ἐν τούτῳ ἡ ἀγάπη τοῦ θεοῦ

τετελείωται,[4] ἐν τούτῳ γινώσκομεν ὅτι ἐν αὐτῷ ἐσμεν.

2.6 ὁ λέγων ἐν αὐτῷ μένειν[5] ὀφείλει[6] καθὼς ἐκεῖνος

περιεπάτησεν καὶ[7] αὐτὸς [οὕτως] περιπατεῖν.

---

[3]The ὃς δ' ἂν is an idiom for *whoever*; see, "Relative Pronoun," *NTG*, 337.
[4]From τελειόω, "I fulfill," "finish," "make complete," "make perfect."
[5]See *NTG*, 275, the infinitive as direct object of indirect discourse.
[6]Requires infinitive to finish the verb ("complementary infinitive," *NTG*, 275–76).
[7]Take the καί here as "also" or "even." Review *NTG*, 191–92.

FIGURE 14. Puteoli Amphitheater. The Flavian amphitheater at Puteoli, built by the same architects and engineers as the Colosseum in Rome, is in a much better state of preservation. The arena floor reveals the portals from which a vast system of pulleys and cranes lifted gladiators and wild beasts into the arena. Paul stayed in Puteoli for seven days on his way to Rome (Acts 28:13–14).

FIGURE 15. Puteoli Amphitheater: Subterranean Passageways. Unlike the Colosseum in Rome, the subterranean passageways and storage vaults of the Puteoli amphitheater are beautifully preserved and can be accessed by visitors to the site. From these passageways animals and contestants were raised in cages to the arena floor. Fights with wild beasts in the morning (called *venationes*) were prelude to the bloody gladiatorial contests in the afternoon, the bloodlust sport Rome exported to the world. Paul evoked these contests of the amphitheater in his Corinthian imagery, "For even if with merely human hopes I fought with beasts in Ephesus, what have I gained?" (1 Cor 15:32).

LESSON 33

(τριάκοντα τρεῖς)

MI Verbs—First Principal Part

μιμνήσκομαι, *I remember*, **amnesia** (partial or total lost of memory; literally, "without memory"), **amnesty** (a general pardon for offenders by a government; literally, "not remembered"), **anamnesis** (a recollection or a complete case history of a patient; literally, "to recall again"), **mnemonic** (something which aids memory)

χαρίζομαι, *I give, grant, pardon, forgive*, **charisma** (charm or personal magnetism; literally, "favor" or "a divine gift"), **charismatic** (emphasizing spiritual or divine gifts; literally, "divine gifts"), **Charissa** (literally, "grace"), **Eucharist** (Christian communion; literally, "thanksgiving" or "good favor")

ἀπόλλυμι, *I destroy, perish*, **Apollyon** (the angel of the bottomless pit in Revelation; literally, "the Destroyer")

δείκνυμι, *I show*, **apodictic** (clearly proven or shown; literally, "shown away from"), **paradigm** (a list of all inflectional forms of a word; literally, "shown alongside")

δίδωμι, *I give, grant, allow*, **antidote** (a remedy to counteract a poison; literally, "given against"), **apodosis** (the clause which states the consequence of a conditional statement; literally, "given away"), **dose** (the amount of medicine taken at one time; literally, "given")

τίθημι, *I put, place, lay*, **antithesis** (direct contrast; literally, "set against"), **bibliotheca** (a library or book collection; literally, "book case"), **hypothesis** (an assumption or explanation; literally,

placed under"), **metathesis** (the transposition of letters or sounds in a word; literally, "transposed" or "place after"), **parenthesis** (punctuation marks used to set off explanatory remarks; literally, "set in alongside"; cf. παρά, + ἐν + τίθημι), **synthesis** (the combination of separate elements to form a whole; literally, "placed together"), **thesis** (a proposition; literally, "something placed")

φημί, *I say*, **aphasia** (a total or partial loss of the power to speak; literally, "without speech"), **blasphemy** (a profane act or utterance against something sacred), **emphasis** (speaking with the force of the voice on; literally, "speaking on"), **euphemism** (using a less direct word or phrase for one considered offensive; literally, "speaking well")

ἵστημι, *I place, set, cause to stand*, **apostasy** (abandoning something formerly believed; literally, "to stand away from"), **apostate** (a person who abandons a former belief; literally, "one standing away from"), **dynasty** (a family or group that maintains power for several generations; literally, "standing in power"), **ecstasy** (a state of intense joy; literally, "to drive out of one's senses" or "to stand out"), **epistemology** (the branch of philosophy that investigates the nature and origin of knowledge; literally, "the study of knowledge"; cf. ἐπί, + ἵστημι + λόγος, **hypostasis** (the substance or essence of something; literally, "standing under")

CONJUGATIONS

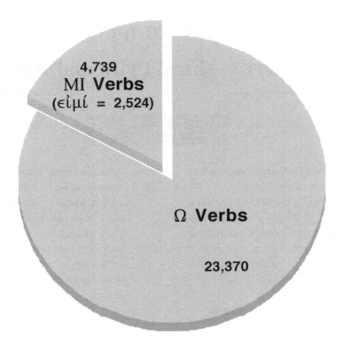

4,739
MI **Verbs**
(εἰμί = 2,524)

Ω **Verbs**

23,370

MI VOICES

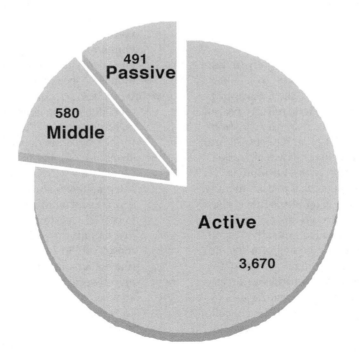

491
Passive

580
Middle

Active

3,670

OBJECTIVE QUESTIONS

1. The primary and secondary endings for -μι verbs are:

Num.	Per.	Primary Active	Primary Mid/Pass.	Secondary Active	Secondary Mid/Pass.
sing.	1st				
	2nd				
	3rd				
plural	1st				
	2nd				
	3rd				

2. Identify the four listed features of the *present* active indicative -μι verb:

$$(2)\text{-}(1)\text{-}(3)\text{-}(4)$$

δί-δω-μι

   2.1 _____

   2.2 _____

   2.3 _____

   2.4 _____

3. What -μι verb mood *does* incorporate a thematic vowel in resultant endings?

   ☐ Indicative   ☐ Subjunctive   ☐ Imperative

4. Identify the five listed features of the *imperfect* active indicative -μι verb:

$$(3)\text{-}(2)\text{-}(1)\text{-}(4)\text{-}(5)$$

ἐ-δί-δου-ν

   4.1 _____

   4.2 _____

4.3   _____

4.4   _____

4.5   _____

5. Locate the following -μι verb forms of τίθημι:

5.1 τιθέασι(ν)

Tense	Voice	Mood	Person	Number

5.2 τίθενται

Tense	Voice	Mood	Person	Number

5.3 τιθῶμεν

Tense	Voice	Mood	Person	Number

5.4 τιθέτω

Tense	Voice	Mood	Person	Number

5.5 ἐτίθεσθε

Tense	Voice	Mood	Person	Number

6. Translate the following:

6.1 οὐχ ὑμεῖς κεκοπιάκατε = _____

6.2 ἀπολλύμεθα = _____

6.3 δείκνυσιν αὐτῷ = _____

6.4 ἐχαρίσατο ὑμῖν = _____

6.5 Τοῦτο δέ φημι = _____

6.6 ἐμνήσθη ὁ Πέτρος = _____

6.7 τὴν ψυχήν μου τίθημι = _____

6.8 ἐδίδου τοῖς μαθηταῖς = _____

6.9 νόμον ἱστάνομεν = _____

6.10 τιθέασιν αὐτόν = _____

TRANSLATION

7. Translate the following, using the translation aids provided below:

O   *Translation Aids*   O

παραδίδωμι, *I deliver over,*   ὦσιν, *from* εἰμί
    hand over   ἐὰν μὴ, *unless, except*

7.1 παντὶ αἰτοῦντί σε δίδου

_____

7.2 ὅταν παραδιδῷ τὴν βασιλείαν τῷ θεῷ

_____

7.3 καὶ δείκνυσιν αὐτῷ πάσας τὰς βασιλείας τοῦ
     κόσμου

_____

7.4 καὶ τὴν δύναμιν καὶ ἐξουσίαν αὐτῶν τῷ θηρίῳ
     διδόασιν

_____

7.5   ὁ ποιμὴν ὁ καλὸς τὴν ψυχὴν αὐτοῦ τίθησιν ὑπὲρ
τῶν προβάτων

7.6   ἵνα ὦσιν μετ' αὐτοῦ καὶ ἵνα ἀποστέλλῃ
αὐτοὺς κηρύσσειν

7.7   οὐδεὶς γὰρ δύναται ταῦτα τὰ σημεῖα ποιεῖν ἃ σὺ
ποιεῖς, ἐὰν μὴ ᾖ ὁ θεὸς μετ' αὐτοῦ

 1 JOHN

8.   Translate 1 John 2:7–11 (be ready to answer questions in footnotes in class):

2.7 Ἀγαπητοί, οὐκ ἐντολὴν καινὴν γράφω ὑμῖν ἀλλ'

ἐντολὴν παλαιὰν ἣν εἴχετε[1] ἀπ' ἀρχῆς· ἡ ἐντολὴ ἡ

παλαιά ἐστιν ὁ λόγος ὃν ἠκούσατε. **2.8** πάλιν ἐντολὴν

καινὴν γράφω ὑμῖν, ὅ ἐστιν ἀληθὲς ἐν αὐτῷ καὶ ἐν

ὑμῖν, ὅτι ἡ σκοτία παράγεται καὶ τὸ φῶς τὸ ἀληθινὸν

---

[1]From ἔχω; an unusual imperfect augment; see p. 163, n. 4.

ἤδη φαίνει. **2.9** ὁ λέγων ἐν τῷ φωτὶ εἶναι[2] καὶ τὸν

ἀδελφὸν αὐτοῦ μισῶν ἐν τῇ σκοτίᾳ ἐστὶν ἕως ἄρτι.

2.10 ὁ ἀγαπῶν τὸν ἀδελφὸν αὐτοῦ ἐν τῷ φωτὶ μένει καὶ

σκάνδαλον ἐν αὐτῷ οὐκ ἔστιν· **2.11** ὁ δὲ μισῶν τὸν

ἀδελφὸν αὐτοῦ ἐν τῇ σκοτίᾳ ἐστὶν καὶ ἐν τῇ σκοτίᾳ

περιπατεῖ καὶ οὐκ οἶδεν[3] ποῦ ὑπάγει, ὅτι ἡ σκοτία

ἐτύφλωσεν[4] τοὺς ὀφθαλμοὺς αὐτοῦ.

---

[2]See *NTG*, 275, the infinitive as direct object of indirect discourse.

[3]From οἶδα, *I know*, an old second perfect that translates as present tense; see *NTG*, 263. Be able to locate this verb.

[4]From τυφλόω, *I blind*. Be able to locate this verb.

FIGURE 16. Iliad Sarcophagus at Ostia. The Ostia Antica Archeological Museum holds this magnificent Roman sarcophagus of Greek marble from the necropolis of Pianabella, dated AD 160. The carving is a collage of famous scenes from Homer's *Iliad*. Foregrounded is the poignant burial scene of Troy's hero, Hector, after his dead body ingloriously was dragged outside the gates of Troy behind the chariot of the Greek warrior, Achilles. Troy finally falls due to the infamous wooden war horse ruse by the Greeks. Another Trojan hero, Aeneas, divinely conceived of the goddess Venus (Aphrodite), escapes the burning city with his son, Lulus, aided by Aphrodite, and finally settles in Italy. In the Roman poet Virgil's *Aeneid*, Aeneas is claimed as the ancestor of Romulus and Remus, the two brothers suckled by a she-wolf and founders of Rome. Thus, Aeneas becomes legendary not only as the first and foremost of Roman heroes, but, with his son, Lulus, as progenitors of the imperial families of Julius and Augustus. Augustus was hailed by Virgil as world savior who brought universal peace after Rome had convulsed for centuries in civil war. In imperial propaganda, the emperors of Rome not only are connected to the gods of Olympus, but are the inheritors of glorious Troy and one of the most famous war stories ever told. Note how Luke is careful to date the birth of Jesus, true son of God and savior of the world, in the days of Augustus, emperor of Rome (Luke 2:1).

LESSON 34

(τριάκοντα τέσσαρες)

MI Verbs—Other Principal Parts

ἀποδίδωμι, *I give back*, **apodosis** (the clause which states the consequence of a conditional statement; literally, "given away")

ἀφιτημι, *I permit, forgive*, **aphesis** (the loss of a vowel from the beginning of a word; e.g., "squire" for "esquire"; literally, "sent away")

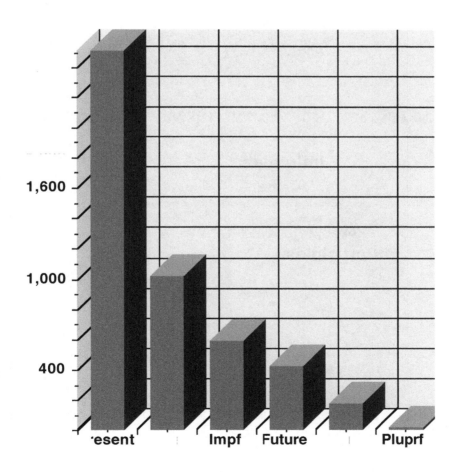

MI VERB MOOD

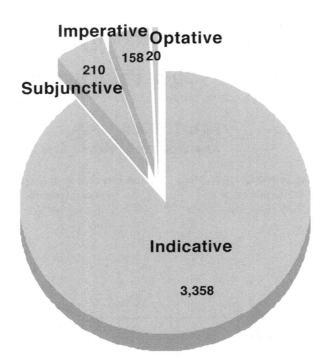

Imperative Optative
158 20
210
Subjunctive

Indicative

3,358

MI VERBAL FORMS

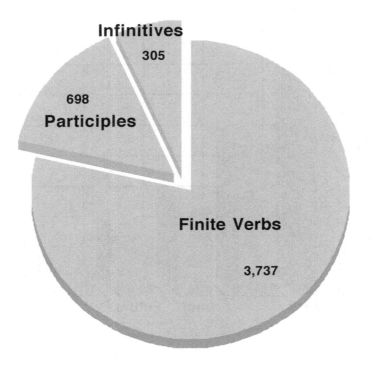

Infinitives
305

698
Participles

Finite Verbs

3,737

OBJECTIVE QUESTIONS

1. In locating -μι verbs outside the first principal part, one key is to notice that for any -μι verb that reduplicates in the first principal part, their non-reduplicated stems are either _____ or _____ tense. Another helpful hint: assume δω- or δο- = δίδωμι; θη- or θε- = τίθημι; στη- or στα- = ἵστημι.

2. Locate the following -μι verb forms of δίδωμι:

   2.1 διδῶμαι

Tense	Voice	Mood	Person	Number

   2.2 δῶμαι

Tense	Voice	Mood	Person	Number

   2.3 δίδονται

Tense	Voice	Mood	Person	Number

   2.4 δώσονται

Tense	Voice	Mood	Person	Number

3. The phrase "_____ aorist" is applied to the three verbs _____, _____, and _____ because the aorist forms replace the -σα tense suffix pattern with a _____ pattern.

4. Locate the following -μι verb forms of δίδωμι:

4.1 ἔδωκας

Tense	Voice	Mood	Person	Number

4.2 δέδωκας

Tense	Voice	Mood	Person	Number

4.3 δέδοσθε

Tense	Voice	Mood	Person	Number

4.4 ἔδοσθε

Tense	Voice	Mood	Person	Number

5. "Non-thematic" second aorists such as _____ and _____, though part of the thematic conjugation, do not use a _____ vowel in the aorist _____ (voice) _____ (mood).

6. Locate the following -ω verb forms:

6.1 ἀνέβη

Tense	Voice	Mood	Person	Number

6.2 ἔγνως

Tense	Voice	Mood	Person	Number

7. Locate the following -μι verb forms:

7.1 ἐδόθημεν

Tense	Voice	Mood	Person	Number

7.2 δοθῶμεν

Tense	Voice	Mood	Person	Number

7.3 διδόντας

Tense	Voice	Kind	Case	Person	Number

7.4 δούς

Tense	Voice	Kind	Case	Person	Number

7.5 δεδωκώς

Tense	Voice	Kind	Case	Person	Number

8. Translate the following:

8.1 ὁ καθήμενος = _____

8.2 ἐπέθηκαν = _____

8.3 ἀποδώσει σοι = _____

8.4 τετελείωται ἡ ἀγάπη = _____

8.5 Πάντα μοι παρεδόθη = _____

8.6 ἁμαρτίας ἀφίησιν = _____

8.7 ἀναστὰς ἐβαπτίσθη = _____

8.8 μακάριοι οἱ πεινῶντες = _____

8.9 μὴ κωλύετε αὐτόν = _____

8.10 γράφω ὑμῖν, νεανίσκοι = _____

TRANSLATION

9. Translate the following, using the translation aids provided below:

○ *Translation Aids* ○

ἠκολούθησεν, from ἀκολου-
θέω; do not let the contract
verb fool you on prin. part
παριστάνετε, negative in μηδέ,
so negative = what mood?

μέλος, -ους, τό, *body part, member*
ὅπλον, *weapon, instrument*

9.1 ἐπέθηκαν αὐτῷ τὸν σταυρὸν

_____

9.2 καὶ ἀναστὰς ἠκολούθησεν αὐτῷ

_____

9.3 ὁ δὲ Ἰησοῦς εἶπεν, "Ἄφετε τὰ παιδία καὶ μὴ
κωλύετε αὐτὰ ἐλθεῖν πρός με

_____

_____

9.4   μηδὲ παριστάνετε τὰ μέλη ὑμῶν ὅπλα ἀδικίας τῇ
ἁμαρτίᾳ, ἀλλὰ παραστήσατε ἑαυτοὺς τῷ θεῷ

_____

_____

▰▰▰▰▰▰▰▰▰   I JOHN   ▰▰▰▰▰▰▰

10. Translate 1 John 2:12–17 (be ready to answer footnote questions in class):

2.12 Γράφω ὑμῖν, τεκνία,

_____

ὅτι ἀφέωνται[1] ὑμῖν αἱ ἁμαρτίαι διὰ τὸ ὄνομα
αὐτοῦ.

_____

2.13 γράφω ὑμῖν, πατέρες,

_____

ὅτι ἐγνώκατε τὸν ἀπ᾽ ἀρχῆς.

_____

γράφω ὑμῖν, νεανίσκοι,

_____

ὅτι νενικήκατε τὸν πονηρόν.

_____

―――――――――――――――

[1]From ἀφίημι; perfect, passive, indicative.

2.14 ἔγραψα[2] ὑμῖν, παιδία,

ὅτι ἐγνώκατε τὸν πατέρα.

ἔγραψα ὑμῖν, πατέρες,

ὅτι ἐγνώκατε τὸν ἀπ' ἀρχῆς.

ἔγραψα ὑμῖν, νεανίσκοι,

ὅτι ἰσχυροί ἐστε

καὶ ὁ λόγος τοῦ θεοῦ ἐν ὑμῖν μένει

καὶ νενικήκατε τὸν πονηρόν.

2.15 Μὴ ἀγαπᾶτε τὸν κόσμον μηδὲ τὰ ἐν τῷ κόσμῳ.

---

[2]Probably this form that reoccurs in this verse should be taken as an "epistolary aorist" (see *NTG*, 218). Why? Be able to explain the context of the epistolary aorist.

ἐάν τις ἀγαπᾷ[3] τὸν κόσμον, οὐκ ἔστιν ἡ ἀγάπη τοῦ

πατρὸς ἐν αὐτῷ· **2.16** ὅτι πᾶν τὸ ἐν τῷ κόσμῳ, ἡ

ἐπιθυμία τῆς σαρκὸς καὶ ἡ ἐπιθυμία τῶν ὀφθαλμῶν καὶ

ἡ ἀλαζονεία τοῦ βίου, οὐκ ἔστιν ἐκ τοῦ πατρὸς ἀλλὰ ἐκ

τοῦ κόσμου ἐστίν. **2.17** καὶ ὁ κόσμος παράγεται καὶ ἡ

ἐπιθυμία αὐτοῦ, ὁ δὲ ποιῶν τὸθέλημα τοῦ θεοῦ μένει εἰς

τὸν αἰῶνα.[4]

---

[3]What is the mood of this verb? What class conditional sentence?

[4]This εἰς τὸν αἰῶνα is an idiom in Greek; a dynamic translation has to substitute an equivalent expression in English. Read the appendix, "On the Art of Translation" in *NTG*, 373–76.

FIGURE 17. Arch of Titus. The Arch of Titus was erected in AD 82 by emperor Domitian to honor his deceased brother, Titus, who destroyed Jerusalem and its temple in the First Jewish War in AD 70. The arch stands fifty feet high, forty-four feet wide, and almost sixteen feet deep. The north panel relief shows Winged Victory crowning Titus in his quadriga chariot with a laurel wreath. The arch was the first time in Roman architecture that gods and humans were pictured together in one scene having the same divine status. The inscription on the front reads: "The Roman Senate and People (dedicate this) to the divine Titus Vespasianus Augustus, son of the divine Vespasian."

FIGURE 18. Arch of Titus: South Panel. The south panel depicts spoils of the Jewish temple in Jerusalem, featuring most prominently in deep relief the great Menorah golden candelabrum. Other items include the gold trumpets, the table of Shew bread, and fire pans for ash removal from around the altar. These items likely were highlighted in gold paint against a blue background. The Arch of Titus is a notable, rare, first-century depiction of actual artifacts from the Jewish temple.

ENGLISH GRAMMAR

(A Primer for the Meek)

The Basics of Words and Sentences

INTRODUCTION

G IVEN THE SORRY STATE OF BASIC English grammar in our secondary school systems, studying foreign languages is a frightening thought. This chapter is intended as a primer of English grammar on the basics of words and sentences for the meek or faint of heart, or those for whom the educational system failed miserably but granted a degree anyway. You are not at fault. Yet, now that you have decided to study Greek, understanding grammar *is* your responsibility. How in the world can you possibly understand the grammar of a foreign language if you do not even understand your own? Take charge. Take control. Get a grip. You only are talking about improving your entire speaking and writing ministry here. One key benefit of studying New Testament Greek, then, is not to make you a Greek scholar. One key benefit is to make you a better minister in practical ways that affect your ministry every day — in better writing, speaking, teaching, and preaching. Even mundane matters like your weekly bulletin insert will improve dramatically.

The approach taken here is traditional, pragmatic, and visual. Traditional terms and categories have been used to stimulate latent memories of long-lost grammar lessons. Modern theory, however, has not been ignored. The pragmatics of getting from basic English structure to Greek structure set the agenda for how the material is presented. A comprehensive treatment of English grammar is not intended, nor would one say by any stretch of the imagination that all the bases are covered. Visual layout is designed for both pedagogical and mnemonic effect. Such layout may appear somewhat unconventional, but, hopefully, not maverick.

Our goal is to understand the basics of words and sentences in English as a bridge for understanding the basics of Greek words and sentences. Some basics are held in common. The distinctions are more significant, though, and provide the challenge of Greek for the meek. We start with the smaller elements of words, then build to the larger elements of sentences. Remember: *in grammar, terminology is crucial and definitions are essential.*

WORDS

Understanding grammar begins by classifying the basic units of communication, words, into their functional categories, called the "parts of speech." We have eight parts of speech.

Parts of Speech

Table 1: The Eight Parts of Speech

	Parts of Speech			
Primary	Noun	Verb	Adjective	Adverb
Secondary	Pronoun	Preposition	Conjunction	Interjection

The eight parts of speech are: (1) noun, (2) verb, (3) adjective, (4) adverb, (5) pronoun, (6) preposition, (7) conjunction, and (8) interjection. The first four of these (noun, verb, adjective, adverb) are the workhorses; they provide the primary functions of speech. The last four sometimes are grouped together into a category called "function" words; these provide secondary functions that enhance the meaning of the primary parts of speech. These eight parts are defined and illustrated.

Primary Parts of Speech

Nouns

Nouns name a person, place, or thing. A *common noun* names a common class of person, place, or thing: man, house, document. A *proper noun* names a particular person, place, or thing: Thomas Jefferson, Monticello, Declaration of Independence. A grammatical element that functions like a noun is called a *substantive*. Thus, an adjective that has the role of a noun is functioning "substantively," that is, like a noun. We generally will mean "substantive" when using the word "noun" in the following discussion.

Verbs

Verbs (V) express action or state. An action can be activity ("running the bases") or event ("caught the ball"). A state is a condition ("tired") or a mode of being ("competitive"). An *auxiliary verb* helps another verb express action in certain forms. Examples include: *be, do, did, have, may, can, must, will, shall, might, could*, *should*, and *would*. So, another form of "run" is "*have* run." The auxiliary verb "have" is used to create the perfect tense form of "run." The agent performing the action of the verb is the *subject* (S) of the verb. The *complete subject* is the subject of the verb and all related words used to complete the meaning of the subject. The *predicate* is the verb, its auxiliaries, and all related words used to complete its meaning that predicates the action of the subject.

The verb's *complement* is a noun or adjective located in the predicate required to complete the meaning of the verb. The five types of complements are: (1) the *direct object* (O_1), the receiver of the verb's action, (2) the *object complement* (O_2), a second direct object that fills out the meaning of the first direct object, (3) the *predicate nominative* (C_N), a noun that renames the subject, used with "copulative" verbs (below), (4) the *predicate adjective* (C_A), an adjective that modifies, describes, or points out the subject, used with "copulative" verbs, and (5) the indirect object (O_i), the indirect receptor or benefactor of the verb's action.

Table 2: The Complete Subject and the Predicate

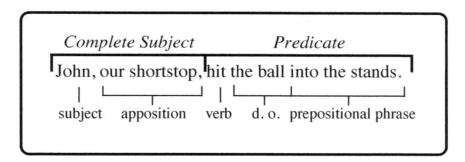

Verbs can be classified in various ways. Two classifications pertinent at this point are the nature of their action and their basic forms.

Action. Verbs classified by the nature of their action are transitive or intransitive. *Transitive* verbs (V_t) transfer the verb's action onto an object. Thus, transitive use requires a direct object for completion. *Intransitive* verbs do not require a direct object for completion. The verb's action is not transferred to an object. Whether a verb is transitive or intransitive is by use—that is, is not necessarily inherent to the verb itself. Some verbs can be used either way. For example, "I *run*" is intransitive, but "I *run* the bases" is transitive ("bases" is object of the action "run").

The intransitive verb has two types. The *basic intransitive* (V_i) verb makes a complete statement by itself without need for any other words in the predicate to complete the meaning: "Athletes *play*." The *copulative intransitive* verb (V_c) requires a predicate noun or predicate adjective in the predicate to complete its meaning. The main English copulative is *to be*: "He *is* our shortstop." ("Shortstop" is a predicate noun that renames the subject.) Other verbs used as copulatives are: *seem*, *become*, *appear*, *prove*, *look*, *remain*, *feel*, *taste*, *smell*, *sound*, *turn*, and *grow*.

Forms. Verbs classified by their forms are finite or infinite. A *finite verb* is a verb that is grammatically limited by a subject: "John *hit* the ball." The verb "hit" is finite because "hit" is limited by a subject, "John." An *infinite verb*, also called a "verbal," is a verb that is not grammatically limited by a subject: "I want *to play*." The verbal "to play" is infinite because the form is not limited by any subject. English has three verbals: infinitive, participle, and gerund. An *infinitive* verbal is unlimited by a subject and has properties of verbs and nouns. The form is associated with the preposition "to" (*to speak*, *to run*, *to vote*). A *participle* is a verbal unlimited by a subject that has properties of verbs and adjectives. The form is associated with the ending "-ing" (*speaking*, *running*, *voting*). A *gerund* is a subcategory of the participle, that is, an "-ing" form of the participle specifically used as a noun: "*Running* is healthy exercise."

Verbals basically transform verbs into other parts of speech. For example, the infinitive can transform a verb into a noun: "*To hit* was his goal"; or, into an adjective: "The ball *to hit* was the fast ball"; or, into an adverb: "John played *to hit the ball*." Similarly, participles transform verbs into adjectives: "The player *hitting the ball* is John"; gerunds function as nouns: "*Hitting the ball* was his goal."

Adjectives

Adjectives modify nouns and pronouns; they describe further or limit meaning. A descriptive adjective expresses a quality of a noun: "the *good* speaker." A limiting adjective restricts a noun from other nouns in its class: "*this* good speaker" (not any good speaker). Examples of limiting adjectives are indefinite, demonstrative, and possessive pronouns, numerals, and articles.

Adjectives have three uses: (1) attributive, (2) substantive, and (3) predicative. The *attributive* adjective is the adjective used as a direct modifier usually positioned immediately before the noun modified: "The *good* player receives a reward." The *substantive* adjective takes any role of a noun—subject, for example: "The *good* will receive their reward." The *predicative* adjective completes the meaning of a copulative verb with a descriptive quality of the subject: "The shortstop is *good*." The predicate adjective provides only an additional description about the subject and is not equal to the totality of the subject. In contrast, the predicate noun completely renames the subject and could stand on its own to represent the totality of the subject: "Mary is our *president*."

Adjectives also are used to express comparisons. Comparisons have three *degrees*: positive, comparative, and superlative. The *positive* degree expresses the basic adjective quality without comparison. The *comparative* degree expresses a relative higher or lower degree when comparing persons or things. The *superlative* degree expresses the highest or lowest degree in comparing persons or things. The comparative and superlative degrees are formed three ways: (1) adding the endings "-er" or "-est" to the adjective itself (high*er*, high*est*), or (2) prefixing auxiliary words "more," "most," or "less," "least" (*more* beautiful, *most* beautiful), and (3) irregular word changes (*bad*, *worse*, *worst*).

The adjectives "a," "an," and "the" are termed *articles*. Both "a" and "an" are *indefinite articles* because they do not point to any particular person, place, or thing. (The form "an" is used before the vowels a, e, i, o, u.) "The" is the *definite article* and points to a particular person, place, or thing. The indefinite article grammatically is unnecessary. The definite article, on the other hand, is grammatically necessary.

Four rules govern the use of the definite article to clarify function (two rules for adjectives, two for nouns). First, two or more adjectives modifying the same noun do not repeat the article after the first adjective; thus, "*the* yellow, white, and blue uniform" means one uniform, whereas "the yellow, the white, and the blue uniform" means three uniforms. Second, an adjective with an understood noun gets the article: "the tall and the tanned player" means two players. Third, two or more nouns denoting the same person or thing requires only one article with the first noun; thus, "the shortstop and captain of the team" means one person. Fourth, two or more nouns denoting different entities require the repetition of the article with each noun; thus, "the shortstop and the captain of the team" means two persons.

Adverbs

Adverbs often are modifiers of verbs. In fact, however, adverbs are nearly global modifiers—in English they can modify just about anything, bottom line. The most typical formation pattern is the addition of "-ly" to the positive adjective form: sad, sad*ly*, joyful, joyful*ly*. Here are examples of adverb modifiers:

1. Substantive: *nearly* all
2. Verb: sings *beautifully*
3. Infinitive: to study *faithfully*
4. Participle: working *diligently*
5. Adjective: *very* large
6. Adverb: *rather* sadly
7. Preposition: *closely* with
8. Conjunction: *just* before I left

Adverbs have three uses: (1) simple, (2) interrogative, and (3) conjunctive. The *simple adverb* modifies: "She sings *beautifully*." Simple adverbs have five classes. The adverb of *manner* specifies how the action occurs: "He spoke *sadly*."

The adverb of *time* indicates when the action occurs: "He studies *daily*." The adverb of *place* shows where the action occurs: "She performs *there*." The adverb of *degree* specifies how much: "He was interrupted *rather* rudely." The adverb of *number* indicates order or frequency: "He came *first*"; "The bell rang *twice*."

Interrogative adverbs ask questions: "*Where* have you been?" Others words that can be interrogative adverbs are *when?*, *how?*, and *why?* when used within questions.

Conjunctive adverbs connect modifying clauses (defined under "Sentences"): "He worked *until the sun went down*." Conjunctive adverbs include *where, whence, whither, wherever, when, whenever, while, as, how, why, before, after, until*, and *since*.

Adverbs, like adjectives, can express degrees of comparison. An adverb comparison simply adds a helping word. The positive adverb degree is the simple adverb: "slowly." The comparative adverb degree adds "more": "*more* slowly." The superlative adverb degree adds "most": "*most* slowly."

Secondary Parts of Speech

Pronouns

Pronouns typically are noun substitutes that help avoid monotonous word repetition. The *antecedent* is the substituted noun. "John plays hard. *He* is a good athlete." "He" is a personal pronoun that substitutes for the antecedent noun, "John." Pronoun use, however, goes beyond simple noun substitution. The pronoun classes are: (1) personal, (2) possessive, (3) relative, (4) interrogative, (5) demonstrative, and (6) indefinite.

Personal pronouns substitute for personal nouns. They are first, second, and third person. First person is the person speaking (*I, we*), second person the person spoken to (*you, you*), and third person the person spoken about (*he, she, it, they*).

The personal pronouns can be compounded by adding the ending "-self" or "-selves": *myself, ourselves; yourself, yourselves; himself, herself, itself, themselves*. The compound forms are used two ways: (1) as *reflexive* to refer back to the subject of the verb: "She helped *herself*." (2) as *intensive* to create emphasis: "John *himself* did the work."

Possessive pronouns indicate possession: "I bought *my* book." The forms are: first person (*my, our*), second person (*your, your*), and third person (*his, her, its, their*). The *absolute possessive pronoun* indicates simultaneously the possessor and the thing possessed: "The book is *mine*." Notice that "mine" expresses possession, yet, at the same time, is equivalent to "my book." The absolute possessive pronouns are: first person (*mine, ours*), second person (*yours, yours*), and third person (*his, hers, its, theirs*).

Relative pronouns connect clauses. Specifically, they join dependent adjective clauses to their antecedent substantives in the main clauses in which they are found: "Our coach *whom we support* is good to us." The main clause is "Our coach is good to us." The dependent clause is "whom we support." The relative pronoun "whom" has as its antecedent "coach" in the main clause. The entire dependent clause functions as an adjective modifying the noun "coach." Words that function as relative pronouns are, for persons, *who, whose,* and *whom,* for animals or things, *which,* and in general for any category, *that* and *what* ("what," however, does not have an antecedent).

Certain relative pronouns can be compounded by adding "-ever" or "-soever": *whoever, whosoever, whomever, whomsoever, whichever, whatever, whatsoever:* "*Whoever* comes will be accepted." This use generalizes the antecedent.

Interrogative pronouns ask questions: "*Who* is coming to dinner?" Other words that can be interrogative pronouns are *who? whom? whose? which?* and *what?* when used within questions.

The last two pronoun classes are set apart. The demonstrative and indefinite pronouns are like the first three classes covered above (personal, relative, interrogative) in that they are pronouns. That is, when used alone, demonstrative and indefinite pronouns act as simple pronouns. Unlike the first three classes, however, these pronouns when used with substantives act as adjectives.

Demonstrative pronouns point out a particular person, place, or thing: "*This* is my book." Demonstrative pronouns are of two kinds, proximate and remote. *Proximate* demonstrative pronouns (*this, these*) point out a person, place, or thing at a relatively close distance to the speaker. *Remote* demonstrative pronouns (*that, those*) point out a person, place, or thing relatively far from the speaker.

Demonstrative pronouns can be used as adjectives. This use is in connection to a substantive: "*This* book is mine." Contrast the earlier pronoun example: "*This* is my book." In this earlier example, the demonstrative "this" is used alone, so acts as a simple pronoun. In the current example, the demonstrative "this" is used in connection with the noun "book," so functions as an adjective.

Indefinite pronouns are weaker forms of demonstrative pronouns. That is, indefinite pronouns point out persons, places, or things, but less definitely than demonstrative pronouns: "*Each* should do his own work." Words commonly used as indefinite pronouns are, as singular: *each, either, neither, one, none, everyone, anyone, someone, no one, nobody, everybody, another,* and, as plural: *some, other, few, all, many, several,* and *both.*

Parallel to demonstrative pronoun use, the indefinite pronouns act as simple pronouns when used alone. When used with substantives, though, these indefinite pronouns act as adjectives: "*Each* student should do his own work." In this example, "each" is used in connection with the noun "student," so functions as an adjective.

Prepositions

Prepositions show relationship. A preposition takes an object and is "pre-positioned" before its object: "*on* the grass." Here, "on" is the preposition, and "grass" is its object. Prepositions can be a simple word (*by*), a compound (*according to*), or an entire phrase (*with regard to*; for "phrase," see the section "Sentences"). They relate their objects to some other word or grammatical unit. The prepositional phrase can be used as an adjective modifying a noun or pronoun. "The man *on the grass* is in trouble." The phrase "on the grass" acts as an adjective modifying the noun "man." The prepositional phrase can be used as an adverb modifying a verb, adjective, or adverb: "The man walking *on the grass* is in trouble." The phrase "on the grass" acts as an adverb modifying the verbal "walking." A prepositional phrase even can be used as a substantive: "'On the grass' was his slogan." The phrase "on the grass" here functions as a noun acting as subject of the verb "was."

Table 3: Commonly Used Prepositions

aboard	before	for	out of	under
about	behind	from	outside	underne
above	below	from	over	ath
across	beneath	among	round	unto
after	beside	from	round	up
against	between	under	about	upon
along	beyond	in	since	with
amid	by	into	through	within
among	down	of	through	
around	during	off	out	
at	except	on	to	

Conjunctions

Conjunctions connect words or groups of words: "John *and* Jane play ball." The conjunction "and" joins the two proper nouns "John" and "Jane." The two classes of conjunctions are coordinate and subordinate. *Coordinate conjunctions* join words, phrases, or clauses of equal grammatical rank, such as two nouns, two infinitives, etc. The word "and" used in the example above is a coordinate conjunction. The most commonly used coordinate conjunctions are: *and, but, or, nor, for, however, moreover, then, therefore, yet,* and *still.* A *correlative* is a paired sequence of coordinate conjunctions that sets up comparison or contrast: "*Both* John *and* Jane play ball." The paired conjunctions used as correlatives are: *both . . . and, not only . . . but also, either . . . or,* and *neither . . . nor.*

Subordinate conjunctions join clauses of unequal rank. Specifically, the subordinate conjunction joins a dependent clause to an independent clause: "Elizabeth makes good grades *because* she studies diligently." Here, the word "because" is a subordinate conjunction that joins the dependent clause "because she studies diligently" to the independent clause, "Elizabeth makes good grades." Words used as subordinate conjunctions include *as*, *as if*, *because*, *before*, *if*, *since*, *that*, *till*, *unless*, *when*, *where*, and *whether*.

Interjections

Interjections insert strong feeling into a statement. Though part of a sentence, interjections formally have no grammatical relationship with any other sentence element: "*Oh*, how I want to win that game!" The word "Oh" is an interjection that has no relation to any other part of the statement. At the same time, the depth of feeling on the part of the speaker is enhanced through the use of "oh."

Summary Observations

Relationships

Table 4: Parts of Speech—Nouns, Verbs, and Their Modifiers

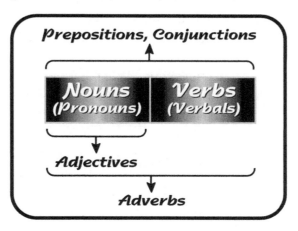

The most basic parts of speech are nouns and verbs. Without these, speech is mute. Nouns name and verbs predicate. Thus, actor and action represent the most fundamental elements of communication. All else is modification. Adjectives modify the meaning of nouns and pronouns. Adverbs modify verbs, adjectives, and other adverbs. So, nouns and verbs, and their modifiers, adjectives and adverbs, form the primary parts of speech.

The secondary parts of speech, prepositions and conjunctions, simply enhance further the basic parts, nouns and verbs. Interjections, on the other hand, exist autonomously. They are not connected to any other part of speech; however, interjections still enhance the overall impact of the sentence. The table above is a visual representation of these relationships.

Functional Category

"Part of speech" is a *functional* category, not an inherent property of a word. The *use* of a word determines its part of speech. The same word can be a noun, a verb, an adjective, an adverb, or some other part of speech—depending on just how that word is used in a particular sentence. The word "down" can illustrate. Observe the different parts of speech for which "down" is used in the following sentences:

1. Noun: In football, ten yards makes a first *down*.
2. Verb: The gun crew could not *down* the attacking plane.
3. Adjective: You should use first gear on that *down* grade.
4. Adverb: Go *down* the mountain.
5. Preposition: The house *down* the mountain is mine.

Even in one part of speech, "down" can have various meanings, or semantic range. The noun "down" can refer to a football game. Yet, "down" could refer to the fluffy plumage of a young bird too.

So, one might be asked, "What part of speech is so-and-so word?" This question has two possible answers. One answer responds with dictionary information about that word. The dictionary entries for a word often are organized around the various parts of speech for which that word typically is used. These are arranged in the order of the most frequently used part of speech to the least frequently used. If the word is by itself, then the primary dictionary entry probably is in view.

The other answer to the question "What part of speech is this word?" responds to the *use* of that word in a *given sentence*. If the word is in composition then one would identify the specific role, or part of speech, that word plays within the particular sentence in question. The five sentences using "down" given above illustrate that the one word "down" can serve as many parts of speech.

Word usage in a given sentences makes all the difference in the world in the meaning of words. Words without context fundamentally are without meaning. Understanding sentences, then, is the next step in getting a grip on grammar.

SENTENCES

Sentences combine words into meaningful statements based on conventions of word relationships peculiar to any given language. Nouns and verbs are the key parts of speech, so meaningful statements depend on ordered relationships among nouns and verbs, accomplished two ways: inflection and word order.

Inflection

Inflection is word changes to indicate grammatical function. Substantives are inflected for: (1) gender, (2) person, (3) number, and (4) case. *Gender* is distinction as to masculine, feminine, or neuter. Thus, nouns associated with feminine gender, such as *sister* or *woman*, would show *feminine grammar*. Nouns associated with masculine gender, such as *brother* or *man*, would show *masculine grammar*. Nouns that do not distinguish gender show *neuter grammar* (*book*, *tree*). Gender is cultural association. English associates "road" as neuter, but Greek associates "road" as feminine. The only way to know gender association in a language is to memorize as part of vocabulary acquisition. English inflection for gender is given by: (1) change of word: *man*, *woman*, (2) adding a word: *grandfather*, *grandmother*, and (3) adding a suffix: *host*, *hostess*.

Person indicates the person speaking (first), the person spoken to (second), and the person spoken about (third). Person is used in connection with the subject of the verb.

Number is distinction between one or more than one person, place, or thing. *Singular number* refers to one person, place, or thing. *Plural number* refers to more than one person, place, or thing. English shows plurals by adding suffixes such as *-en*, *-ren*, *-s*, *-es*, *-ies*, or *-ves* according to various spelling rules, or by changing internal vowels. Interestingly, the demonstrative pronouns are the only English adjectives inflected for number (*this*, *these*; *that*, *those*).

Declension is inflection of nouns arranged in an ordered sequence of gender, number, and case. What is case? Case is function in a sentence. In discussing nouns as words, we actually bumped into several case functions: for example, subject and direct object. Sometimes the same word will be spelled differently ("inflected") to show that that word is subject or object of a verb. For example, the spelling "he" indicates the subject function of this pronoun: "*He* hit the ball." What would the spelling be if this pronoun were the *object* of this verb? "The ball hit ___." Right: "*him*." Notice how the word's spelling changed to indicate a different *function* in the sentence, direct object of the verb rather than subject of the verb. That change is inflection. Here is another sentence: "He hit the ball to ___." Right again: "*him*." Why the same spelling? The *function* is still the same. This word is still an *object*, not an object of a verb, but an object of a preposition, "to." We can summarize both illustrations as the "object function" of the pronoun "he," in which "object" means either object of a verb or object of a preposition. We then could summarize this *object function* as shown by a changed inflection from "he" to "him" by calling this use the *objective case* of the pronoun. What are the English noun cases?

Noun Cases

Nominative Case

English has three cases for its substantives: (1) nominative, (2) possessive, and (3) objective. The *nominative case* is that word inflection that is used to indicate certain grammatical functions such as: subject, predicate nominative, vocative, exclamation, absolute, and apposition. The subject use is the subject of the verb: "*John* hit the ball." A *compound subject* is two or more simple subjects: "*John and Jane* hit the ball." (A *compound predicate* is two or more simple predicates: "hit and run.") The predicate nominative is the complement in the predicate of a copulative verb that renames the subject: "Our shortstop is *John*." The vocative is a person or thing directly addressed by the speaker: "*John*, catch the ball!" The exclamation is interjection of strong feeling into a statement. "*Yea*, he caught the ball!" The absolute is a nominative related in thought to the sentence but not grammatically related to any word, usually in English formed by a noun and a participle: "*John* having arrived, we left for the game." The appositive is a nominative placed immediately after another nominative to explain the first word without the use of a verb; apposition is set off by commas: "Our shortstop, *John*, will play today." The appositional word "John" renames the noun "shortstop."

Possessive Case

The *possessive case* (or, "genitive") shows ownership or possession. This case is simple to spot because the inflection is common to all nouns, the letter "s" with an apostrophe in some form, or just the apostrophe, according to English conventions of forming possessives. Here are examples: *John's*, one *student's*, three *students'*, *conscience'* sake, *Jesus'*. The other signal of possessive case is a noun as the object of the preposition "of": "the music *of Hayden*." English also has *possessive pronouns* that show possession: "this is *my* book."

Objective Case

The *objective case* (sometimes called "accusative") is that word inflection that is used to indicate grammatical functions such as: direct object, object complement, cognate object, object of a preposition, indirect object, adverbial nouns (time, distance, measure, weight, value), the objective subject of the infinitive, the object of a participle, and apposition. The direct object is object of the verb: "John hit the *ball*." The object complement is a second direct object that fills out the meaning of the first: "The coach selected John *shortstop*." The cognate object is a direct object that has common lexical roots as the verb: "Johns sleeps a restful *sleep* before any game." The object of a preposition is an objective noun in a prepositional phrase: "John hit the ball *into the stands*." The indirect object indirectly receives the action or the benefit of the action of the verb: "He hit *John* the ball." The indirect object also can be indicated by the object of the prepositions "to" or "for": "He hit the ball *to John*." (Indirect object also is called *dative case*.) The adverbial noun is used without a preposition to express time, distance, etc.: "John ran three *miles*." The objective subject of the infinitive gives a noun to which the verbal action of the infinitive can be associated: "We wanted *John to play short-stop*." The object of a participle is the noun that is object of the participle in a verbal clause: "Throwing the *ball*, John made the last out." The appositive is an objective immediately after another objective to explain the first word without use of a verb; apposition is set off by commas: "We like our shortstop, *John*."

Table 4: English Case and Inflection—Examples

	Pronoun Example		Noun Example	
Case	Singular	Plural	Singular	Plural
Nominative	he	they	student	students
Possessive	his	their, theirs	student's	students'
Objective	him	them	student	students

By these inflectional changes, words indicate their function in a sentence. But, you may ask, you used the proper noun "John" in most of your illustrations, and that word did not change its spelling to indicate those cases. Right you are. The problem with English is that many nouns are not inflected for various cases. Inflection can be seen better in a pronoun in English. Compare a masculine pronoun's inflection with that of a noun in the table. So, while nouns *can* be inflected, remember that some words show little or no inflection for each case function. Now we turn to verb inflection.

Verb Inflection

Verbs are inflected to show five grammatical elements: (1) tense, (2) voice, (3) mood, (4) person, and (5) number. These elements are overviewed briefly.

Tense

Tense in English is the time of action indicated by the verb. English, therefore, has three basic tenses: past, present, and future. Each tense can be made perfect, yielding a total of six tenses. Tense can be used in certain situations other than the name of the tense indicates. Auxiliary verbs are used to create the future and perfect tenses. The verb "to be" can be used as an auxiliary verb with the present participle to indicate progressive action for transitive verbs: "John *is hitting* the ball," or, in the past, "John *was hitting* the ball." A *verb phrase* is a verb with its helping verbs.

Table 5: The Six English Tenses

	Tenses		
Basic	Past	Present	Future
Perfect	Past Perfect	Present Perfect	Future Perfect

Present tense indicates action that takes place in present time, or action that occurs repeatedly: "John *hits* the ball." This action occurs in present time. "John *hits* the ball every day." This action occurs repeatedly. Present tense, however, also can be used for future time: "The bus *leaves* for the game in five minutes!" The present tense can be used to refer to the past, called the "historical present," used for dramatic impact: "In the last game, John *catches* the last out and *saves* the season." In terms of verbals, the present tense infinitive is formed by "to" and the present tense of the verb (*to hit*). The present participle is formed by adding the ending "-ing" to the present tense (*hitting*).

Past tense denotes action in past time: "John *caught* the last out to end the game." The tense is formed by adding a suffix to the present tense form or by a change in spelling. Verbs can be classified by the manner of their formation of the past tense as regular or irregular. A *regular verb* does not change its basic spelling to make the past tense, but simply adds the endings "-d," "-ed," and "-t" or does not change at all (*hear, heard*; *work, worked*; *deal, dealt*; *hit, hit*). An *irregular verb* changes its spelling to make the past tense (*begin, began*; *go, went*). In terms of verbals, the past participle is formed by the past tense of regular verbs; irregular verbs show various formations. The past participle becomes part of the formation of perfect tenses.

Future tense indicates action that is anticipated in the future. This tense is formed using the auxiliary verb, "will" ("shall" for first person in formal writing), and the present tense form: "John *will play* in the game tomorrow."

Perfect tense emphasizes the completed nature of the verbal action. The time frame of the completed action distinguishes the basic tense modified. The *present perfect* expresses action completed at some specific point in the past. The tense is formed using the auxiliary verb "has" or "have" and the past participle: "John *has played* many games." For verbals, the perfect infinitive is formed by "to" plus the auxiliary "have" and the past participle: "John wanted *to have played* twenty games by the time of the playoffs." The perfect participle is formed by the auxiliary "having" and the past participle: "*Having played* twenty games, John was in the playoffs."

The *past perfect* expresses action completed before a specific time in the past. The tense is formed using the past tense auxiliary verb "had" and the past participle: "John *had played* twenty games by the time of playoffs last year."

Future perfect indicates action that will be completed before a certain time in the future. The tense is formed using two auxiliary verbs, the future auxiliary "will" and the perfect auxiliary "have," with the past participle: "John *will have played* twenty games by the playoffs next week." We can summarize these tense formation patterns in a table.

Table 6: Tense Formation Patterns (Indicative Mood)

Tense	Formation—Active Voice	Formation—Passive Voice
Past: regular	suffixes: *-d*, *-ed*, *-t*, or pres. ten.	*was, were* + past part.
irregular	various forms, spelling changes	*was, were* + past part.
perfect	*had* + past participle	*had been* + past part.
participle	past participle	
Present	present tense	*am, are, is* + past part.
perfect	*has, have* + past participle	*have, has been* + pp
infinitive	*to* + present tense	*to be* + past part.
participle	present tense + *-ing*	*being* + past part.
Future	*will (shall)* + present tense	*shall, will be* + past p.
perfect	*will (shall) have* + past part.	*will, shall have been* + p

Formation patterns reveal that knowledge of three key components can generate any English verb form: (1) present tense, (2) past tense, and (3) past participle. These three keys are called the *principal parts* of a verb: present tense in first person singular, past tense in first person singular, and the past participle. So, the principal parts of the regular verb "love" are *love, loved, loved*. The principal parts of the irregular verb "go" are *go, went, gone*.

Voice

Voice is the relationship of the verb's action to the verb's subject. *Active voice* is the verb's subject *performing* the verb's action: "John *hit* the ball." The subject, "John" performs the action of hitting the ball. *Passive voice* is the verb's subject *receiving* the verb's action: "John *was hit* by the ball." Passive voice requires an auxiliary verb (a form of "to be") plus a past participle: "John *was hit* by the ball." (The active voice form would have been: "The ball *hit* John.")

Mood

Mood represents the manner of a verb's action. English has three: indicative, imperative, and subjunctive. The *indicative mood* either makes a statement or asks a question: "John

Table 6: English Moods

Mood	Application
Indicative	statement, question
Imperative	command, request
Subjunctive	doubt, wish, contrary to fact condition

is our shortstop"; or "*Is* John our shortstop?" The *imperative mood* issues a command or request: "*Catch* the ball!" or "Please *give* me the ball." The *subjunctive mood* expresses doubt, wish, or contrary to fact condition: "John *might play* tomorrow"; or "I wish John *would play* tomorrow"; or "If I were a shortstop, I *would play* tomorrow." The present tense has all three moods and verb forms, past tense only indicative and subjunctive, and future only indicative.

Person and Number

A verb shows inflection for the subject's person and number. Notice forms of "to be." First singular is "I *am*," but first plural is "we *are*"; third

Table 7: Verb Form Distribution

Form	Tense					
	Pre	PreP	Past	PstP	Fut	FutP
Indicative	●	●	●	●	●	●
Subjunctive	●	●	●	●		
Imperative	●					
Infinitive	●	●				
Participle	●	●	●	●		

singular is "he *is*." All of these forms are the same tense, but have different inflections for person and number. Verbs agree with their subjects in person and number. Thus, "I *is*" is the wrong person, while "I *are*" is the wrong number. An unspecified subject assumes the appropriate personal pronoun agreeing with the verb's person and number.

Conjugation is listing a given verb's forms through all its tenses, voices, moods, persons, and numbers. A *synopsis* is an abbreviated conjugation of a given verb through its tenses, voices, and moods in just one person and number.

Table 8: Present and Present Perfect Conjugation

Form	Person	Present		Present Perfect	
		Act.	Passive	Active	Passive
Indicative	I	go	am gone	have gone	have been gone
	you	go	are gone	have gone	have been gone
	he, etc.	goes	is gone	has gone	has been gone
	we	go	are gone	have gone	have been gone
	you	go	are gone	have gone	have been gone
	they	go	are gone	have gone	have been gone
Subjunctive	I	go	be gone	(If) have gone	(If) have been gone
	you	go	be gone	(If) have gone	(If) have been gone
	he, etc.	go	be gone	(If) have gone	(If) have been gone
	we	go	be gone	(If) have gone	(If) have been gone
	you	go	be gone	(If) have gone	(If) have been gone
	they	go	be gone	(If) have gone	(If) have been gone
Imperative	(you)	go	be gone	--------	--------
Infinitive	--------	to go	to be gone	to have gone	to have been gone
Participle	--------	going	being gone	having gone	having been gone

Table 9: Past and Past Perfect Conjugation

Form	Person	Past		Past Perfect	
		Active	Passive	Active	Passive
Indicative	I	went	was gone	had gone	had been gone
	you	went	were gone	had gone	had been gone
	he, etc.	went	was gone	had gone	had been gone
	we	went	were gone	had gone	had been gone
	you	went	were gone	had gone	had been gone
	they	went	were gone	had gone	had been gone
Subjunctive	(If) I	went	were gone	had gone	had been gone
	(If) you	went	were gone	had gone	had been gone
	(If) he, etc.	went	were gone	had gone	had been gone
	(If) we	went	were gone	had gone	had been gone
	(If) you	went	were gone	had gone	had been gone
	(If) they	went	were gone	had gone	had been gone
Imperative	--------	--------	--------	--------	--------
Infinitive	--------	--------	--------	--------	--------
Participle	--------	gone	--------	gone	--------

Table 10: Future and Future Perfect Conjugation

| Form | Pers. | Future | | Future Perfect | |
		Active	Passive	Active	Passive
Indic.	I	shall go	shall be gone	shall have gone	shall have been gone
	you	will go	will be gone	will have gone	will have been gone
	he, etc.	will go	will be gone	will have gone	will have been gone
	we	shall go	shall be gone	shall have gone	shall have been gone
	you	will go	will be gone	will have gone	will have been gone
	they	will go	will be gone	will have gone	will have been gone
Subj.	--------	--------	--------	--------	--------
Imper.	--------	--------	--------	--------	--------
Infin.	--------	--------	--------	--------	--------
Part.	--------	--------	--------	--------	--------

Order

Besides inflection, the other method of indicating grammatical relationships in English is word order. *Order* is the ordered placement of parts of speech in a sentence to generate meaning. For languages that are not highly inflected, such as English, *word order is crucial* for indicating word relationships. Notice this principle with English nouns, which are not inflected as much as in other languages. "John hit the ball!" is very different in meaning than "The ball hit John!" Notice that nothing changed in these two sentences besides word order. On the other hand, whenever an English word *is* inflected (e.g., pronouns), word order is not so crucial to meaning. Thus, "I hit him!" and "Him, I hit!" have the same meaning, even though the word order is different; this result is because the third personal pronoun's *inflection* for the *objective* case indicates the grammatical function of *direct object*, not the position after the verb. Thus, we need to know about English word order principles as much as inflection of words.

We already have met some word order observations. An appositive is a direct modifier located *after* the substantive: "Our shortstop, *John*, will play today." Adjectives are placed immediately *before* the noun they modify: "John is a *good* shortstop." To put the adjective after the noun modified just "sounds wrong": "John is a shortstop *good*." What? you would ask. The adjective is out of conventional order, so the sentence "sounds funny" and its meaning is obscured.

Further, most language conventions go beyond individual words! What are some other grammatical units besides individual words that bring ordered meaning to sentences? One would be groups of words taken together for their meaning. These groups of words would include phrases and clauses, the basic difference based on whether the verb does or does not have a subject.

Word Units

Phrases

Sentences have two basic word units: phrases and clauses. Traditionally in English grammar, a *phrase* is a group of grammatically related words that *may* have a verb but is *without* a subject. Two basic types of phrases are prepositions and verbals, with their modifiers, which create prepositional phrases (*outside the park*) and verbal phrases (*to hit a home run*). Phrases

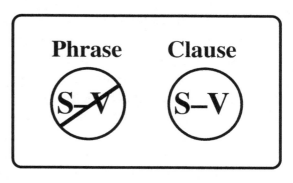

function as three parts of speech: noun, adjective, and adverb. A *noun phrase* is a unit of words used in the role of a noun: "*Outside the park* was his only goal as he stepped up to the plate." Here, the noun phrase functions as subject. One could use a verbal phrase for the same noun function: "*To hit a home run* was his only goal as he stepped up to the plate." An *adjective phrase* is a unit of words used in the role of an adjective: "The ball hit a window *outside the park*." An *adverb phrase* uses a unit of words in the role of an adverb: "The ball John hit *outside the park* broke a window."

Clauses

A *clause* is a group of grammatically related words with a subject and a predicate. The two basic forms of clauses are independent and dependent. An *independent clause* is a subject-predicate unit that makes sense by itself. The independent clause, then, by definition is the most basic sentence: "John hit the ball." The subject is "John." The predicate is "hit the ball." The clause makes a meaningful statement by itself.

A *dependent clause* is a subject-predicate unit that does not make sense by itself: "because John hit the ball." This clause depends upon another verb to modify in order to make sense; for example: "The coach cheered *because John hit the ball*." Now, the clause makes sense by giving an explanation for why the coach cheered. Thus, the clause "because John hit the ball" is a *dependent* clause—the clause depends upon modifying the verb "cheered" for its significance. How are dependent clauses used? Parallel to the use of phrases, dependent clauses are used as nouns, adjectives, and adverbs.

The *noun clause* is a subject-predicate unit that functions as subject, object (of prepositions and verbals), predicate noun, or in apposition to subject, object, or predicate noun. For example, "*That John hit the ball* was the coach's desire."

The subject-predicate unit "That John hit the ball" functions as subject of the verb "was."

An *adjective clause* is a subject-predicate unit that takes on the role of an adjective. The adjective clause is introduced by a relative pronoun, conjunctive adverb, or subordinate conjunction. For example, "John was the player *who hit the home run*." Or again, "The ball *that John hit out of the park* won the game."

An *adverb clause* is a subject-predicate unit that takes the role of an adverb. The adverb clause is introduced by a conjunctive adverb or a subordinate conjunction: "John celebrated his home run *until the next season rolled around*." Or, with the subordinate conjunction, the sentence above illustrates: "The coach cheered *because John hit the ball*."

We can summarize the discussion of words, phrases, and clauses with an illustration on various incarnations of an adverbial expression whose meaning is the same but whose form is different. The adverbial idea *joyfully* can be expressed with one word: *joyfully*, with an adverb phrase: *with joy*, or with an adverb clause: *because they had joy*.

Sentence Classification

The words "compound" and "complex" traditionally have been used to classify sentences by their clause structure. A *simple sentence* is an independent clause with no dependent clause. A *compound sentence* is two or more independent clauses used as a single sentence connected by words or punctuation: "John hit the ball, and Mary scored the run." A *complex sentence* is one independent clause with at least one dependent clause: "The coach cheered because John hit the ball." The *compound-complex sentence* is a compound sentence of two independent clauses with one of the independent clauses having at least one dependent clause: "John hit the fast ball that the relief pitcher threw, and his home run won the game." The independent clauses are "John hit the fast ball" and "his home run won the game." The dependent clause is "that the relief pitcher threw."

Sentence Structure

The most basic sentence structures in English involve the ordering of the subject and the predicate within the independent clause in the normal pattern of subject (S) first, verb (V) second. When this basic pattern is expanded with verb complements in the predicate (direct object, object complement, predicate nominative, predicate adjective), then the basic ordering of English sentence structure is in place. These patterns become the building blocks of all other sentences. Modifiers maintain close proximity to the words, phrases, or clauses they modify, but do not change the basic sentence structural order.

Before launching into these patterns, a good reminder is that not all English structures explicitly express the subject or predicate. *Ellipsis* is leaving out words that are understood in the context. The subject may not be expressed, as in the structure of English commands: "Go!" leaves off the subject. ("*You* go!") The predicate may not be expressed, as in the structure of answers to questions: "Who hit the home run? John." Some answers leave *both* subject and predicate understood: "What did Jane give you? A glove." With these observations in hand, then, what are the basic English ordering patterns for sentences?

Intransitive Patterns

English has two main sentence patterns: one for intransitive verbs, and one for transitive. The intransitive verb pattern is subdivided into two forms based upon the nature of the intransitive verb. The first is the basic intransitive verb (V_i):

> ### Basic Intransitive
> ## $S-V_i$

An example would be: "John runs." Here "John" = S and "runs" = V_i. Observe that the order is subject first, then verb.

The second pattern is the copulative intransitive (V_c), which requires a complement (C) to complete its meaning. The copulative intransitive pattern is:

> ### Copulative Intransitive
> ## $S-V_c-C$

The complement would be either a predicate nominative (C_N), a noun that renames the subject, or a predicate adjective (C_A), an adjective that modifies, describes, or points out the subject. For example: "John is shortstop." Here "John" = S, "is" = V_c, and "shortstop" = C_N. Another example is: "John is good." Here "John" = S, "is" = V_c, and "good" = C_A. Observe in both examples that the order is subject first, then verb, then complement.

Transitive Patterns

The other main English sentence pattern is for transitive verbs (V_t). The transitive verb by nature requires a complement in the predicate (direct object, O or O_1, object compliment, O_2). The normal word order for an English object is subject, verb, object. Thus:

$$\boxed{\begin{array}{c} \text{Basic Transitive} \\ \text{S--V}_t\text{--O} \end{array}}$$

An example would be: "John hits the ball." Here "John" = S, "hits" = V_t, and "ball" = O. This basic transitive pattern is what generates two different meanings out of the same words: "John hit the ball" or "The ball hit John." By word position related to the verb, one can determine what is subject and what is object.

Other transitive sentences are variations on this basic pattern. One common variation is the transitive verb with indirect object (O_i):

$$\boxed{\begin{array}{c} \text{Indirect Object} \\ \text{S--V}_t\text{--O}_i\text{--O} \end{array}}$$

"O_i" is the indirect object, and "O" is the direct object. The normal indirect object position is *between* the verb and the direct object: "He hit *John* the ball." Eliminate the direct object here ("the ball"), and the indirect object "John" becomes direct object by position (no noun follows to function as direct object): "He hit *John*." However, if the indirect object is a prepositional phrase using "to" or "for," then its position is *after* the direct object: "He hit the ball *to John*." This indirect object position after the verb is an example of different word order conventions depending on whether the unit is an individual word or a phrase.

Another transitive pattern (S--V_t--O) is the transitive verb with an object complement (O_2), a second object that fills out the meaning of the direct object. The object complement immediately follows the direct object:

$$\boxed{\begin{array}{c} \text{Object Complement} \\ \text{S--V}_t\text{--O}_1\text{--O}_2 \end{array}}$$

Here, "O_1" is the direct object of the verb, and "O_2" is the object complement. An example would be: "Coach nicknamed John 'Shorty.'" In this example, "John" is the direct object (O_1), and "Shorty" is the object complement (O_2).

Variations

The *passive voice* typically is just a conversion of the basic transitive pattern into an intransitive pattern. The transitive pattern is modified three ways: (1) the active voice verb is made passive voice, (2) the direct object is made subject, (3) the subject is made object of the preposition "by" and positioned after the verb. Take, for example, the transitive, active voice sentence: "John hit the ball." First, the active voice verb, "hit," is made passive voice, "was hit." Second, the direct object, "ball," is made the subject, "The ball was hit." Note that, now, the verb is intransitive. Third, the subject, "John" is made object of the preposition "by" and placed after the verb, "The ball was hit by John." Thus, the passive voice is just a tortuous inversion of the basic transitive pattern into intransitive ($S–V_t–O \rightarrow S–V_i$). Some verbs, however, retain their transitive force even after this transformation.

Other types of sentences simply vary normal word order or drop an element. *Questions* invert the normal subject, verb order by placing the verb first. The opening verb of a question is one of the auxiliaries "do," "does," or "did," or the helping verbs "has" or "have": "*Do* you understand English?"; "*Have* you studied your lesson?" For stress, even the auxiliary and the subject can be dropped: "Understand?" *Commands* use imperative mood and drop the subject, whether intransitive or transitive verbs. The intransitive command "Run!" implies a second person subject: "*You* run!" A transitive verb command would be: "Study the lesson!" *Poetry* is a complex feature of any language, but one obvious element is the scrambling of normal word order patterns: "Love I gave, yet hope I lost." Here, the transitive pattern subject, verb, object has been scrambled into object, subject, verb. This unexpected turn on word order helps creates a "poetic feel."

Diagramming Sentence Structure

Diagramming represents word relationships visually. Notice that diagramming is built on English word order. The subject is first, the verb second, and the direct object third. The line that holds these slots is called the *base line*. Various strokes through or on the base line indicate word function.

Intransitive Patterns

A vertical line through the base line separates subject and verb, here intransitive:

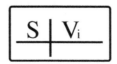

A back-slanted line not through the base line separates a copulative verb from its complement:

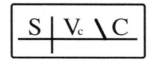

Transitive Patterns

A vertical line not through the base line separates transitive verb and object:

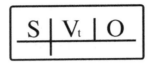

A back-slanted line not through the base line separates direct object and object complement:

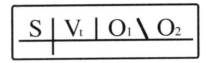

A subordinated line extending off a slanted line under the verb is used for the indirect object:

Other Grammatical Functions

Other diagramming variations do not change the basic structure of sentences above. These deal with primary and secondary modifiers (adjectives and adverbs; prepositions and conjunctions). *Compound subjects* and *compound verbs* simply split the base line:

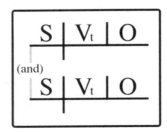

Compound sentences join two base lines at the subject end:

Attributive adjectives, *modifying adverbs*, and *prepositional phrases* are handled like an indirect object, but under the particular word, phrase, or clause modified:

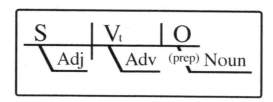

Modifying clauses also are handled similarly to the indirect object as well, only their slanted line holds the subordinate conjunction and their horizontal line creates a subordinate base line for their own subject and predicate units:

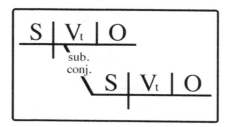

Substantival clauses take the slot of their sentence function (subject, direct object, etc.), but are placed on a standard to give them their own base line for their own subject and predicate units. A subordinate conjunction is placed on the standard:

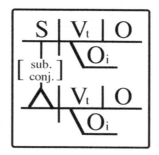

Discourse, both direct and indirect, functions as direct object. The quotation is a substantival clause. The clause is placed on a standard in the direct object slot:

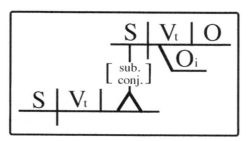

Relative pronouns open clauses, so require their own base line. They are joined by a dotted line back to their antecedent. Their diagramming might be confusing because the direct object or object complement relative pronoun *still occurs first in its clause, even though the object of a verb*. For example: "He nominated the candidate *whom you knew*." The relative pronoun clause, "*whom* you knew," modifies "candidate" in the main clause. "Whom" is in the objective case as a direct object in its own clause ("You knew *whom*."); however, though direct object, notice that "whom" occurs *first* in its own clause in the example sentence ("*whom* you knew"). A diagram represents *function*, so the correct slot for a relative pronoun acting as *direct object* in its own clause is *after* the verb:

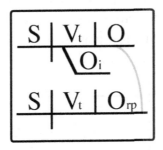

Absolute constructions are independent, so are set out in brackets by themselves:

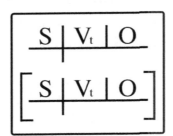

Appositive constructions are independent, but explain further the word to which they are in apposition, so are given their own base line with an equals mark to the element explained. Thus, "Our shortstop, *John*, plays well" would diagram with the appositional element of "John" equal to "shortstop," the subject:

$$\text{App} = \text{S} \mid \text{V}_t \mid \text{O}$$

Verbals combine elements of nouns, verbs, adjectives and adverbs. Their diagramming mixes these grammatical features. The *infinitive*, substantival or adverbial, always has a standard with double vertical lines through the base line separating the infinitive verbal and the objective subject, which is placed in brackets (not a true grammatical subject). A substantival infinitive is placed on a normal upright standard; the adverbial infinitive is placed on an inverted standard underneath the grammatical element modified:

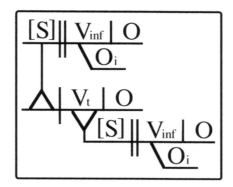

Participles require a standard only if part of a phrase or clause; otherwise they just take the diagramming slot appropriate to their grammatical function. Thus, a simple adjective participle would go on a line underneath the noun modified. So, "the *shining* star" would put "shining" as an adjective on a line underneath "star." When the participle is a phrase that includes its own grammatical elements, the substantive associated in a subject relationship with the participle is placed in brackets (not a true grammatical subject):

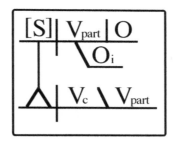

Conclusion

Whenever your head is spinning trying to analyze a sentence, repeat this mantra: "English is as simple as 1–2–3." The 1–2–3 is subject, verb, object, in that order. That's the whole ball of yarn, no matter how intricately your weave the tapestry. All sentences can be reduced down to 1–2–3. All else is embroidered lace to enhance the artistry. Take a breath, back away a moment, and then relook at the words in front of you. First find the 1–2–3. Circle the subject, underline the verb, double-underline the object. The rest modifies.

Diagramming is so useful in studying English because diagramming focuses on this fundamental core of the sentence: 1–2–3. You have a linear line. The subject is first; the verb is second; the direct object is third. Even entire strings of words can be compacted down to fill each of the 1–2–3 slots. That whole string of words over there? Just your subject, that's all. Just your direct object, that's all. "He said that he was going to study his Greek grammar." What about that string of words: "that he was going to study his Greek grammar"? Just the 3 of 1–2–3.

Further, when analyzing both phrases and clauses, almost every one of them boils down to either a noun, an adjective, or an adverb role in the sentence. The noun role typically would fill slot 1 or slot 3 on the linear line. The adjective or adverb roles would modify 1–2–3, so would diagram under the linear line in the appropriate slot. Again, compounds of any kind simply split the baseline or join two baselines together.

So, remember: "English is as simple as 1–2–3." Done. Let yourself believe that you *can* conquer English grammar. By doing so, you are miles ahead of the pack in conquering Greek grammar. Knowing God's Word more deeply is worth the work. You will be repaid a hundredfold, and your ministry enriched in ways beyond knowing.

ANSWER KEY
(Exercises and Helps)
Stevens Greek Workbook

Lesson 1: Writing and Pronouncing Greek

1. αι, οι, ει
   αυ, ου, ευ
   υι, ηυ, ᾳ
   ωυ, ῃ
   ῳ
2. ε, ο, αι and οι
3. η, ω, diphthongs
4. ᾰ, ῐ, ῠ
5. ng, nk, nx, nc
6. uncial, majuscule
7. minuscule
8. Scripto continua
9. uncial, minuscule
10. Line 1: rough with acute, rough, smooth, diaeresis with acute, circumflex, acute, circumflex
    Line 2: rough with grave, circumflex with smooth, colon, acute, comma, acute, smooth, acute, circumflex, smooth, circumflex
    Line 3: rough, circumflex, question mark, grave, rough, acute, acute, acute, smooth, acute, question mark
11. crasis, coronis
12. elision, rough breathing
13. A. capital letter
    B. *hoti* recitative
14. the formalized writing style of the Hellenistic period
15. the common, or koine, spoken Greek of the Hellenistic period
16. Non-literary
17. Adolf Deissmann
18. 1900s
19. lexicons
20. Εἰ ἀπεθάνετε σὺν Χριστῷ ἀπὸ
    τῶν στοιχείων
    τοῦ κόσμου, τί ὡς ζῶντες ἐν
    κόσμῳ
    δογματίζεσθε, Μὴ ἅψῃ μηδὲ
    γεύσῃ
    μηδὲ θίγῃς, ἅ ἐστιν πάντα εἰς
    φθορὰν
    τῇ ἀποχρήσει, κατὰ τὰ
    ἐντάλματα καὶ
    διδασκαλίας τῶν ἀνθρώπων;
    ἅτινά ἐστιν
    λόγον μὲν ἔχοντα σοφίας ἐν
    ἐθελοθρησκίᾳ
    καὶ ταπεινοφροσύνῃ [καὶ]
    ἀφειδίᾳ σώματος,
    οὐκ ἐν τιμῇ τινι πρὸς
    πλησμονὴν τῆς σαρκός.
21. 2.13 kai hymas nekrous ontas [en] tois paraptōmasin kai tēi akrobystiai tēs sarkos hymōn, synezōopoiēsen hymas syn autōi charisamenos hēmin panta ta paraptōmata 2.14 exaleipsas to kath' hēmōn cheirographon tois dogmasin ho ēn
22. buyer = βαιερ; pouting = παυτιγγ; cave = χειφ; fool = φουλ; tweed = τυιδ

Bonus:
ἐνέγκαι = enenkai
Ἰακώβ = Yakōb

Lesson 2: Consonants, Syllables, and Accents

1. λ, μ, ν, ρ
2. ἑωράκαμεν τοῖς ὀφθαλμοῖς ἡμῖν
3. π, β, φ
4. ἡμεῖς οὖν ὀφείλομεν ὑπολαμβάνειν
5. κ, γ, χ
6. χρῖσμα ἔχετε ἀπὸ τοῦ ἁγίου καὶ
7. τ, δ, θ
8. τῷ σκότει περιπατῶμεν, ψευδόμεθὰ
9. σ, ψ, ξ, ζ
10. ποιήσεις προπέμψας ἀξίως τοῦ
11. •τεσ-σα-ρες: 2 consonants, single vowel, last consonant
    •θνη-σκω: consonant unit, first and internal
    •βλε-πω: consonant unit, first
    •εἰ-μι: simple, diphthong
    •στι-γμα: consonant unit, first and nasal -μ unit, internal
    •ἀ-κου-ω: double vowel
    •δι-υ-λι-ζω: double vowel
    •γνω-σις: nasal -ν unit, first
    •λυ-στρα: consonant unit, internal
    •ορ-θρι-ος: three consonants or consonant unit, internal
    •ἐκ-λυ-ω: compound
    •ἐχ-θρος: three consonants or consonant unit, internal
12. antepenult, penult, ultima
13. vowel, diphthong
14. long, antepenult
15. last, long
16. long
17. circumflex
18. acute
19. persistent, the accent tends to stay in the syllable of the lexical form
20. recessive, the accent tends to recede back from the ultima as far as possible
21. 1. ἀκούωσιν, ἀκούετε, ἀκουέτω
    2. βλέπομεν, βλέπει, βλεπομένη
    3. λέγωμεν, λεγόμενοι, λεγομένοις
22. 1. ἄνθρωποι, ἀνθρώπου, ἄνθρωπον
    2. λόγοι, λόγοις, λόγῳ
    3. κύριοι, κυρίου, κύριον
23. 1. γραφόμεν = verb accent is recessive; ultima is short; nothing prevents acute receding to the antepenult (γράφομεν)
    2. βλῆπουσιν = verb accent is recessive; ultima is short, but only acute allowed on antepenult (βλέπουσιν); circumflex can stand over long syllables only
    3. λὲγει = verb accent is recessive; however, grave accent may stand over ultima only; ultima is long, so penult must be accented as acute (λέγει)
    4. ἄκουσει = verb accent is recessive; ultima is long; antepenult cannot be accented; penult is acute (ἀκούσει)
    5. λὲγεις = verb accent is recessive; but ultima is long, so penult must be acute (λέγεις); also, circumflex can stand over long syllables only
    6. ἀνθρῶπου = noun accent is persistent; lexical form is accented in the antepenult;

however, with long ultima, accent is drawn back to the penult and also must be acute

7. ἀνθρῶπον = noun accent is persistent; lexical form is accented on antepenult; ultima is short, so the antepenult may retain accent (ἄνθρωπον)

8. κυριοῖς = noun accent is persistent; lexial form is accented on the antepenult; however, ultima is long (the οι is not final)—so antepenult cannot retain accent and moves to penult; penult could be long or short, but long ultima requires accented penult to be acute (κυρίοις)

9. κύριου = noun accent is persistent; lexical form is accented on the antepenult; however, ultima is long—so antepenult cannot retain accent and acute moves to penult; penult could be long or short, but long ultima requires accented penult to be acute (κυρίου)

10. λογοῦς = noun accent is persistent; lexical accented on penult, so persists in penult position, but with long ultima, penult must be acute (λόγους); also, the short penult could not take a circumflex anyway

Lesson 3: Present Active Indicative
Assignment 1
1. six, stems
2. present, imperfect
3. thematic vowel
4. aspect (kind)
5. durative
6. perfect
7. Voice
8. middle
9. εἰμί
10. passive
11. reality, time
12. indicative, οὐ
13. present, future
14. primary, secondary
15. a system of word endings to indicate word relationships
16. pronominal suffixes
17. thematic vowel
18. movable nu, vowel
19. Tense
20. ο, ε, ε; ο, ε, ο
21. pronominal suffix
22. -ω = "I"
    -εις = "you" (sg.)
    -ει = "he," "she," "it"
    -ομεν = "we"
    -ετε = "you" (pl.)
    -ουσι(ν) = "they"
23. ἀκούω, *I am hearing*
    ἀκούεις, *you are hearing*
    ἀκούει, *he is hearing* (etc.)
    ἀκούομεν, *we are hearing*
    ἀκούετε, *you are hearing*
    ἀκούουσι(ν), *they are hearing*

    λέγω, *I am saying*
    λέγεις, *you are saying*
    λέγει, *he is saying* (etc.)
    λέγομεν, *we are saying*
    λέγετε, *you are saying*
    λέγουσι(ν), *they are saying*

    βλέπω, *I am seeing*
    βλέπεις, *you are seeing*
    βλέπει, *he is seeing* (etc.)
    βλέπομεν, *we are seeing*
    βλέπετε, *you are seeing*
    βλέπουσι(ν), *they are seeing*

ἔχω, *I am having*
ἔχεις, *you are having*
ἔχει, *he is having* (etc.)
ἔχομεν, *we are having*
ἔχετε, *you are having*
ἔχουσι(ν), *they are having*

24. to provide the inflection pattern of a verb in a given tense, voice, and mood

25. you specify a particular verb's six component parts

26. ἔχουσιν: present, active, indicative, 3rd, plural, ἔχω
λαμβάνεις: present, active, indicative, 2nd, singular, λαμβάνω

Assignment 2

27. 1. *they are hearing*
2. *he (she, it) is seeing*
3. *you (pl.) are writing*
4. *you (sg.) are saying*
5. *we are loosing*
6. *I am knowing*
7. *he (she, it) is teaching*
8. *they are having*
9. *you (sg.) are receiving*
10. *you (pl.) are hearing*
11. *I am seeing*
12. *we are writing*

28. 1. *God is seeing*
2. *a brother and an apostle are teaching*
3. *you (pl.) are receiving and are teaching*
4. *three houses and two angels*
5. *you (sg.) are sending and we are knowing*
6. *they are hearing the word* [Mark 4:20]
7. *You know our brother Timothy* [Heb. 13:23]
8. *he has the Father and the Son* [2 John 1:9]

9. *You are speaking and teaching correctly and you do not show partiality* [Luke 20:21]

29. Diagram

1.
ὁ θεός | πέμπει

2.
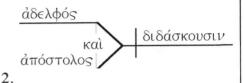

3.
λαμβάνετε
(you)
καὶ
διδάσκετε

Lesson 4: Second Declension

Assignment 1

1. word order, prepositions, inflection

3. *Nominative* = designation, naming = subj.
Genitive = description, possession = of
= separation, origin, source = of, from, by
Dative = personal interest = ind. obj., to, for
= location = in, at, on, by, among
= means, agency = by, with
Accusative = extension = direct object
Vocative = direct address = not connected

5. 1. True, 2. False, 3. False, 4. True, 5. False, 6. True

7. τέκνον   τέκνα
τέκνου   τέκνων
τέκνῳ   τέκνοις
τέκνον   τέκνα
τέκνον   τέκνα

ἱερόν   ἱερά
ἱεροῦ   ἱερῶν
ἱερῷ   ἱεροῖς
ἱερόν   ἱερά
ἱερόν   ἱερά

9. ultima
11. point
13. 1. False, 2. False, 3. False, 4. False
15. τὸ   ἔργον   = *the work*
    τοῦ   ἔργου   = *of the work*, etc.
    τῷ   ἔργῳ   = *to the work*, etc.
    τὸ   ἔργον   = *the work*
       ἔργον   = *O Work!*
17. persistent
19. ἀγγέλοις: dative, masculine, plural, ἄγγελος, *angel*
    ἀποστόλων: genitive, masculine, plural, ἀπόστολος, *apostle*
    δῶρα: nom./acc., neuter, plural, δῶρον, *gift*

Assignment 2

20. 1. *we are preaching*
   3. *of a gospel*, etc.
   5. *you are finding*
   7. *of death*, etc.
   9. *Do you (sg.) believe?*
   11. *of heaven*, etc.
   13. *to temples*, etc.
   15. *they are finding*
   17. *you (sg.) are receiving*
   19. *you (pl.) are baptizing*
21. 1. *the four angels*
   3. *even as I am sending you*
   5. *and Jesus finds Philip and says to him*
   7. *the apostles of the Lord are teaching brothers the word in the house*
22. Diagram

| τὰ τέκνα | ἄκουει | τὸ εὐαγγέλιον |

1.

οἱ ἀπόστολοι | διδάσκουσιν | ἀδελφούς \ τὸν λόγον
2.   \ τοῦ κυρίου   \ τῷ οἴκῳ

Lesson 5: First Declension

1. ε, ι, ρ stems, nominatives in η, sibilants, all the same
3. -α   -η   -α   -αι
   -ας   -ης   -ης   -ων
   -ᾳ   -ῃ   -ῃ   -αις
   -αν   -ην   -αν   -ας
5. ε, ι, ρ stems, -ας, genitive, accusative, genitive singular
7. ὥρας: genitive (acc.), feminine, singular (pl.), ὥρα, *hour*
   ψυχάς: accusative, feminine, plural, ψυχή, *soul*
   ἡμέραν: accusative, feminine, singular, ἡμέρα, *day*
   θάλασσαι: nominative, feminine, plural, θάλασσα, *sea*
8. 1. *tongue* (sub.)

3. *to voices*, etc.
5. *of glory*, etc.
7. *of teaching*, etc.
9. *to peace*, etc.
11. *of an hour* or *hours* (dir. obj.)
13. *to souls*, etc.
15. *of life*, etc.
17. *kingdom* (sub.)
19. *church* (dir. obj.)
21. *to joy*, etc.
9. 1. *I am the bread of life*
   3. *the hour of glory is the hour of death*
   5. *first say, "Peace to this house!"*
   7. *in the days of the son of man*

9. *for the son of man is saving the souls of men from sin in their hearts, and they are writing the teachings of his commandment in a book*

10. Diagram

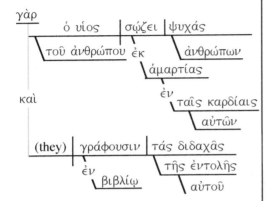

Lesson 6: Adjectives and Εἰμί

1. three, concord
3. attributive, substantive, predicative
5. 1. *the teaching is good*
   3. *the evil angels*
   5. *the children are righteous*
7. 1. ἀγαθός ἐστιν, #3: acute ultima does not revert to grave
   3. δίκαιοί εἰσιν, #1: acute antepenult adds an acute to the ultima
9. πιστούς: accusative, masculine, plural, πιστός, *faithful*
   ἰδίᾳ: dative, feminine, singular, ἴδιος, *one's own*
   μικρόν: nom./acc., mas./neu., sg., μικρός, *small, little*
11. 1. *my son was dead*
    3. *Jesus is the word*, predicate nominative, proper name precedence
    5. *the evil one comes* [Matt. 13:19]

7. *who is my beloved child and faithful in the Lord* [1 Cor. 4:17]

12. Diagram

Lesson 7: Contract Verbs and Conjunctions

2. 1. εὐλογεῖτε = ε + ε = *you (pl.) are blessing*
   3. ζητεῖ = ε + ει = *he (sg.) is seeking*
   5. ἀγαπῶμεν = α + ο = *we are loving*
   7. ποιεῖς = ε + ει = *you are doing*
   9. σταυρῶ = ο + ω = *I am crucifying*
   11. καλοῦμεν = ε + ο = *we are calling*
   13. λαλεῖ = ε + ει = *he is speaking*
   15. φιλοῦσιν = ε + ου = *they are loving*
   17. πληροῖς = ο + ει = *you (sg.) are fulfilling*
   19. τιμῶ = α + ω = *I am honoring*
3. 1. *he does not honor the Father* [John 5:23]
   3. *they are seeking my life* [Rom. 11:3]
   5. *David calls him Lord* [Matt. 22:45]
   7. *we are keeping his commandments* [1 John 3:22]
   9. *(it is) no longer I who lives, but Christ (who) lives in me* [Gal. 2:20]

11. *Therefore, brothers, we are asking and urging you in the Lord Jesus* [1 Thess. 4:1]

4. Diagram

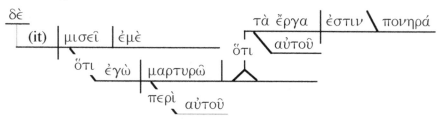

Lesson 8: Gender, Contraction, Adverbs, Comparisons

1. ης or ας

-ης	-αι	-ας	-αι
-ου	-ων	-ου	-ων
-η	-αις	-ᾳ	-αις
-ην	-ας	-αν	-ας

3. -ος

5. modifiers, substantives, clarifiers, verbal, place

7. ablative, accusative, παρά and ὑπέρ, ἤ

9. 1. *to the only wise God* [Rom. 16:27]

   3. *"Simon, son of John, do you love me?"* [John 21:16]

   5. *they put new wine into fresh wineskins* [Matt. 9:17]

   7. *for our salvation is nearer now than when we first believed* [John 21:16]

10. Diagram

1.

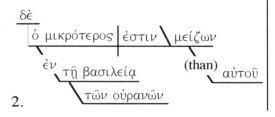
2.

Lesson 9: Prepositions and Compounds

1. adverbs

3. 1. ἀνά, *up, through, in, each one*

   3. ἀπό, *away from, from, by, because of*

   5. εἰς, *into, in, resulting in*

   7. ἐν, *in, to, with respect in, among*

   9. κατά, *down, by, against, as, according to*

   11. παρά, *beside, from, by, with*

   13. πρό, *before, from, above*

   15. σύν, *with*

   17. ὑπό, *under, by*

5. Directional prepositions

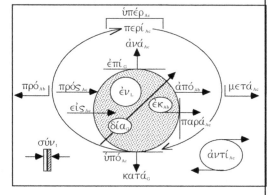

7. 1. ἀπό   7. ἐπί

   3. κατά   9. κατά

   5. παρά

9. 1. *after six days* [Matt. 17:1]

3. *we have fellowship with him* [1 John 1:6]

5. *evil for evil* [1 Thess. 5:15]

7. *you do not hear, because you are not from God* [John 8:47]

9. *the blind are seeing and the lame are walking about* [Matt. 11:15]

11. *we have peace with God through our Lord Jesus Christ* [Rom. 5:1]

13. *Paul, an apostle not from men nor through man but through Jesus Christ* [Gal. 1:1]

10. Diagram

(we) | ἔχομεν | εἰρήνην
πρός τὸν θεὸν
διὰ τοῦ κυρίου = Ἰησοῦ Χριστοῦ
ἡμῶν

Lesson 10: Present Middle/Passive Indicative

1. subject

3. self interest
-μαι, -μην, -μεθα, -νται, -ντο,
-σαι, -σθε, -σο, -ται, -το

5. συνάγομαι = *I am being gathered together*

συνάγῃ = *you are being gathered together*

συνάγεται = *he is being gathered together* (etc.)

συναγόμεθα = *we are being gathered together*

συνάγεσθε = *you are being gathered together*

συνάγονται = *they are being gathered together*

7. deponent
1. βούλεται = *he is wishing*
3. πορεύομαι = *I am going*
5. ἔρχῃ = *you (sg.) are going*

9. assume passive unless context dictates middle

11. divine passive

13. 1. *now the field is the world* [Matt. 13:38]
3. *it does not regard the wrong* (or *evil*, i.e., *wrong done*) [1 Cor. 13:5]
5. *but the hour comes, and now is* [John 4:23]
7. *they are entering into the kingdom of God* [Luke 18:24]
9. *And the apostles gather themselves together to Jesus* [John 4:23]

Lesson 11: Pronouns—A Summary

1. ἐγώ = *I*
ἐμοῦ = *of me*, etc.
ἐμοί = *to me*, etc.
ἐμέ = *me* (d.o.)

ἡμεῖς = *we*
ἡμῶν = *of us*, etc.
ἡμῖν = *to us*
ἡμᾶς = *us* (d.o.)

σύ = *you*
σοῦ = *of you*, etc.
σοί = *to you*
σέ = *you* (d.o.)

ὑμεῖς = *you*
ὑμῶν = *of you*, etc.
ὑμῖν = *to you*
ὑμᾶς = *you* (d.o.)

3. gender, number, case, grammatical function

5. preposition

7. anarthrous, nominative, emphatic

9. genitive
11. 1. *he receives me* [Matt. 18:15]
    3. *your Lord is coming* [Matt. 24:42]
    5. *and we proclaim good news to you* [Acts 13:32]
    7. *and I tell you that you are Peter* [Matt. 16:18]
    9. *And masters, you do the same to them* [Eph. 6:9]

Lesson 12: Imperfect Active Indicative

1. secondary, secondary, durative, present

-ω	-μαι	-ν	-μην
-εις	-σαι (η)	-ς	-σο (ου)
-ει	-ται	---(εν)	-το
-ομεν	-μεθα	-μεν	-μεθα
-ετε	-σθε	-τε	-θσε
-ουσι	-νται	-ν, -σαν	-ντο

3. Identify verbal components:

tense stem ↓   pronominal suffix ↓

ἔ-λυ-ο-ν

↑ augment   ↑ thematic vowel

5. ἤκουον = *I was hearing*
   ἤκουες = *you were hearing*
   ἤκουε(ν) = *he was hearing*, etc.
   ἠκούομεν = *we were hearing*
   ἠκούετε = *you were hearing*
   ἤκουον = *they were hearing*

7. τούτου, τούτων, letter τ, rough
   1. *this (man) is*
   3. *these words* (dir. obj.)
9. τοι- prefix
   1. *I hear such things*
11. function
12. 1. *she was dying* [Luke 8:42]
    3. *therefore, the crowd was testifying* [John 12:17]

5. *I am sending my messenger* [Mark 13:24]
7. *when he was in Galilee they were following him* [Mark 15:41]
9. *but the crowds were saying, "This one is the prophet"* [Matt. 21:11]
11. *the son of man has authority upon earth* [Luke 5:24]
13. *But in those days after that tribulation* [Mark 13:24]
15. *the one who does righteousness is righteous, just as that one is righteous* [1 John 3:7]

Lesson 13: Imperfect Middle and Conditional Sentences

1. ἐφοβούμην = *I was fearing*
   ἐφοβοῦ = *you were fearing*
   ἐφοβεῖτο = *he (etc.) was fearing*
   ἐφοβούμεθα = *we were fearing*
   ἐφοβεῖσθε = *you were fearing*
   ἐφοβοῦντο = *they were fearing*
3. personal pronoun is not inflected for gender as is the possessive pronoun
5. ἐμ-, σε-, same, ἐ, rough
   1. *from themselves (or 1ˢᵗ, 2ⁿᵈ person)*
7. Conditional sentence graphic

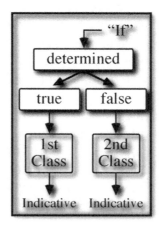

8. 1. *in your field* [Matt. 13:27]
  3. *my commandments* [John 14:15]
  5. *and he was following him along the road* [Mark 10:52]
  7. *his disciples are following him* [Mark 6:1]
  9. *but he was still in the place where Martha was* [John 11:30, adapted]
  11. *if I am speaking truth, for what (reason) do you not believe me?* [John 8:46] indicative, first, true
  13. *the fear of God is not before their eyes* [Rom. 3:18]
  15. *You are witnessing concerning yourself; your testimony is not true* [John 8:13]

Lesson 14: Third Declension—Stop and Sibilant Stems

Assignment 1
  1. consonant, theme, stem, nominative, dative, sigma
  3. feminine, same, drop
  5. π, β, φ + σ = ψ
     κ, γ, χ + σ = ξ
     τ, δ, θ + σ = σ
  7. 1. *and a certain woman named Lydia, . . ., was listening* [Acts 16:14]
    3. *which is Christ in you, the hope of glory* [Col. 1:27]
    5. *in my flesh for his body, which is the church* [Col. 1:24]

Assignment 2
  8. definite article concord:
    1. ἡ ἐλπις   7. αἱ χάριτες
    3. τὸ ὄρος   9. τὸν ἄρχοντα
    5. τῇ σαρκί   11. τῷ πνεύματι

9. c 1. χάριν   a. λόγους   = a, m, p
   e 2. σαρκός   b. δώρου   = g, n, s
   d 3. σῶμα   c. καρδίαν   = a, f, s
   a 4. ἄρχοντας d. δῶρον   = n, n, s
   b 5. ἔθνους   e. γραφῆς   = g, f, s

10. 1. *sons of the generation of Abraham* [Acts 13:26]
  3. *and he goes up into the mountain* [Mark 3:13]
  5. *love covers a multitude of sins* [1 Pet. 4:8]
  7. *the rulers of the gentiles have power over them* [Matt. 20:25]
  9. *on the one hand, I am baptizing you with water unto repentance, . . ., he will baptize you with the Holy Spirit* [Matt. 3:11]

Lesson 15: Third Declension— Liquid and Vowel Stems

  1. syncopation, πατήρ (or ἀνήρ)
  3. ἱερεύς, ευ-, nominative and accusative, ἱερεῖς, ἱερέως
  5. c 1. πίστεως a. λόγους = a, m, p
     d 2. πίστεις   b. λόγοις = d, m p
     a 3. ἱερεῖς   c. καρδίας = g, f, s
     b 4. πατράσι   d. καρδίαι = n, f, p
  7. rough, ὁ, ὅ, gender and number, not case
  8. 1. *from city unto city* [Matt. 23:34]
    3. *both men and women were being baptized* [Acts 8:12]
    5. *he is stronger than I (am), of whom I am not worthy* [Matt. 3:11]
    7. *a large multitude of the priests were being obedient to the faith* [Acts 6:7]
    9. *a savior, who is Christ, the Lord, in the city of David* [Luke 2:11]

11. *Do you not believe that I am in the Father and the Father is in me?* [John 14:10]

13. *for the righteousness of God is being revealed in it from faith to faith* [Rom. 1:17]

9. Diagrams

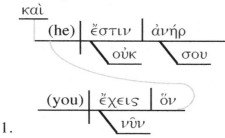

1.

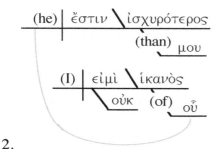

2.

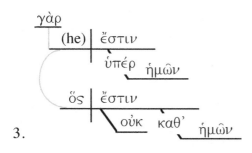

3.

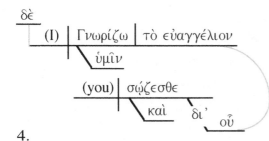

4.

Lesson 16: Adjectives and Comparisons—Again

1. 1. *you are true (sincere)* [Mark 12:14]

   3. *you have words of eternal life* [John 6:68]

   5. *they were saying he has an unclean spirit* [Mark 3:30]

   7. *a woman who was a sinner in the city* [Luke 7:37]

   9. *and every thing which is not from faith is sin* [Rom. 14:23]

   11. *he was in the desert places and they were coming to him* [Mark 1:45]

   13. *the (one who is) faithful in the least also is faithful in much* [Luke 16:10]

   15. *but the least in the kingdom of heaven is greater than he (is)* [Matt. 11:11]

   17. *glory in the highest to God and on earth peace among men of good will* [Luke 2:14]

Lesson 17: Numerals

1. *who?*, *which?*, or *what?*, *somebody*, *something*, or *a certain*, accent, third

3. subject, nominative

   1. ὅστις, οἵτινες

   3. ὅτι, ἅτινα

   who, whoever, which ones

5. nominative absolute

6. noun of action

   1. *the fear of God*, objective [Rom. 3:18]

   3. *the perseverance of Christ*, subjective [2 Thess. 3:5]

7. measure, time, space, manner, cause

   1. *the devil takes him* ***to a mountain*** [Matt. 4:8]

9. μή, indicative, οὐ

1. *you are not greater than our father Jacob, are you? [John 4:12]*
11. parentheses, absolute, equals
13. 1. *about three thousand lives [Acts 2:41]*
    3. *from the sixth hour . . . until the ninth hour [Mark 15:33]*
    5. *and he was in the wilderness forty days [Mark 1:13]*
    7. *the fourth angel . . . a third of the stars [Rev. 8:12]*
    9. *now the Jerusalem above is free, which is our mother [2 Cor. 12:8]*
    11. *the first man is of earth, earthly, the second man is from heaven [1 Cor. 15:47]*
14. Diagram

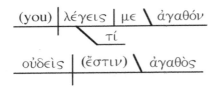

Lesson 18: Future and Liquid Future

1. primary, fut. passive built on another stem
3. λ, μ, ν, ρ, -εσ, σ drops, contract, circumflex
5. Identify tense components

future suffix

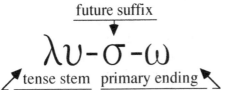

λυ-σ-ω

tense stem   primary ending

7. τοσ-, -οῦτος, -οῦτο, -αύτη, as, as much as, rough
9. **R**egular, **S**top, **H**idden, **L**iquid, **D**eponent, **I**rregular, **C**ontract
    1. λαλέω   C   *he will speak*
    3. διδάσκω H   *he will teach*

5. ἔρχομαι   I   *I will go*
7. ὁράω   I, D   *he will see*
9. λαμβάνω   D, H *he will receive*
10. 1. *whatsoever he will hear (hears) he will speak [John 16:13]*
    3. *all will believe in him [John 11:48]*
    5. *and I will be their God, and they will be my people [2 Cor. 6:16]*
    7. *the stones will cry out [Luke 19:40]*
    9. *that one will teach you all things [John 14:26]*
    11. *and I will come to you quickly [1 Cor. 4:19]*
    13. *and all flesh will see the salvation of God [Luke 3:6]*
    15. *but someone will say, "How are the dead raised? And with what sort of body do they come?" [1 Cor. 15:35]*

Lesson 19: First Aorist and Liquid Aorist

1. active and middle, the passive voice is built on a different stem
3. λ, μ, ν, ρ, σ drops, α, asigmatic, lengthening
5. Identify tense components:

tense stem   tense suffix

ἐ-λυ-σα-ν

augment   secondary ending

7. punctiliar, undefined
9. epistolary, present
10. 1. *he is not here [Mark 16:6]*
    3. *they ask him [Mark 7:5]*
    5. *Lord, where are you going? [John 13:36]*

7. *they were observing the signs which he was performing* [John 6:2]

9. *the devil sins from the beginning* [1 John 3:8]

11. *they reported all these things to the eleven* [Luke 24:9]

13. *we preached the good news of God to you* [1 Thess. 2:9]

15. *but men loved the darkness more than the light, for their deeds were evil* [John 3:19]

Lesson 20: Second Aorist and Indirect Dis.

1. regular, -ed; irregular, *I went*

3. σ, εἶπον, εἶδον

5. ἐλίπου, -σο, intervocalic, εο, ου

7.
1.	γνω-	-ν	ἔγνων
3.	εἰπ-	---- (-εν)	εἶπεν
5.	φαγ-	-τε	ἐφάγετε
7.	ἀγαγ-	-τε	ἠγάγετε
9.	ἐνεγκ-	---- (-εν)	ἤνεγκεν

8.
1.	βαλ-	-μην	ἐβαλόμην
3.	πεσ-	-το	ἐπέσετο
5.	εὑρ-	-σθε	εὕρεσθε
7.	γεν-	-το	ἐγένετο

9. 1. *we persuade men* [2 Cor. 5:11]

3. *we preach good news to you* [Acts 13:32]

5. *But if any one of you lacks wisdom* [James 1 :5]

7. *he enters where the child was* [Mk. 5:40]

9. *for he said he was* [indirect dis.] *the son of God* [Matt. 27:43]

11. *the time of the promise neared* [Acts 7:17]

13. *Jesus heard that they had thrown* [indirect dis.] *him outside* [John 9:35]

15. *Isaiah said these things because he saw his glory* [John 12:41]

17. *"I believed, therefore I spoke," and we believe, therefore we also speak* [2 Cor. 4:13]

10. Diagram

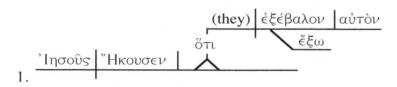

1.

Lesson 21: The Passive System — Aor., Fut.

1.
$$\pi, \beta, [\phi] + \theta = \phi\theta \ [\theta \text{ drops}]$$
$$\kappa, \gamma, \chi + \theta = \chi\theta$$
$$\tau, \delta, \theta + \theta = \sigma\theta$$

3.

    tense stem   passive suffix

$$\overset{}{\text{ἐ}}\text{-}λυ\text{-}θη\text{-}ν$$

  augment pronominal suffix

5.
ἐπέμφθην	πεμφθήσομαι
ἐπέμφθης	πεμφθήσῃ
ἐπέμφθη	πεμφθήσεται
ἐπέμφθημεν	πεμφθησόμεθα
ἐπέμφθητε	πεμφθήσεσθε
ἐπέμφθησαν	πεμφθήσονται

7. True. Well, *mostly* true. The epsilon and alpha contracts wind up with the same resultant

look (compare φιλήσομαι, τιμήσομαι, with γραφήσομαι). The omicron spoils the point a little with an omega result (cf. δηλώσομαι).

9.

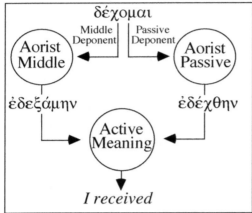

δέχομαι

Aorist Middle — Middle Deponent | Passive Deponent → Aorist Passive

ἐδεξάμην   ἐδέχθην

Active Meaning

I received

10. 1. *strong (men)* — nmp
3. *animal* — n/ans
5. *need* — afs
7. *of a beast* — gns
9. *in a prison* — dfs
11. 1. *we sowed* — aa1p
3. *you persecuted* — aa2s
5. *they reported* — aa3p
7. *he was amazed* — ia3s
9. *they were carrying* — ia3p
11. *you received* — aa2p
13. *you are living* — pa2s
15. *he is being manifested* — pp3s
12. 1. *I will be saved* [Mark 5:28]
3. *Elijah was sent* [Acts 13:32]
5. *for in hope we have been saved* [Rom. 8:24]
7. *a great crowd followed him* [Matt. 20:29]
9. *and the beast which I saw was like a leopard* [Rev. 13:2]
11. *and they said, "The master has need of it."* [Luke 19:34]

13. *this already was the third time Jesus was manifested to the disciples* [John 21:14]
15. *they seized John and bound him in prison* [Mark 6:17]
17. *and its deadly wound was healed. And the whole earth marveled after the beast* [Rev. 13:12]

Lesson 22: Perfect Active and Fut. Perfect

1. active, middle and passive are built on another principal part
2. 1. single consonant δεδικαίωκα
   3. stop consonant πεφώνηκα
   5. Attic ἀκήκοα
   7. irregular ἐλήλυθα
3. Identify tense components:

tense stem   tense suffix

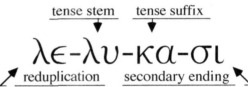

λε-λυ-κα-σι

reduplication   secondary ending

5. continuing effects, have or has
7. 1. *door* — afs
8. 1. *he touched* — am3s
   3. *you prepared* — aa2s
9. 1. *I am not worthy* [Mark 1:7]
   3. *what I have written, I have written* [John 19:22]
   5. *I thank my God* [1 Cor. 1:4]
   7. *I suffered much today* [Matt. 27:19]
   9. *the evil one does not touch him* [1 John 5:18]
   11. *a person is not justified out of works of (the) law* [Gal. 2:16]
   13. *the world is passing away and its lust* [1 John 2:17]
   15. *I have testified that this one is the son of God* [John 1:34]

17. *and we have believed and have known that you are the Holy One of God* [John 6:69]

Lesson 23: Perfect Middle Indicative

1. middle and passive, fourth, tense suffix, thematic vowel
3.
   1. χμ   γμ   δέδεγμαι
   3. φτ   πτ   γέγραπται
   5. ρσ   ρθ   ἤρηθε
   7. λσ   λθ   ἤγγελθε
5. third, -νται, periphrastically
7.
   1. *of (the) devil*   gms
   3. *in wrath*   dfs
   5. *of stones*   gmp
8.
   1. *he will turn*   fa3s
   3. *they were ministering* ia3p
   5. *they have hated*   pa3p
   7. *I came*   am1s
9.
   1. *Lazarus was sick* [John 11:2]
   3. *they had (were having) a few fish* [Mark 8:7]
   5. *you also have not been deceived, have you?* [John 7:47]
   7. *they did not repent from their works* [Rev. 16:11]
   9. *the way of truth will be blasphemed* [2 Peter 2:2]
   11. *he rolled a stone over the tomb* [Mark 15:46]

Lesson 24: Pluperfect Indicative

1. fourth, fifth, secondary
3. secondary

-ν	-μην
-ς	-σο
---(εν)	-το
-μεν	-μεθα
-τε	-σθε
-ν or -σαν	-ντο

5. Identify tense components:

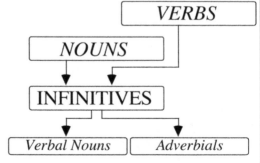

reduplication   tense stem   tense suffix

ἐ-λε-λυ-κει-ν

augment   secondary ending

7. is not, imperfect, aorist or pluperfect, mood, protasis, conjunction
8.
   1. *of a covenant*   gfs
   3. *desires*   gfs/afp
9.
   1. *he owes (was owing)* ia3s
10.
   1. *and another book was opened* [Rev. 20:12]
   3. *at the ninth hour of prayer* [Acts 3:1]
   5. *but each one is tempted by their own desire* [James 1:14]
   7. *they went out from us, but they were not of us, for if they were of us, they would have remained with us* [1 John 2:19]

Lesson 25: Infinitives

Assignment 1
1. substantive

```
              ┌──────────┐
              │  VERBS   │
      ┌───────┴──┐       │
      │  NOUNS   │       │
      └───┬──────┘       │
          ▼              ▼
      ┌──────────────────────┐
      │    INFINITIVES       │
      └──────────────────────┘
          ▼              ▼
  ┌───────────────┐ ┌──────────────┐
  │ Verbal Nouns  │ │  Adverbials  │
  └───────────────┘ └──────────────┘
```

3. subject, accusative
5. subject, direct object, modifier
7. εἶναι, ἔσεσθαι
8.
   1. *they were seeking to seize him* [Mark 12:12]; direct object
   3. *do we not have authority not to work?* [1 Cor. 9:6]; modifier; yes (οὐ)

5. *I have much to say and to judge concerning you* [John 8:26]; modifier

7. *you say that I cast out demons by Beelzebub* [Luke 11:18]; direct object, indirect discourse; accusative of general reference

9. *no one worthy was found to open the book nor to see it* [Rev. 5:4]; modifiers

9. Diagrams

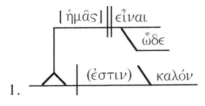

1.

2.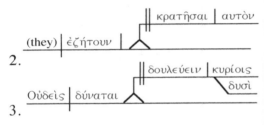

3.

4.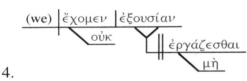

Assignment 2

10. 1. *they deny the Lamb*
     3. *the sun shines*
     5. *it is lawful to buy*
     7. *the only true God*
     9. *he made the water wine*

11. main verb

12. 1. time *while buying*
     3. purpose *in order to shine, to shine*
     5. purpose *in order to deny, to deny*

13. 1. *and now I have told you before it happens* [John 14:29]

3. *now it happened that while they were there* [Luke 2:6]

5. *he says to him, "Yes, Lord, you know that I love you"* [John 21:15]

7. *likewise also the second (man) and the third until the seventh* [Matt. 22:26]

9. *after I am raised, I will go before you into Galilee* [Mark 14:28]

11. *but they perform all their works in order to be seen by men* [Matt. 23:5]

13. *I am sending you to open their eyes, to turn (them) from darkness to light and from the authority of Satan to God, in order that they receive forgiveness of sins* [Acts 26:17b–18]

14. Diagrams

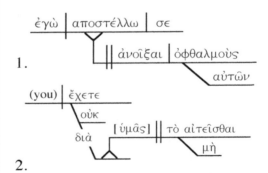

1.

2.

3.

Lesson 26: Present Active Participle

Assignment 1

1. adjectival

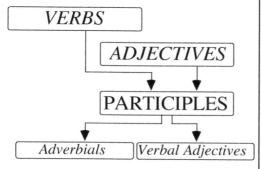

3. -ντ, -ουσ, third, ἄρχων, first, δόξα

5. article, adjectival, without article, adverbial

6. concord
   1. *those hearing, the men who hear*
   3. *to those asking, to those who ask*
   5. *of the word which says*

7. 1. *those who marry*
   3. *he wore no garment*
   5. *he calls the twelve*
   7. *they consider (regard)*
   9. *he rebuked them*

8. 1. *to those who are in Rome* [Rom. 1:7]
   3. *I am speaking to you who listen* [Luke 6:27]
   5. *the truth that abides in us* [2 John 1:2]
   7. *but they heard not the voice of the one speaking to me* [Acts 22:9]
   9. *in order that he be the father of all those who believe* [Rom. 4:11]
   11. *Not every one who says to me, "Lord, Lord," will enter into the kingdom of heaven* [Matt. 7:21]

Assignment 2

9. ambiguous, attributive, *a living God* (or a prepositional phrase: *to a living God*, etc.),

adverbially, ἔρχομαι, *after, while*, or *as*

10. 1. *while he was teaching*
    3. *because she is*
    5. *though he desires*
    7. *he went rejoicing*
    9. *and they said*

11. 1. *I come to him while he is saying these things*

13. genitive, genitive, independent of
    1. λέγοντος αὐτοῦ ἐξέρχονται

14. 1. *you are my friends*
    3. *the end is not yet*
    5. *what reward do you have?*
    7. *whether knowledge*
    9. *because of the consolation*

15. 1. *for he went on his way rejoicing* [Acts 8:39]
    3. *the Pharisees came to him to test him* [Luke 6:27]
    5. *they were disbelieving and spoke evil of the way before the multitude* [Acts 19:9]
    7. *because the hour already was late, he went out to Bethany with the twelve* [Mark 11:11]
    9. *this man does not stop speaking words against this place and the law* [Acts 6:13]
    11. *For if we freely sin after we have received the knowledge of the truth, no longer is a sacrifice left for sins* [Heb. 10:26]

Lesson 27: Present Middle Participle

1. -μεν, ο, ἀγαθός
3. true
4. 1. indirect object or dative of direct object, depending on the understood verb
   3. locative of place
   5. locative of point in time
   7. instrumental of cause

9. instrumental of manner

5. false

6. 1. *a widow's village in the country*
   3. *he conquers with the sword*
   5. *I make known to the sisters*
   7. *you are clean*
   9. *you go out from there*
   11. *he will be healed*
   13. *you command me?*

7. 1. *they think the things of the flesh* [Rom. 8:5]
   3. *the altar which sanctifies the gift* [Matt. 23:19]
   5. *he went alway grieving, for he had many possessions* [Mark 10:22]
   7. *for if I have grieved you, who is the one who makes me glad except the one who was grieved by me?* [2 Cor. 2:2]
   9. *For the wrath of God is being revealed from heaven against every ungodliness and unrighteousness of men* [Rom. 1:18]

11. *For the word of the cross to those who are perishing is foolishness, but to us who are being saved it is the power of God* [1 Cor. 1:18]

8. Diagrams

1.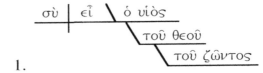

2.

3.

4.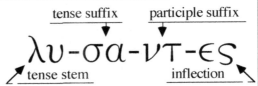

5.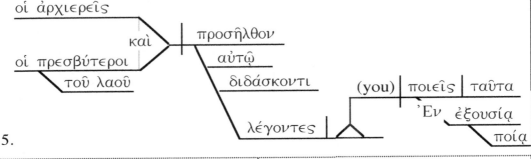

Lesson 28: Aorist and Future Participles

1. -σα, -ντ, -σας, -μεν, -θεντ, -θεισ

3. Identify verbal components:

$$\overset{\text{tense suffix}}{\downarrow} \quad \overset{\text{participle suffix}}{\downarrow}$$

λυ-σα-ντ-ες

tense stem   inflection

5. Identify verbal components:

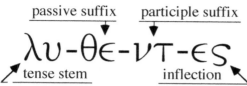

passive suffix   participle suffix

λυ-θε-ντ-ες

tense stem   inflection

7. θ, -εἰς, -εῖσα, -έν
9. 1. *he comes with the clouds*
   3. *of her fornication*
10. 1. *and when they saw the star, they rejoiced* [Matt. 2:10]
    3. *she did not desire to repent from her fornication* [Rev. 2:21]
    5. *this is the victory which conquers the world, our faith* [1 John 5:4]
    7. *this already was the third time Jesus was manifested to the disciples after he had been raised from the dead* [John 21:14]
    9. *this one, after he had summoned Barnabas and Saul, sought to hear the word of God* [Acts 13:7]

Lesson 29: Perfect Participles

1. Identify verbal components:

tense stem   resultant participial suffix

λε-λυ-κ-οτ-ος

reduplication perfect suffix inflection

3. λελυκυι, α pure, καρδία
5. periphrastic, εἰμί, perfect participle
7. 1. *therefore, I testify to you*
   3. *unto their Sanhedrin*
   5. *in our weakness*
   7. *you will hear a report*
   9. *to whom all were giving heed*
8. 1. *and he left them and went away* [Matt. 16:4]

3. *for many are called, but few are chosen* [Matt. 22:14]
5. *therefore, Jesus was saying to those Jews who believed in him* [John 8:31]
7. *for I am an old man and my wife has advanced in her days* [Luke 1:18]
9. *he is clothed in a garment which has been dipped in blood, and his name is called, "The Word of God"* [Rev. 19:13]

Lesson 30: Subjunctive Mood

1. potentiality, probable
3. first, -ωμεν, *let us*
5. *shall we*
7. Conditional Sentences:

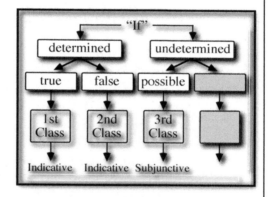

8. 1. *the teacher has arrived*
   3. *I have seen the Spirit*
   5. *leads you unto repentance*
9. 1. *do not believe* [Matt. 24:23, subjunctive of prohibition]
   3. *and whenever they hear, immediately Satan comes* [Mark 4:15]
   5. *he says to his disciples, "Let us go again into Judea"* [John 11:7]
10. 1 John 1:1–4

   1.1 *What was from the beginning, what we have heard, what we* *have seen with our eyes, what we have observed and our hands handled concerning the word of life*

1.3 *what we have seen and have heard, we are proclaiming also to you, in order that you might have fellowship with us. And our fellowship is with the Father and with his Son, Jesus Christ.*

Lesson 31: Imperative Mood

1. contingency, potential
3. present, durative, progress
5.
   | ----- | ----- |
   | --, ς, θι | -σο |
-τω	-σθω
-τε	-σθε
-τωσαν	-σθωσαν

6. 1. *he (she, it) is free from the law*
   3. *we set sail in a boat*
   5. *And the child grew*

7. 1. *the one who has ears, let him hear* [Matt. 11:15]
   3. *let them flee into the mountains* [Mark 13:14]
   5. *he saved others, let him save himself* [Luke 23:35]
   7. *and all were weeping and mourning her. But he said, "Stop weeping!"* [Luke 8:52]

10. 1 John 1:5–10
    1.5 *And this is the message which we have heard from him and we are proclaiming to you, that God is light and darkness is not in him at all.*
    1.7 *but if we are walking in the light as he is in the light we have fellowship with one another and the blood of Jesus his Son cleanses us from every sin.*

1.9 *If we confess our sins he is faithful and just to forgive us our sins and to cleanse us from every unrighteousness.*

Lesson 32: Optative Mood

1. contingency, possible
3.
-ιμι	-ιμην
-ις	-ιο
-ι	-ιτο
-ιμεν	-ιμεθα
-ιτε	-ισθε
-ιεν	-ιντο

5. μὴ γένοιτο, *may it never be!*
7. *if, may, might*
9. Conditional Sentences:

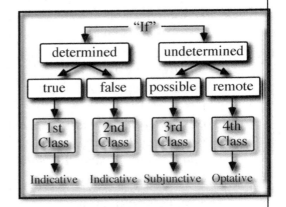

10. 1. *I beg you*
    3. *we accuse him*
    5. *a vessel of wrath*

7. 1. *the whole world lies in (the power of) the evil (one)* [1 John 5:9]
   3. *and they were discussing with one another what they might do with Jesus* [Luke 6:11]
   5. *Let it not be! But let God be true, and every person a liar* [Rom. 3:4]

10. 1 John 2:1–6
    2.1 *My children, these things I am writing to you in order that you not sin. And if anyone sins,*

we have an advocate with the Father, Jesus Christ, the righteous

2.3 *And by this we know that we have known him, if we keep his commandments.*

2.5 *Whoever keeps his word, truly in this one the love of God has been perfected; by this we know that we are in him*

Lesson 33: MI Verbs—First Principal Part

1.
-μι	-μαι	-ν	-μην
-ς	-σαι	-ς	-σο
-σι(ν)	-ται	---(εν)	-το
-μεν	-μεθα	-μεν	-μεθα
-τε	-σθε	-τε	-θσε
-ασι	-νται	-ν, -σαν	-ντο

2. 1. lengthening (singulars)
    3. athematic (except future, subjunctive, & pres. act. impr. 2s)
3. subjunctive
4. 1. lengthening (singulars)
    3. augment (-ω verb patterns)
    5. secondary endings
5. 1. present, act., indicative, 3p
    3. present, act., subjunctive, 1p
    5. imperfect, mid., indicative, 2p
6. 1. *you have not toiled*
    3. *he shows to him*
    5. *Now this I say*
    7. *I lay down my life*
    9. *we establish the law*
7. 1. *give to everyone who asks you* [Luke 6:30]
    3. *and he shows to him all the kingdoms of the world* [Matt. 4:8]
    5. *the good shepherd lays down his life for the sheep* [John 10:11]
    7. *for no one is able to do these signs which you are doing,*

unless God be with him [John 3:2]

8. 1 John 2:7–11

    2.7 *Beloved, I do not write to you a new commandment but an old commandment which you were having from the beginning; the old commandment is the word which you heard.*

    2.9 *The one who says he is in the light and hates his brother is in the darkness until now.*

    2.11 *But the one who hates his brother is in the darkness and walks in the darkness and does not know where he is going, because the darkness blinded his eyes.*

Lesson 34:   MI Verbs—Other Prin. Parts

1. aorist or future
2. 1. present, mid., subjunctive, 1s
    3. present, mid., indicative, 3p
3. kappa, δίδωμι, τίθημι, ἵημι, -κα
4. 1. aorist, active, indicative, 2s
    3. perfect, middle, indicative, 2p
5. ἀναβαίνω and γινώσκω, thematic, active indicative
6. 1. aorist, act., indicative, 3s
7. 1. aorist, pass., indicative, 1p
    3. present, act., participle, amp
    5. perfect, act., participle, nms
8. 1. *the one who sits*
    3. *he will pay back to you*
    5. *All things have been delivered to me*
    7. *when he arose, he was baptized*
    9. *do not hinder (forbid) him*
9. 1. *they placed the cross upon him* [Luke 23:26]
    3. *but Jesus said, "Permit the children and do not hinder*

them from coming to me."
[Matt. 19:14]

10. 1 John 2:12–17

2.12 *I am writing to you, children, because your sins have been forgiven because of his name.*

2.14 *I am writing (have written) to you, children, because you have known the Father. I am writing (have written) to you, fathers, because you have known the one from the beginning. I am writing (have written) to you, young men, because you are strong and the word of God abides in you, and you have conquered the evil one.*

2.16 *because everything that is in the world, the lust of the flesh and the lust of the eyes and the pride of life, is not from the Father but from the world.*

Made in the USA
Coppell, TX
19 April 2021